To Judith
A delightfully different Dark Lady

Shakespea
Mistr

Shakespeare's Mistress

The Mystery of the Dark Lady Revealed

AUBREY BURL

AMBERLEY

First published 2012

Amberley Publishing
The Hill, Stroud
Gloucestershire, GL5 4EP

www.amberley-books.com

ISBN 978 1 4456 0217 2

British Library Cataloguing in Publication Data.
A catalogue record for this book is available
from the British Library.

Typeset in 11pt on 14pt Palatino.
Typesetting and Origination by Amberley Publishing.
Printed in the UK.

Contents

The Dark Lady of the Sonnets

Shakespeare's sonnet sequence has been treated as a conundrum and the poems as items of forensic evidence. Scholars have thought about, written about and argued about the sonnets for entire lifetimes, but they still retain their mystery, because they are not meant to be solved. They are meant to be as mysterious as life itself. Hundreds of very clever people have laboured mightily to arrive at versions of the story that the sonnets tell, only to convince their readers that the sonnets cannot be made to tell a story at all.
Germaine Greer, *William Shakespeare. Sonnets*, 2009, vii.

The Dark Lady:
A whitely wanton with a velvet brow.
With two pitch-balls stuck in her face for eyes.
Ay, and by heaven, one that will do the deed
Though Argus were her eunuch and her guard.
Love's Labours Lost, III, I, 153-6.

Preface

Shakespeare's Dark Lady is a mystery without a name. The years when she brought delight, desire and despair to the poet came in the years after the Spanish Armada of 1588 and before the Gunpowder Plot of 1605, a long, unsettled period of competition between theatres, personal rivalries, warfare and brutal death.

For Shakespeare those years were dramatically rich. He wrote comedies, tragedies and histories, including *Romeo and Juliet, Hamlet, Twelfth Night, A Midsummer Night's Dream, Richard III* and *King Lear*. His acting company was successful and prospered. But for him, privately, it was an emotionally demanding time, the torment of the years when he met his Dark Lady, his incubus, his horrifying nightmare. She was musical, alluring, married with children, but without honour and faithless, a tantalus.

Shakespeare never identified her in his sonnets. In those enigmatic poems no one was given a name, neither the youth; nor the Rival Poet, nor the 'Mr. W. H.' who stole the sonnets, nor, most tantalising, the Dark Lady. Everything, every one, was left in a mist. Candidates for that woman have been many. They have included maids of honour to Queen Elizabeth, attractively nubile young women who were tempting targets for courtiers like Sir Walter Ralegh as John Aubrey laughingly described:

He was a tall, handsome and bold man ... He loved a wench well; and one time getting up one of the Maids of Honour up against a tree in a Wood (twas his first Lady) who seemed at first boarding to be something fearfull of her Honour, and modest, she cryed, 'sweet Sir Walter, what doe you me ask? Will you undoe me; Nay, sweet Sir Walter! Sweet Sir Walter! Sir Walter!' At last, as the danger and the pleasure at the same time grew higher, she cryed in the extacey, 'Switter Swatter Switter Swatter'. She proved with child, and I doubt not but this Hero tooke care of them both, as also that the Product was more than an ordinary mortal.[1]

If the Dark Lady had not been one of those susceptible girls then several other women have been 'credibly' identified as her including a married countess; an unmarried Lady, and an assortment of respectable wives as well as a musician and a prostitute who may have been a negress. Those women are feasible possibilities unlike three improbabilities that have been proposed: Elizabeth Tudor, Queen of England; and Mrs Winifred Burbage, the wife of Shakespeare's leading actor. The third woman, Jeanne de Ketulle, has to be rejected because she never existed.

There are no agreed identities for any of the people in Shakespeare's sonnets. The fair youth may have been a nobleman. Several writers have been claimed as the rival poet; and just as many thieves for the man who stole the sonnets. Most frustrating in this masked identity parade is the Dark Lady. The quest to discover her name began in Elizabethan times, became an obsession in the nineteenth and twentieth centuries and continues, optimistically, today.

She is a challenge. Card-sharps ask passers-by to 'find the lady', the queen in the three court-cards displayed face up, swiftly shuffled and held out upside down. Similarly this book challenges readers to find the Dark Lady. She lurks there, mockingly, somewhere in Shakespeare's shuffled sonnets. But she was not his first elusive love. Years earlier there had been another 'invisible' woman, Anne Whateley, a rival to Anne Hathaway. Did she exist? Did Shakespeare love her?

Or was she just the spelling mistake of an overworked clerk?

Note to the reader
Shakespearian quotations are from J. Bate & E. Rasmussen, *The RSC Shakespeare. William Shakespeare. Complete Works*, Macmillan, London, 2007.

Finding Places in Shakespeare
An indispensable guide to Shakespearian connections in London is *The A to Z of Elizabethan London*, Harry Margary, Lympne Castle, Kent, 1979, compiled by Adrian Prockter and Robert Taylor. Its detailed maps and place name index make it easy to discover the former situation of houses, brothels and taverns mentioned in this story.

Old House Books of Moretonhampstead, Devon, have produced a detailed map on a single folded sheet, 'The City of London Five Hundred Years Ago', showing the major streets, lanes, churches, great houses, monasteries and public buildings of *c*. 1520. The sheet is accompanied by a useful gazetteer locating places on the map.

For the adventurous explorer there are helpful guidebooks: Nicholas Robins' *Walking Shakespeare's London*, Interlink, Northampton, Mass., 2005, contains itineraries for 'twenty original walks in and around London'; Sarah Kettler's and Carole Trimble's *The Amateur Historian's Guide to Medieval & Tudor London*, Capital Books, Sterling, Virginia, 2001, provides information about interesting places to visit in the city.

Details about sixteenth-century life in the capital can be found in Liza Picard's *Elizabeth's London*, Weidenfeld & Nicolson, London, 2003; and in Stephen Porter's *Shakespeare's London, Everyday Life in London, 1580–1616*, Amberley Press, Stroud, 2009.

A guidebook, *London Plaques*, Shire, Oxford, 2010, by Derek Sumeray and John Sheppard locates places with memorial plaques with Shakespearian associations.

Outside London places connected with Shakespeare are listed in Keith Cheetham's *On the Trail of William Shakespeare*, Luarth, Edinburgh, 2006.

Introduction

It began in a mist and ended in darkness. During the 1590s Shakespeare composed a long set of sonnets. In them, but giving no names for the people, was a youth, a poet, and a she-devil inhabiting human flesh, the woman known as his Dark Lady. She enticed him, seduced him and discarded him. Despairingly, he deceived himself that she had never betrayed him:

> When my love swears that she is made of truth,
> I do believe her though I know she lies ... Sonnet 138, 1-2.

He was caught at a corner of life's notorious triangle, a man with a young friend and with a woman who used them, tormented both of them – and laughed.

> Two loves I have, of comfort and despair,
> Which like two spirits do suggest me still;
> The better angel is a man right fair,
> The worser spirit a woman coloured ill ... Sonnet 144, 1-4

His only comfort was his own self-deception. He longed for her, lusted for her, persuaded himself that she loved him. But that 'love' was no more than a flicker of sunshine in a world without light. She was his lady of the night.

> Past cure I am, now reason is past care ...
> For I have sworn thee fair, and thought thee bright,
> Who art as black as hell, as dark as night. Sonnet 147, 9, 13-14.

Today she is a wraith, an insubstantial shade. Who she was, which year Shakespeare met her, for how long, what she did day by day, what happened to her, these are wisps of history that seem beyond our recovery. She is one of the four anonymous people in the sonnets, the only woman, and she is the most exasperatingly elusive, as Katherine Duncan-James remarks:

> The 'Dark Lady' ... may be one of a dozen or more known women of the period, such as Mary Fitton or Emilia Lanyer; or she may be one of the many about whom no evidence survives; or she may a fictitious figure, possibly compounded of several real or literary models. Paradoxical praise of 'black' beauty was fashionable in the later Elizabethan period: it is, for instance, mocked by Shakespeare in *Love's Labours Lost*. To what extent the Sonnets – life experiences – which could include the experience of reading other poets – we shall never know.[1]

Long generations of writers have scoured the sonnets line by cryptic line for the identities of those nameless participants. Writers have provided different solutions to the problem, each suggestion as feasible as any offered by other researchers. And most elusive of those ghostlike people in the poems is the woman known as the Dark Lady.

In his one-act play of 1910, *The Dark Lady of the Sonnets*, Bernard Shaw said 'he did not care a jot about the identity of the Dark Lady. She might have been Maria Tompkins for all he cared'.[2] She was not. Shaw was wrong. It is now generally agreed that 'textual hints in Sonnets 127-152 support Rowse's insistence' that the 'woman coloured ill' was 'a well known person' of 'superior social standing'[3] who enjoyed making love. Those Dark Lady sonnets were so obsessed with sexual infatuation that 'it is impossible to believe that Shakespeare wished them [the entire sequence] to be published'.[4] But the poems were published. Twice. On both occasions without permission.

At some time in the late sixteenth century Shakespeare composed those sonnets. Most of them, if not all, must have been written by 1598 because in that year they were mentioned by Francis Meres, a Cambridge graduate, in his poetical anthology, *Palladis Tamia, Being the Second Part of Wits Treasury*. It contained his comments on more than a hundred English writers from Chaucer onwards. Meres was only briefly in London, just two years from 1597 to 1598, living in Botolph Lane just north-east of London Bridge at a time when Shakespeare was staying near the Clink just south of the Bridge. Hardly a quarter of a mile apart the two men were almost neighbours and may have met. It is a tempting but unprovable thought that the poetically-minded Meres may even have been shown some of the sonnets.

Meres considered Sir Philip Sidney was the rarest poet, and that Michael Drayton was Shakespeare's equal in verse. But Shakespeare was praised as:

> the most passionate among us to bewaile and bemoane the perplexities of loue', excellent for both comedy and tragedy, and, most commendable of al, 'The sweete wittie sole of Ovid lives in mellifluous and hony-tongued Shakespeare witness his Venus & Adonis, his Lucrece and his sugrd Sonnets among his priuate friends &c ...[5]

The public but illicit history of those sonnets began with a theft. A year after Meres two of the poems were plagiarised in 1599. An opportunistic printer, William Jaggard, illicitly printed sonnets 138, 'I know she lies', and 144, 'my female evil', in his *The Passionate Pilgrime*, adding three excerpts from the third act of Shakespeare's *Love's Labours Lost* and finally inserting other unauthorised poems to pad out his thin book.[6] Worse followed. Ten years later, again without permission, the entire set of 154 sonnets was published by Thomas Thorpe in a slim paperback, *SHAKE-SPEARES SONNETS Never Before Imprinted* of 1609, printed by G. Eld and sold in the London bookshops of William Apsley and John Wright. The book's dedication read, word for word as it was punctuated:

TO.THE.ONLIE.BEGETTER.OF
THESE.INSUING.SONNETS.
Mr. W. H. ALL. HAPPINESSE.
AND.THAT.ETERNITIE.
PROMISED.
BY.
OUR.EVER-LIVING. POET.
WISHETH.
THE.WELL-WISHING.
ADVENTURER.IN.
SETTING.
FORTH.
T.T

'T. T' obviously was Thomas Thorpe. But 'Mr. W. H.' is yet another of the queue of anonymous persons contained in those exasperatingly coded poems.[7]

Most Elizabethan sonnet sequences were dedicated to an apparently unnamed anonymous woman but the accepted convention was that behind her pseudonym the poet would provide clear hints to her identity. All the sonneteers did so, whether Barnaby Barnes, or Samuel Daniel or Michael Drayton or Thomas Lodge, even Sir Philip Sidney whose 'Stella' in his *Astrophel and Stella*, was the lovely, ardent but unobtainable Penelope Devereux. She was one of many women meant to be recognised behind her coded title. Superficially nameless all those 'concealed' phantoms were living human beings intended to be revealed.[8]

Samuel Daniel's sonnet sequence, *Delia*, of 1592, was written for Muriel, a woman living somewhere in Somerset close to the River Avon. Daniel was faithful to her for years but was rejected, almost disdained, because he had neither power nor prestige. But behind the artifice of his sonnets was a genuine love and it was remembered that when he was rejected he cried.[9]

Another frustrated poet was Michael Drayton who had been brought up in the household of Sir Henry Goodere. Drayton idolised Goodere's daughter, Anne, who was eventually profitably married off to Sir Henry Rainsford of Clifford Chambers not far south of Stratford-upon-Avon. In 1594 Drayton's adoration for her inspired his *Idea's Mirror* sonnets. They were updated in his *Idea* 1619. In that sequence was his famous and lovely 'Since there's no help, come let us kiss and part ...'.[10]

Samuel Daniel and Michael Drayton were two of many writers of sonnets: Thomas Lodge and his *Phillis*, 1593, that 'female-voiced lament'; Richard Barnfield's *Cynthia*; Edmond Spenser's *Amoretti*, both of 1595. Sonnet sequences were written by Barnabe Rudge, Gervase Markham and others and dedicated to members of the nobility in the hope of patronage. Many of the poems were good but they were works of imagination, lovely musically ingenious poetical fictions. Shakespeare's sonnets were not. The poems in his sequence were different. The majority of those 'sugred sonnets' were probably written within two or three brief years, they were personal, and they were unique. Neither in the title nor in any of the sonnets was there one personal name. Every participant, whether man or woman, was a mystery – especially the woman. She was his prize both in mind and in body but she remained nameless in every one of the sonnets about her. Marchette Chute wrote:

> Many attempts have been made to interpret the sonnets as autobiographical, and no doubt the desire to discover something about Shakespeare's private life is legitimate enough. But each reader finds a different story in the sonnets and reaches a different conclusion, and perhaps it is just as well. No single theory can safely be formed about them, and in the meantime William Shakespeare remains securely in possession of his privacy.[11]

A great obstacle in any attempt to find her is to know the original order of the sonnets. It is probably not the one known today. It could be compared to a shelf of books that once was neatly arranged by date of publication. The shelf collapsed. The scattered books were replaced haphazardly by someone ignorant to the original sequence. Similarly for Shakespeare's sonnets the dozens of handwritten sheets of paper, a haphazard mélange, was put together by a well-meaning printer attempting to make a sensible sequence out of apparent contradictions. The poet, W. H. Auden, understood:

> The first thing which is obvious after reading through the one hundred and fifty-four sonnets as we have them, is that they are not in any kind of planned sequence. The only semblance of order is a division into two unequal heaps. Nor in the two sets considered separately is it possible to believe that the order is chronological.[12]

There are seemingly logical groups in the sonnets. Some at the beginning urge a young man to marry. Later, others are addressed to a 'Fair Friend'. They are followed by a short group about a rival poet. It is only near the end of the series that the Dark Lady poems appear – almost thirty of them. That woman, whether physically dark-skinned or just dark of hair or merely dark in the poet's mind, is a mystery. Whoever she was, she ensnared the poet with her loveliness, teased him, tempted him, then tortured him with wanton infidelity, scornfully flaunting her successful seduction of his young friend.

Who she was, her name, her occupation, even her nationality has been argued for more than four hundred years. Brown called her 'The Embarrassing Phantom'.[13] A guesswork of women 'identified' as that elusive siren has included two former maids of honour to the queen, Mary Fitton and Lucy Morgan. Others who have been 'proved' to be the Dark Lady include Jane Davenant, wife of an Oxford innkeeper; the lovely, well-born Penelope Devereux, later Lady Rich; Jacqueline Field, French wife of a printer; Mrs Florio, Christian name uncertain, wife of John Florio the famous Italian scholar and lexicographer; Emilia Lanier, a skilful player of the virginals, daughter of an Italian family of musicians; Marie Mountjoy, wife of a wig-maker of expensively fashionable hair-pieces. Shakespeare lodged with her family in Silver Street, Cripplegate in the north of London.

Whether any of them can be identified as Shakespeare's Dark Lady is considered individually in the chapters that follow. To that eight, however, less critical enthusiasts have added three extremely unlikely dark ladies: Winifred Burbage, wife of Shakespeare's leading actor; a non-existent Jane Daniel, formerly Jeanne de Ketulle, a woman as insubstantial as the anagram that 'proves' her existence; and Elizabeth Tudor, the red-headed Queen of England. Both 'Jane Daniel' and Queen Elizabeth can be ignored as whimsies fashioned from over-imaginative minds.[14]

Even Winifred Burbage has only been put forward unenthusiastically, a shrug of the shoulders, little more than, 'if not them, then what about her?' Not much is known about her other than that she was the wife of a great Elizabethan actor. Born around 1579 Winifred was an almost elderly spinster of twenty-three when she married Richard Burbage, the celebrated star of Shakespeare's theatrical company. He was famous for his realistic performances that enthralled audiences. When he died in 1619 one of his epitaphs read simply but poignantly: 'Exit Burbage'. His widow was the only executrix of his will. A witness was Richard Robinson, a former boy actor. Winifred Burbage married him on 31 October 1622 and they lived in Shoreditch until her death thirty years later. With so little known about her, her appearance, manner, her social life, she must remain an 'outsider' as Shakespeare's Dark Lady,[15] even Kerrigan complains:

No editor can tell you ... how many Wills the dark lady is supposed to have slept with. Nor can he tell the reader the name of that dark lady and whether she was 'Mary Fitton, or Lucy Negro, Jacqueline Field, Emilia Lanier, or, to back an outsider, Mistress Winifred Burbage.[16]

Shakespeare tells us that, besides deceiving him and ensnaring his friend, she has been unfaithful to her 'bed-vow', from which we might perhaps infer that she was the wife of some rich City merchant, one of the 'beauties of the Cheap and the wives of Lombard Street' whose vanity, promiscuity and taste for fashion scandalized Elizabethan critics.[17]

Perhaps she was a lady, or a maid of honour, or a Londoner's wife, or a trollop. The challenge is to find the lady. It has even been doubted that there ever was a real, human Dark Lady rather than an evocation of Shakespeare's creative mind. The intensely personal tone of the sonnets argues against such pessimism as Sonnet 127, the first of the Dark Lady group, shows:

In the old age black was not counted fair,
Or if it were, it bore not beauty's name;
But now is black beauty's successive heir,
And beauty slander'd with a bastard shame:
For since each hand hath put on nature's power,
Fairing the foul with art's false borrow'd face,
Sweet beauty hath no name, not holy bower,
But is profaned, if not lives in disgrace.
Therefore my mistress' eyes are raven black,
Her eyes so suited, and they mourners seem
At such who, not born fair, no beauty lack,
Slandering creation with a false esteem:
Yet so they mourn, becoming of their woe,
That every tongue says beauty should look so.

That Dark Lady was his triumphant prize both in mind and in body but she remained unnamed in every one of the many sonnets about her.

The short fourteen-line poems known as sonnets were created in fourteenth-century Italy. Their greatest exponent was Petrarch who arranged their lines into two parts, the octet of eight lines asking a question being followed by a six-line sestet providing an answer. His sonnets idealised 'Laura', the unattainably married Laura de Noves of Carpentras near Avignon. In 1325 she wed a gloomy husband, Hugh de Sade. It was an unfortunate surname centuries later made infamous by the libidinous Marquis de Sade whose sexual perversions added the word 'sadistic' to modern vocabulary. Many years before him the innocent Laura had died in 1348, probably of the Black Death if not of marital boredom and dejection.

Over the years the sonnet became popular in Europe, reaching England in the early sixteenth century. Fine poets such as Sir Thomas Wyatt changed the complex Italian structure of the sonnet, merging the octet/sestet scheme into a continuous fourteen lines with an easier rhyme scheme of abab cdcd efef gg. Those lines were written in iambic pentameters: a driving beat of the iambic di-da, di-da sound, ten light/heavy syllables of a rhythm that fell naturally into English speech patterns. It was the form in which Shakespeare wrote:

> When forty winters shall besiege thy brow,
> And dig deep trenches in thy beauty's field ... Sonnet 2, 1-2.

He followed that pattern in all but three of the 154 sonnets of his sequence. Sonnet 99 had fifteen lines. Sonnet 126 was written in rhyming couplets. Sonnet 145 was unique. It was probably very early, its lines not written in pentameters of ten syllables, but in short octameters of eight syllables. The differences suggest that Shakespeare's sonnet sequence was not a true succession of poems written one after another but a 'compilation' of poems composed at different times, some of them many years apart, that were finally put together in a readable series but probably not the one composed by the poet. There have been attempts to assemble that original order of composition whose sonnets may have begun as early as 1581 and ended as late as the beginning of the seventeenth century, some twenty years or more. It is probable, however, that the majority were written in a short period of three or four years.

The original order of composition is unknown. So is the

number of alterations and cancellations to which that order was subjected over a decade or more after 1600.[18] Thorpe's pirated edition of 1609, the first to be printed in the sonnets' entirety, has been accepted by scholars as the basis for research into the poems. For the entire sequence a facsimile of its original layout and typography has been provided in Giroux.[19] It is almost certainly not in the order that Shakespeare had written.

Sonnet 145 provides a good example of the problems confronting today's reader. It is unique among the long sequence in its construction and use of language as its first version shows:

> Those lips that Louves owne hand did make
> Breath'd forth the sound that said I hate,
> To me that languisht for her sake:
> But when she saw my wofull state,
> Straight in her heart did mercie come,
> Chiding that tongue that euer sweet,
> Was vsede in giuing gentle dome:
> And tought it thus a new to greete:
> I hate she alterd with an end,
> That follow'd it as gentle day,
> Doth follow night who like a fiend
> From heauen to hell is flowne away.
> I hate, from hate away she threw,
> And sau'd my life saying not you.

But today's scholarly version in modern spelling, punctuation and inverted commas reads rather differently:

> Those lips that love's own hand did make,
> Breathed forth the sound that said 'I hate',
> To me, that languished for her sake;
> But when she saw my woeful state
> Straight in her heart did mercy come,
> Chiding that tongue that ever sweet,
> Was used in giving gentle doom:

And taught it thus anew to greet:
'I hate' she altered with an end
That followed it as gentle day
Doth follow night, who like a fiend
From heaven to hell is flown away.
'I hate', from 'hate' away she threw,
And saved my life, saying 'not you'.

Termed 'a pretty trifle', and 'the slightest of sonnets', using 'you' rather than the 'thou' of the Dark Lady poems it may have been composed as early as 1581–2. This was long before Shakespeare reached London and met his fateful woman of the night. If that is correct then years later someone placed that old sonnet very ingeniously between two others in the later sequence, linking 145's own 'fiend' and 'hell' with Sonnet 144's 'fiend', 'heaven', 'hell'; and its own 'gentle day doth follow night' with Sonnet 146's , 'afterlife'. That is an interesting poetical technicality. Far more significant in evidence of Shakespeare's emotional life are the sonnet's final two lines:

'I hate', from 'hate' away she threw,
And saved my life, saying 'not you'.

Line 13's, 'hate away', a line written without inverted commas in Thorpe, I hate, from hate away, could be a clumsy pun, 'hate–way', meaning 'Hathaway'. But line 14's 'And saved ...' could also read 'Anne saved my life' by releasing Shakespeare from his woeful state of being trapped by his pledges to two different young women, both of them named Anne. If so, the 'Anne' of line 14 might have been an entirely different woman, not the historical Anne Hathaway but the elusive Anne Whateley.

1

Anne Whateley: Wraith or Rival to Anne Hathaway?

Sigh no more, ladies, sigh no more,
Men were deceivers ever:
William Shakespeare, *Much Ado about Nothing*, Act II, 3, 50-1.

Fate has many faces. Two, perhaps three, women changed Shakespeare's life. One from Shottery near Stratford-upon-Avon became his wife. Years later another in London taunted him, scarred his heart. The third, near Stratford, may never have existed, no more than the faintest of names in fading ink. So it is thought. It is unproved.

In 1897 H. G. Wells wrote his short story, *The Invisible Man*. Three hundred years earlier there was an unwritten story of another invisible woman, the myth who became known as Anne Whateley. She disappeared, lost in clouds of wishful disbelief. In a recent collection of scholarly essays by a score of contributors about Shakespeare's sonnets not once in over 500 pages was there any reference to her, not even in the index. Any possibility that Sonnet 145 might refer to her was unconsidered. Instead, the poem, 'perhaps written in youth', was considered to be a tribute to another woman, Anne Hathaway of Shottery, who became his wife.[1]

History has many 'buts'. But Anne Whateley, daughter of a family whose name was widespread in the English Midlands, may have been a real woman who lived a few miles from

Shottery in the village of Temple Grafton. But that 'may have been' has been transformed into 'never was' by defenders of Anne Hathaway who refuse to accept that their lady may once have had a competitor. Those defenders erased Anne Whateley from Shakespeare's life, transforming her into nothing more than a misspelling, a calligraphic hiccough.[2] In place of that awkward hallucination Michael Wood proposed another woman who helped Shakespeare: 'He was vulnerable. Anne [Hathaway] was twenty-six and knew the world. Reading between the lines, she would be the rock upon whom he relied through his life, supporting his career in London'.[3] Perhaps.

Half-truths muddle the story of William Shakespeare and his wife, Anne Hathaway. Their apparently happy marriage is haunted by the suspected phantom. Most scholarly biographies of Shakespeare do not mention her. Others dismiss her as an aberration, the 'Elizabethan equivalent of a typing error', a spectral doppelgänger rather than a flesh-and-blood person who once lived and loved.[4]

So consistently has her existence been doubted that it has become a 'fact' that Shakespeare had mistakenly been associated with a fiction, a non-woman, a slip of the quill. Sceptics could be mistaken. A document exists that contradicts their scepticism. Late in November 1582 there was marital confusion for clerks in Worcester. On two successive days seventeen-year-old William Shakespeare of Stratford-upon-Avon was recorded by the city's registrar as a man to be married to two quite different Warwickshire young women, one from Temple Grafton, and then, with a different name, a second from Shottery. The youthful Shakespeare personally registered only the first. Rene Weis wrote:

> For reasons that are not now fully understood the church authorities in Worcester accepted a bond for a bride who had two separate names and two different addresses. All sorts of skulduggery has been suggested to account for this ... In fact, the explanation seems to be the simple one of clerical incompetence.

That was the confusion. On Tuesday 27 November 1582, the Bishop of Worcester's Episcopal Registrar granted a special marriage licence with banns for one day only instead of the traditional three between *'item eodem die similie emanavit licensia inter Willelmum Shaxpere et Annam whateley de Temple grafton'*, between William Shakespeare and Anne Whateley of Temple Grafton.[5] Customarily there would have been readings of the banns on three successive Sundays but by Tuesday 27 November, there was only one available Sunday left after St Andrew's Day on Friday the 30th. That day was Advent Sunday on the second of December after which the church's marriage season ended.

The haste for a special licence is usually explained in the belief that a respectable young woman, Anne Hathaway of Shottery, having been made pregnant by William Shakespeare, understandably wanted to be married as quickly as possible. There could be a different explanation. That first registration of the marriage banns on Tuesday 27 November, may have been a desperate attempt by the youth, William Shakespeare, to be married to another Anne, Anne Whateley of Temple Grafton. Entirely on his own that young man made a desperate visit to the registrar in Worcester, an impatient twenty-five mile ride from Stratford through Alcester along unmade roads, once Roman, now long neglected tracks rutted but unchallenging except for the steep Red Hill at Binton three miles out of Stratford just a mile east of Temple Grafton. A further seven miles brought the rider to a steepish rise at Dunnington Heath. After that it was an easy canter to Worcester. On horseback in late November with eight hours of daylight a man could be there and back to Stratford in a day even with the inevitable tedious legal delays in Worcester. That was on Tuesday 27 November 1582.

Immediate pre-marital chaos developed. The very next day, Wednesday 28 November two Warwickshire farmers, Fulk Sandells and John Richardson, husbandmen of Stratford, *'Fulconem Sandells de Straftford in Comitatu warwicensi agricolum et Johannem Rychardson ibidem agricolem ...'*, went to the same registrar in Worcester to stand surety for the legality of a marriage between Anne Hathaway of Stratford and William Shakespeare, leaving a deposit of £40 of 'legal English money'.[6]

Fulk Sandells, a Shottery farmer, represented John Shakespeare, William's father. John Richardson, a witness of Anne Hathaway's will, purportedly represented Anne's father. Whether John Shakespeare was aware of Sandell's highhanded action is unknown. There are reasons for doubt. Forty pounds was a huge sum, twice the yearly income of a Stratford schoolmaster and eight times the wages of a London clothier. More than ten years later the by-then well-to-do actor and playwright, William Shakespeare, was recorded as paying only £60 for his fine house, New Place, in Stratford-upon-Avon. Anne's own dowry for her 'day of marriage', left by her father before his death, was £6 13s 4d, ten silver marks. It was a considerable amount. Some years later Shakespeare as a novice actor in London was paid only ten shillings, half a sovereign weekly. Forty pounds was a lot of money.[7]

Sandells' and Richardsons's money was payment for a shotgun marriage. Anne Hathway was with child. Sandells was very much a Shottery man, being the supervisor of Richard Hathaway's will, Anne's father. Two years later he was to go to Chancery to debate the claim that the Earl of Warwick had made about some of the land in the parish. He certainly would have defended the cause of a local girl like Anne Hathaway. Anthony Holden:

It was a common story. It is estimated that a third of all Tudor women were pregnant when they married ... Official homilies against 'whoredom and uncleanliness' were read on Sundays in every parish church when there was no sermon ... 'Great swarms of vice, outrageous seas of adultery, whoredom, fornication and uncleanliness have overflowed the whole world, so much so that this vice among many is counted no sin at all, but rather a pastime, a dalliance and but a touch of youth; not rebuked but winked at; not punished but laughed at'. For William and Anne their affair was 'a touch of youth'.[8]

To a working-class Warwickshire girl Shakespeare was a desirable young man. He was physically presentable, he came from a good family, his father had been a prominent Stratford citizen, and his son had been well educated at the local grammar school. His prospects were good. He also had the gift of a honeyed tongue.

Fate spins tangled cloth. The young Shakespeare was twice registered to marry an Anne but the second was the emphatically 'with-child' Hathaway not the first 'without' Anne Whateley. Ironically, the Hathaway 'Anne' had been christened 'Agnes'.[9] Sandells and Richardson ensured that the bishop and his officials were indemnified from any action or suit arising from the grant of this special licence ' ... by reason of any precontract'.[10]

Similar bonds were common on payment of a fee to a bishop's commissary. It expedited marriage while protecting the clergy from any breach of canonical law but it was an uncommon legal loophole rarely used by ordinary folk. And the bond itself was unusual. A normal contract stated 'only on consent of parents', and in the case of an 'infant bridegroom', such as a youth like Shakespeare not yet eighteen years old, formal parental consent was essential. But, instead, that particular bond asked only for the consent of 'friends'. There was no mention of Shakespeare's father. Only the two bondsmen – representing the Hathaway family – were named. Neither the father nor the mother of Shakespeare was mentioned in the bond. It appears to have been entered without their consent or knowledge.[11] The bond read:

> that Willm Shagskere on thone ptie, and Anne Hathwey of Stratford in the Dioces of Worcester maiden may lawfully solemnize mirony together and in the same afterward remain and continew like man and wife according to the lawes in that behalf prouided ... And also if the said William do upon his owne proper costes and expenses defend & save harmles the right Reverend father in god Lord John bishop of Worcester and his offycers for Licencing them the said William and Anne be married

togither with once asking of the bannses of matrimony between them ...[12]

That was probably in November 1583. There is no record of where the marriage between William Shakespeare and Anne Hathaway took place. The law demanded that they should marry in a home parish and both came from Stratford. For some reason they rejected the town and the marriage is not listed in St James, the parish church of Stratford. But Anne Hathaway, not Anne Whateley, did become Shakespeare's wife. He was just over eighteen and a half years old, she was eight years older. They may have rejected Worcester because of its fervent Protestant bishop, John Whitgift. And they may also have disliked Stratford for the same reason, its priest, Henry Haycroft, an equally zealous Protestant. Religion divided Elizabethan England. There were local rumours that John Shakespeare was a covert Catholic. It was believed that many others of his family also accepted that dangerous papist religion.

Despite the absence of evidence it is possible, but unlikely, that William and Anne married in Worcester. It could be significant that in the church of St Martin's parish the two leaves of the register 'covering the likely date of the marriage had been cut out: an unscrupulous collector may have snatched this prize. The relic-hunter is sometimes a devotee whose devotion carried him into theft and vandalism'.[13] Since the eighteenth century Shakespearian forgeries have been almost commonplace, and pilfering of pages for copying, even from a church, are not unknown. Thieves existed. Two notorious for their misdeeds, were the mid-eighteenth century father and son, the Irelands, persistent stealers of documents. The father, Samuel, simply plundered for souvenirs. In Stratford-upon-Avon he was duped into buying 'the very oak chair in which the poet used to sit holding Ann upon his knee'. More profitably, the son William-Henry, used historical manuscripts as material on which to write his incompetent forgeries.[14]

If William and Anne did not marry in Worcester then, in special circumstances, a different parish from Stratford was permissible, 'for reasonable security', if the woman was pregnant, or for difficult social differences, even because of cost. Two possible nearby parishes were Luddington only two miles south of Stratford or Temple Grafton five miles to the west. Local folklore claimed that they were married in Luddington on the north bank of the Avon. Thomas Hunt, its curate, was also the schoolmaster in Stratford where Shakespeare had been a pupil. Years later Judith Shakespeare, his daughter, used to love walking in the fields by the river 'and', wrote Arthur Mee in his Warwickshire, 'there can be no doubt that not once nor twice but many times she must have been here with the poet and her mother'.

In 1862 a villager, Mrs Dyke, said that when she was a girl an old lady told her that Shakespeare had married there and that the woman 'had seen the ancient tome in which it was registered'. It 'was in the possession of a Mrs Pickering, who had been housekeeper to Mr Coles, the last curate, and one cold day had burnt the register to boil a kettle.[15] The old church has gone, only one stone remaining, being rebuilt in 1871–2 in an unremarkable Early English style, but at its new doorway is a slab stating that the marriage did take place there.

The absence of any entry for Shakespeare's marriage in Worcester, Stratford or Luddington leaves the possibility, a very ironical one, if Anne Whateley of Temple Grafton did exist and was still alive that William Shakespeare and Anne Hathaway got married in her village church. Shakespeare's family with its suggested Catholic tendencies may have wished it. There were ancestral Catholic affinities with Temple Grafton as its place-name recorded, 'the settlement of the Knights Templar by the small wood'. The village of Victorian houses today has fine views towards the Cotswolds. It was nicknamed 'hungry' because of its poor, dry soil over a bed of thirsty limestone.

In 1586 there was a puritanical report about the village's vicar, 'old John Frith', who had remained faithful to the old religion having been a Catholic priest in Mary's time. Maybe because of his age and obscurity he had escaped persecution though:

an old priest & Unsound in religion ... he can neither prech nor read well, his chiefest trade is to cure hawkes yt are hurt or diseased, for which purpose manie doe usuellie repaire to him.

He was a Catholic, a hard-drinking one, but too unimportant to bother with. There is an irony in his interest in hawks. To make their way about the country less suspicious Jesuits sometimes disguised themselves as hawkers. Puritanical condemnation was understandable. Only two years earlier in 1584, almost exactly the time when Shakespeare married, Frith was 'reported for solemnising marriages illicitly outside the times laid down by the Protestant Church and without proper reading of the banns. So there must be a strong suspicion that Frith was resorted to because he bent the rules and performed the old ceremonies. Anne and William – or more likely their families – probably wanted a marriage in the traditional English style, ending with a Roman mass'.[16]

But wherever the Shakespeares married it was not a promising beginning for the husband and wife. Anne Hathaway was eight years older than him, twenty-six years of age, almost 'on the-shelf'. She had been willingly seduced and in August 1582, she was pregnant. Nine months later on 26 May 1583, the Stratford register recorded, 'C' [christened] 'Susanna daughter to William Shakespeare'.[17] For a young man it was not a good beginning to a marriage. Many years later in his play, *A Winter's Tale*, Shakespeare was to have a shepherd mutter:

I would there were no age between ten and three-and-twenty, or that youth would sleep out the rest, for there is nothing in the between but getting wenches with child, wronging the ancientry, stealing, fighting.

And in *Twelfth Night* the Duke advised Viola, 'Then let thy love be younger than thyself, Or thy affection cannot hold the bent'.[18]

A local legend, or whispered gossip, said that Anne Whateley had been a maidservant to Anne Hathaway but:

while courting the mistress Shakespeare fell in love with the maid. The details of the earlier proposal and the reasons for the sudden change are quite obscure – although Anne Hathaway's pregnancy was presumably not without relevance.[19]

William and Anne Shakespeare remained man and wife for twenty-eight years, she living in Stratford-upon-Avon, he almost always in London, until his return home and death in 1616. She died seven years later on 6 August 1623, aged sixty-seven, forty-one years after the pre-marital predicament. She was buried unobtrusively at Stratford in Holy Trinity Church below the wall-mounted effigy of her husband. Her grave lies on the floor behind the altar-rail of the restored chancel. Her stone names her only as 'Mistress Shakespeare'.[20] That is her known history, the near-anonymous Anne Hathaway who married William Shakespeare. It does not resolve the question of another woman, whether a so-called 'Anne Whateley' ever existed rather than a clerical mispelling for 'Anne Hathaway'.

To her own satisfaction at least Charlotte Stopes resolved those considerable contradictions between the conflicting claims of 'Annam whateley' and Shakespeare's wife:

> Will set out for the licence alone, as bridegrooms were often wont to do, when they could afford the expense of a special licence. He might give his own name, and that of his intended wife, at a temporary address. The clerk made an error in the spelling, which might have been corrected; but meanwhile discovered that Shakespeare was under age, was acting without his parents – that the bride was not in her own home, and that no marriage settlement was in the air. No risk might be run by an official in such a case; the licence was stayed; sureties must be found for a penalty in case of error. So poor Will would have to find, in post-haste, the nearest friends he could find to trust him and his story. And who so likely to ask as Fulk Sandells and John Richardson, friends of the Hathaways – the one supervisor, and the other witness to the will of Anne's father, Richard ... They were both 'good men' in the financial sense.[21]

It is too glib. Stopes was one of the first of many critics eager to erase 'Anne Whateley' from the human race as a misunderstanding, a clerk's incompetence, a blunder, a nothing. In reality she may have lived, an Anne Whateley who lived not in Shottery nor Stratford-upon-Avon but in the more distant Temple Grafton, a young woman with whom Shakespeare had fondled and bedded, and who, in the equivocal two last lines, 13 and 14, of his Sonnet 145 said, 'not you', releasing him, giving freedom to a youthful seducer who had flirted and made love to two girls, got one with child, the Anne from the village of Shottery, and was now desperately looking for a way to escape.

The significance of that fourteenth line, 'And saved my life', lies in Tudor speech patterns. 'And' was customarily pronounced 'An' so that 'And saved my life', saying 'not you', can be read as 'Anne saved my life', saying 'not you' to Shakespeare. But Anne Hathaway did marry William Shakespeare when she was already three months pregnant by him. Desperate for respectability she would never have said, 'not you!' Instead, it is probable that the 'Anne' of the last line was not Anne Hathaway but the other Anne, the no-longer ethereal Anne Whateley.

Ardent, impulsive and unrestrained William Shakespeare had seduced two young unmarried women, Anne Whateley of Temple Grafton and Anne Hathaway of Shottery, made love to both, favoured the first and younger, and proposed marriage to her which explains that first licence to a Whateley rather than a Hathaway. Hathaway's family stepped in. They ignored Anne Whateley and the Worcester licence, and compelled Shakespeare to marry Hathaway because she was three months pregnant.

Family honour and family disgrace have been unhappy bedfellows ever since biblical times. The only surviving evidence of that three-sided entanglement is the recorded actions of Sandells and Richardson and the Shakespeare-Hathaway marriage certificate. It is all Hathaway. There is no Whateley except for that first entry in the Worcester records. It exists but Hathawayites eagerly explain it away. The simplest of 'solutions' and the one generally accepted, is that 'Whateley' was a misspelling for 'Hathaway'. Opponents of a real-life 'other woman' argue that 'Anne Whateley' was just a clerical slip by an overworked clerk who had been dealing with a long running case involving another Whateley on the same day, a William Whateley of Crowle who was involved in a long-prolonged tithe dispute.

It is feasible. It would have been easy to mistake 'Whateley' for 'Hathaway'. But however slipshod the clerk it would not explain the substitution of 'Temple Grafton' for 'Shottery'. Personal surnames could have been confused but not place-names on successive pages in the Worcester Register. Temple Grafton could not be a mistake for Shottery. Shottery was only half a mile west of Stratford whereas Temple Grafton was a full five miles west. Despite the almost universal doubts of Shakespearian scholars Anne Whateley may have been a real young woman rather than a misheard spelling of a surname by an inattentive scribbler. She may not have been the hypothetical 'nothing', a mythical White Lady to haunt his dreams. Quite differently she could be imagined as a delightful Warwickshire girl who enraptured Shakespeare some years before the nightmare of his Dark Lady in London. To dismiss her as the creation of an inattentive clerk may do her an injustice. In his *Women in Shakespeare's Life*, Ivor Brown argued:

> Now however sleepy a clerk may have become during the course of his day's penmanship and its refreshment intervals, it is extremely unlikely that he would transliterate Temple Grafton into Stratford. He might, let us admit, muddle Hathaway into Whateley: the letters are nearly the same in each word. He might have been thus careless, though it is a larger and less likely error than altering Elcock into Edgcock or confusing a couple called Baker and Barbar. What is much less credible is that a clerk could confuse two such wholly different names as those of Stratford and Temple Grafton. If there were any known connection between the Hathaway family and Temple Grafton, the affair would be more explicable on the lines of clerical error. But there is not.

I am inclined to believe that there was an Anne Whateley of Temple Grafton and that she was beaten on the post by Anne Hathaway of Stratford (which included Shottery). The latter lady had the stronger claim and powerful friends. The suspicion that the young man after an 'affair' at Shottery, had lost his heart elsewhere, would give further cause for the haste with which the Hathaway champions descended, money in hand, upon Worcester. It may sound like melodrama to suggest that when Anne Hathaway heard of a rival in Temple Grafton and of William's riding to Worcester, the registral centre of the area, she sent her friends in rapid pursuit, so that the entry for licence on one day was followed by the bond of the next. But melodramas are occasionally realised in life and one has to do a great deal of unsatisfactory explaining in order to reduce poor Miss Whateley of Temple Grafton to the dim, sad status of a shadow born of a misprint.[22]

Such desperate, almost deranged defence of Anne Hathaway and the destruction of Anne Whatley are unnecessary. Both women may have lived. But the insistence that the Whateley woman never existed has demanded almost hysterical arguments about Temple Grafton. Anne Hathaway, it is argued, apparently fled from prying eyes and gossip to Temple Grafton 'because it was her mother's village'. It is desperate speculation. 'Apparently' could be changed to 'it would be convenient if she had gone to'. There is not one word anywhere stating that Anne's mother had lived in Temple Grafton. Ironically, it is very probable that Anne Whateley's mother did live there. There is neither whisper nor whisker of proof to support the guesswork about the Hathaway connection. Instead, there are many doubts.[23]

The sometimes inaccurate and opinionated Mrs Charlotte Carmichael Stopes was one of the first of many critics eager to erase 'Anne Whateley' from the human race as a misheard name, a mistake. But that 'blunder' may be today's wishful thinking 'because the Bishop's Registrar is a neat, fair copy written up later from notes or from files of loose documents and not on the actual day when the licence was issued'. It contained the surname 'Whateley' because that was the name that had been recorded.[24]

Despite scholarly scepticism Anne Whateley probably did live, a person rather than a misheard spelling of a surname by an inattentive scribbler. She may not have been a wraith, a mythical White Lady to haunt Shakespeare's uneasy dreams, but a delightful young woman who had enraptured him in the Warwickshire countryside before his much later nightmare of the Dark Lady in the meandering London streets. Temple Grafton was a short ride on a horse. Even without a mount a young man, could walk the five miles easily, eagerly when there was an alluring and acquiescent young female at the end of them.

All three surnames, Hathaway, Shakespeare, Whateley, were widespread in the Midlands. In the sixteenth century the Shakespeare name was familiar in Warwickshire. Two Shakespeares were known as early as 1369: a felon in Coventry, another, an Adam, in Temple Balsall. In the first half of the sixteenth century there were at least sixteen Shakespeares in Warwickshire and between 1570 and 1616 no fewer than four William Shakespeares were living at Rowington twelve miles north of Stratford. They may have been related to their famous namesake. Both names, 'Hathaway' and 'Whateley', were commonplace in Warwickshire and neighbouring counties. Despite the wishful thinking of modern-day anti-Whateleys 'Whateley' did not have to be a misspelling of 'Hathaway'.

Shakespeare may have may have met Anne Whateley in Stratford. The name was common in the district and there was a prosperous family of Whateleys in the town. 'Whateley' was a well-known Warwickshire surname. One of them, George Whateley, who died in 1593, was a prominent Stratford wool draper wealthy enough to have a house in Henley Street with glass windows in the hall, the parlour and the upper chamber. He also had two brothers who were well-hidden Catholic priests. There are considerable beliefs that the Shakespeares themselves were closet Catholics. They may even have met those surreptitious Whateleys.[25]

That second Anne, Anne Whateley of Temple Grafton, may have encouraged a personable and imaginative young man to enjoy her arms. Promises can be easily forgotten. As Shakespeare was to write in his early Sonnet 151, 'Love is too young to know what conscience is'. And enjoyable flirtation can evolve into serious love – explaining those two frantic days at the end of November 1582. Sexually aroused young men yield to desire but, when satisfied and scared of the possible consequence, blame the woman for her weakness in not resisting him. Years later in his Hamlet Shakespeare understood the dishonesty and the contradiction:

> Alack, and fie for shame!
> Young men will do't, if they come to't.
> By cock, they are to blame.
> Quoth she, 'Before you tumbled me,
> You promised me to wed'.
> 'So would I ha'done, by yonder sun,
> An thou hadst not come to my bed'.[26]

The woman could have been either of the Annes. The evidence is fragile but it seems that the youthful William Shakespeare had flirted with two attractive young spinsters, Anne Whateley of Temple Grafton and Anne Hathaway of Shottery, making love to both but preferring the first and younger. Impulsively he proposed marriage. That the first November licence of 1582 in Worcester was to Anne Whateley, not Anne Hathaway, suggests that it was Miss Whateley whom Shakespeare wanted as his wife. Youth may propose – adults dispose. Hathaway's family stepped in. They ignored Anne Whateley and the first Worcester licence. Instead, ruthlessly highhanded, they took out a second licence, and compelled Shakespeare to marry the three-month-with-child Anne Hathaway.[27]

It was irrevocable. It was irreversible but not necessarily desirable. There was to be a marriage but possibly not one that Shakespeare had intended. A poem that he wrote may hold the truth. Its lines are an Elizabethan hall of mirrors changing from truth to deception as the reader wishes. It was his Sonnet 145, 'Those lips that love's own hand did make', perhaps his very first. It is equivocal. It can be read by Hathawayites as a husband's statement of a happy marriage. Conversely, believers in an Anne Whateley see the poem as an expression of gratitude from Shakespeare that the young woman from Temple Grafton had unselfishly released him from his oath of allegiance to her. The meaning of the sonnet can be taken as one's preference suggests. Whose lips? Whose mercy? Who said, 'not you'?

> Those lips that Love's own hand did make
> Breathed forth the sound that said 'I hate'
> To me that languished for her sake.
> But when she saw my woeful state,
> Straight in her heart did mercy come
> Chiding that tongue that ever sweet
> Was used in giving gentle doom,
> And taught it thus anew to greet:
> 'I hate' she altered with an end
> That followed it as gentle day
> Doth follow night, who, like a fiend,
> From heaven to hell is flown away:
> 'I hate' from hate away she threw,
> And saved my life, saying – 'not you'.

Sonnet 145 is different from the majority of sonnets in the much later sequence of 154 poems. It is the only one with lines of eight syllables rather than the customary ten. Two other sonnets also differ. Sonnet 99 has fifteen rather than fourteen lines. Sonnet 126 was written in rhyming couplets. All the other sonnets have fourteen lines of ten syllables with a rhyme-scheme of ababcdcdefefgg.

Sonnet 145 has been termed a madrigal rather than a sonnet, 'a pretty trifle', and 'the slightest of sonnets', with monosyllables predominating in it, 'a childish tripping movement that seems to make light of claims that the woman has power of life and death over him'; and 'many critics consider this poem so awful they'd like to see it excluded from the sequence, but it's an amusing little curiosity'.[28] It was probably composed around 1582 and is likely to be the earliest of all Shakespeare's published poems. There have been distinguished disagreements about its worth. William Wordsworth considered that 'with this key Shakespeare unlocked his heart'. Robert Browning disagreed: 'Did Shakespeare? If so, the less Shakespeare he'. Germaine Greer added:

> The syntax of this sonnet ... is so baggy that the sense becomes almost dropsical; fourteen lines are needed to convey a single fatuous idea that the beloved said 'I hate' (boo!) and then 'not thou' (hurrah!). The complex rhyme scheme closes each four-stressed-end-stopped line with a definite clunk. Amid this elephantine tiptoeing we arrive at 'hate-away' which has been interpreted by the Shakespearian cryptologists as Hathaway', which goes as near to prove as anything does in these cloudy regions that the poem is about Ann [sic] Hathaway, if not addressed to her. If it is, then according to her husband, Ann Hathaway's heart was merciful, her tongue ever sweet, and her judgement gentle.[29]

That is one interpretation of Sonnet 145, and one that is generally accepted. It is a poem of gratitude. William Shakespeare wrote it to record the kindness of the woman from Shottery who had agreed to marry him. He underlined that benevolence by including her name in the poem, the thirteenth line's 'hate away' being a clumsy pun on the name Hathaway which would have been pronounced 'hat-away' in Tudor times. Perhaps.

There is a different interpretation and a more plausible one. Sonnet 145 can more simply be read as a memory of relief and gratitude to Anne Whateley who released him from his vows when he told her of the other woman's pregnancy. The clumsy poem combines thanks for that release and regret that he had lost his real love. It was not a romantic offering to Anne Hathaway. It makes the sonnet not about a joyful marriage to Anne Hathaway but about the regretted loss of Anne Whateley.

It was possibly written in the dying weeks of 1582. It is a sonnet of bitter resentment describing the despair of being forced apart, rage at the hold Anne Hathaway had over Shakespeare, the hate felt by the woman abandoned by her lover. 'I hate'. She swore. But her hatred diminished and changed to pity as she realised that Shakespeare was trapped in an unwanted marriage. She saw him woeful, helpless, languishing in his realisation that she could never be his wife because he was shackled to her rival, Anne Hathaway. Then there was sorrow. And regret. And resignation. She released him from his promises. And in those drab months he remembered:

'I hate' from hate away she threw,
And saved my life, saying – 'not you'.

Sonnet 145 is not a love-poem to Anne Hathaway. It is an elegy for a lost love, a mourning for Anne Whateley. Many years later that young, immature poem was integrated into the long sonnet sequence, intelligently placed between Sonnet 144, 'Two loves I have of comfort and despair' with its devils, angel and hell, and Sonnet 146, 'Poor soul, the centre of my sinful earth', about death and afterlife. It was a clever interpolation of a very early poem. The placing is so satisfying that it may have been chosen by Shakespeare himself. There may be a deliberate irony in its position. Sonnets 144 and 146 are two of the twenty-six poems, numbers 127 to 152, concerning Shakespeare's later demon, the Dark Lady.

There is a final remark about Sonnet 145. 'It might not be too far-fetched to see the bad seeds of William Shakespeare's less-than-idyllic marriage in this very poem'.[30] There were three sonnets and there were three women in those sonnets but only one of those women, Anne Whateley, gave Shakespeare happiness.

There is an irony. Scholarly critics insist, almost demand, that such a delightful woman as Anne Whateley never lived.[31] As George Bernard Shaw observed, 'Critics, like other people, see what they look for, not what is actually before them'.

2

Ten 'Lost Years', 1582–1591

The very substance of the ambitious
Is merely the shadow of a dream.
William Shakespeare, *Hamlet*, II, 2, 149-50.

Life has its bleak periods. What records there are of the years following his enforced marriage suggest that they had not been good years for William Shakespeare. There was the marriage itself. There were several deaths of his sisters. And there had been a decline in his father's affairs. That once well-to-do distinguished citizen was now in debt, selling property and draining money from his wife's inheritance. There were also rumours that Shakespeare himself had been caught poaching deer from the nearby estate of a rich landowner. He was not yet entangled with his Dark Lady. That fateful meeting would be some years later in London.

Facts are few, fiction flourishes. Some fifty years after Shakespeare's death the ever-curious John Aubrey asked an old man whose son had known the playwright what that dramatist had been like. What he learned was that hybrid term, 'faction', some speckles of fact in a murky stew of fiction.

Mr. William Shakspear was borne at Stratford upon Avon in the county of Warwick. His father was a Butcher, and I have been told heretofore by some of the neighbours, that when he was a boy he exercised his father's Trade, but when he kill'd a Calfe he would doe it in a high style , and make a Speech ...

This William being inclined naturally to Poetry and acting, came to London, I guesse about 18, and was an Actor at one of the Play-houses and did acte exceedingly well ...

He began early to make essayes at Dramatique Poetry and acting, which at that time was every lowe; and his Playes tooke well.

He was a handsome, well-shap't man: very good company, and of a very readie and pleasant smoothe Witt'.

... Though, as Ben Johnson sayes of him, that he had little Latine and lesse Greek, He understood Latine pretty well; for he had been in his younger yeares a schoolmaster in the countrey.
from Mr ... Beeston.[1]

William Beeston who died in London at Shoreditch in 1682 had given Aubrey some gossipy snippets about Shakespeare that he had heard from his father, Christopher, who had acted with the Lord Chamberlain's Men and other companies including Queen Henrietta's. He would have met Shakespeare. But the snippets were unreliable. There were half-remembered stories of Shakespeare's boyhood as he worked with his father. They tittered that, 'When he was a boy he exercised his father's trade, but when he killed a calfe he would doe it in a high style, and make a speech'. There may be some truth in it as the lad cut and dressed the different animal skins, leathers of kid, lamb, suede, perhaps even chamois, and release his poetical imagination. It was not yet high poetry. There was no splendid evocation of:

O for a Muse of fire, that would ascend
The brightest heaven of invention,
A kingdom for a stage, princes to act
And monarchs to behold the swelling scene ...

Those words from *Henry V* would wait to be written for another twenty years but the rhymes and jingles that were created as

Shakespeare worked for his father were the forerunners of passages that were to astonish an audience, that 'clapper-clawed multitude', as Shakespeare's contemporary, John Webster, jeered.

Shakespeare's father had not been a butcher. He was a highly skilled glove-maker who had served a long apprenticeship. He made gloves and he prepared the skins for them being a skilled whittawer, a converter of skins into white leather, by soaking them in a solution of alum and salt. He also dabbled in wool and moneylending. His career had been ambitious but uneven. Moving from Snitterfield to live in Stratford he bought a house in Henley Street. Not many years later in 1558 he was fined for having a malodorous dung-hill outside in the street, the stench reeking from the rotting animal hides that had been discarded once the good leather had been cut from them.

But he was respected. A few years later he was one of the four town constables, although, being only semi-literate, he had to make his mark in the Minutes. But he became one of the two chamberlains in 1565, then one of the fourteen aldermen, then three years later a bailiff, the town's chief official like a modern mayor. It was during those twelve months of 1568–9, that as Stratford's bailiff he welcomed the companies of both the Queen's and the Lord Leicester's Men in the town's Guildhall.

Paradoxically – and prophetically – he was also prosecuted for usury, illicit wool dealings and charging interest on loans. By 1571 he was the chief alderman and in 1575 he was able to pay £40 for two houses in the town. But then his fortunes and his standing collapsed. Between 1568 and 1576 he had regularly attended council meetings. Then he stopped. Only once more, in 1582, did he appear, significantly the year of the Hathaway/Whateley marital contretemps. By that time John Shakespeare had serious financial problems. He owed money. He sold land, mortgaged his wife's inheritance at Wilmcote and was unable to redeem it. There was worse.

Even more serious in those strongly Protestant times in two Warwickshire lists of 1592 he was named with eight others of being a recusant, a Roman Catholic who refused to attend Church of England services even though it was a legal requirement. So few years after the brutal martyrdoms of Protestant bishops being burned at the stake in the Catholic reign of Mary Tudor it was a serious accusation. And one that was probably justified.

John Shakespeare died on 8 September 1601. A century and a half later in 1757 a bricklayer tiling the roof of Shakespeare's house in Henley Street found a six-leaf manuscript in the rafters. Although its first sheet was missing the document was recognisable as the hidden last Will and Testament of John Shakespeare who had clearly died in the Catholic faith.[2] In later years there were to be similar suspicions about the faith of his famous son.

There had been several earlier deaths, untimely ones of children, in the Shakespeare family. Infant mortality was high in Tudor England. A girl, Joan, was born and died in 1560. Margaret born in 1562 was dead a few months later in 1563. Anne, born in 1571 died aged eight in 1579. But a second Joan did survive into the seventeenth century. Many Midland children also died by accident. In 1569, in the Worcestershire village of Upton Warren the two-year old Jane Shaxpere, unrelated to the Stratford family, was picking flowers by a pond when she slipped and drowned. In mid-December ten years later, in the hamlet of Tiddington near Stratford a young spinster, Katherine Hamlet, fetching water from the Avon slipped, fell and died in the freezing river. Shakespeare was fifteen but he never forgot the scandal. There was local gossip of pregnancy and suicide and in January her indignant family had her exhumed. She had not been with child. On 11 February 1580, at Warwick an inquest jury decided that her death was not a suicide. It had been an accident.[3]

Years later in Shakespeare's tragedy, *Hamlet,* her surname and her sad death was remembered when the poet described the death of Ophelia drowning in a stream:

There is a willow grows aslant the brook ...
Therewith fantastic garlands did she make

Of crow-flowers, nettles, daisies, and long purples …
But our cold maids do dead men's fingers call them[4]

Shakespeare's personal family was more fortunate. On 26 May 1583 his daughter, Susanna was born. By theatrical coincidence it was the year when the Queen's Company was formed. Henry Carey, 2nd Lord Hunsdon, was to become its Lord Chamberlain twenty years later.

Two years after the birth of Susanna William Shakespeare and his wife, Anne, had twins. Judith and Hamnet were born in the 'dead of winter' 1585, and were baptised on the second of February. 'Hamnet' was an unusual Christian name, probably chosen as a pleasantry to the parents' friends, Hamnet and Judith Sadler, who became the twins' godparents. It may have been in memory of their births that Shakespeare was to write his 'twin' plays, *The Comedy of Errors* and, in particular, *Twelfth Night* where the twins happen to be a boy and a girl.

In real life there was tragedy rather than laughter. Hamnet died on 11 August 1596, only eleven years old. The burial register recorded *Hamnet, filius William Shakspere*. Shakespeare was not at the funeral. He was far from Stratford on tour with the Lord Chamberlain's Men in Kent.[5]

His daughter Susanna survived childhood but when she was twenty-two she and twenty others stood before the ecclesiastical court in Stratford accused of failing to attend church to receive communion on Easter Day 1605. To the Protestant churchmen she was a suspected 'cupboard' Catholic. To be suspected of papistry only a few months after the Gunpowder Plot was both reckless and dangerous. She protected herself. Within a year she had married a well-respected Puritan, Dr John Hall and eight months later she had given birth to Shakespeare's first grandchild, Elizabeth.[6]

Some twenty years earlier in the mid 1580s, his father penniless, Shakespeare was desperate for work. But there is no history. Between the baptism of his twins in 1585 and Robert Greene's 1592 attack on him as an upstart playwright in London there is no certainty about Shakespeare's whereabouts.

They are empty years for which there are only uncorroborated stories. He may have been a lawyer's clerk, work that would explain his knowledge of erudite legal terms. There was also speculation that Shakespeare had been a tutor to the son of the Catholic Houghton family in Lancashire. Suspicious minds muttered that he was directed there on the recommendation of his former Stratford schoolmaster, John Cottam, a man believed to a secret Roman Catholic. A story of about 1581, perhaps too early, states that Lancastrian tutor's name was 'William Shakeschafte', a feasible alternative for 'Shakespeare' in those years of haphazard spell-it-as-it-sounds creative writing. But the date is very early.[7]

The years 1585 to 1592 are Shakespeare's 'missing years'. There was a mid-eighteenth century rumour that Shakespeare had been caught poaching deer near Stratford. According to Nicholas Rowe in his 1709 *Some Account of the Life, &c. of Mr. WILLIAM SHAKESPEARE*:

He had, by a Misfortune common enough in young Fellows, fallen into ill Company; and amongst them, some that made a frequent practice of Deer-stealing, engag'd him with them more than once in robbing a Park that belong'd to Sir Thomas Lucy of Cherlecot, near Stratford. For this he was prosecuted by that Gentleman, as he thought, somewhat too severely; and in order to revenge that ill Usage, he made a Ballad upon him. And tho' this, probably the first Essay of his Poetry, be lost, yet it is said to have been so very bitter, that it redoubled the Prosecution against him to that degree, that he was oblig'd to leave his Business and Family in Warwickshire, for some time, and shelter himself in London'.

It is at this Time, and upon this Accident, that he is said to have made his first Acquaintance in the Play-house. He was receiv'd into the Company then in being, at first in a very mean Rank.[8]

There may be some truth in it but Lucy did not have a deer park until 1618, only an abundance of small wild game on his large estate: rabbits, hares, pheasants, and the occasional roe deer whose skin would have been ideal for the gloves of Shakespeare's father. Its venison would also have been happily eaten in Henley Street. The youthful Shakespeare may have been caught and punished for the theft of rustling. Nothing is known. There is only suspicion.

But something did happen. Sir Thomas Lucy had an armorial badge of three luces, quartered, twelve freshwater fish known as pikes ornamenting his coat of arms. Years later he was ridiculed as Justice Shallow in *The Merry Wives of Windsor*. Nicknamed 'Justice Clodpate' at the very beginning of the play he was mocked as 'a gentleman born'; his ancestors having a 'dozen white luces in their coat', 'It is an old coat'; 'The dozen white louses do become an old coat well'.

'The luce is the fresh fish; the salt fish is an old coat'. 'Coat' was a play on words. Today it is meaningless. To an Elizabethan audience it was a bawdy joke at Shallow's expense. 'Coat', pronounced 'cod' was slang for the male genitals, and, scoffed Shakespeare, old Justice Shallow's private parts were antiquated. It was slang. A 'cod' was the male penis, and a 'codpiece', was a grossly large bagged addition to a man's close-fitting breeches to exaggerate its contents. It could be decorated with pins. 'Codpiece' was also a crude term for the female vagina. Shakespeare jested about the words coarsely in one of his earliest plays, the *Two Gentlemen of Verona* when the saucy serving-maid, Lucetta, said to her mistress:

a round hose, madam, now's not worth a pin,
Unless you have a codpiece to stick pins on.

'A round hose' was a conspicuous penis. A 'pin' was a diminutive penis too small for a codpiece. Both of the coarse crudities about copulation would have had the audience howling with mirth at the vulgarities. And all of it derided Lucy bringing raucous laughter from a knowledgeable local audience when the play was performed in Stratford close to Lucy's Charlecote Park.[9] Peter Razzell added:

The weight of evidence therefore supports the various traditional accounts of Shakespeare's deer and cony-stealing exploits – sometimes in great detail – and that by breaking into the park he incurred the wrath of Sir Thomas Lucy and was forced to flee to London to avoid further punishment.[10]

Fact or fiction, certainty or speculation, clerk, tutor or poacher, these were 'lost years' that would become a seedbed of experience for William Shakespeare as a playwright. Visits to Stratford of groups of strolling players were part of this missing history. England had a long history of play-watching from its medieval beginning with miracle plays whose religious message was modified over the years by the intrusion of jests on human failings and irreligiously profanely contaminated with bawdy comedy.

Serious drama in England began in medieval times with the performance of Biblical stories inside churches for the Christian education of illiterate congregations. But the gradual insinuation of less godly comedy caused such corrupted plays to be banned from holy premises. It was the beginning of popular theatre in England. From dawn to dusk open-air performances in towns were presented street by street. Individual scenes of Biblical events were acted on wheeled wagons, the 'pagonds', by individual guilds, the Carpenters acting the crucifixion, the Goldsmiths the Magi bearing gifts to the infant Jesus. Scene by scene the decorated carts were dragged from one place to the next to entertain another expectant audience. Each Easter the wagons passed through the town to perform selected parts of the Bible from *Genesis* to the *Last Judgement*. Some complete city texts have survived for Chester; York, and the Towneley or Wakefield plays. Over time some performances developed into the Passion plays about the suffering, death and resurrection of Our Lord. The most famous of all is the version performed at Oberammergau in the Bavarian Alps. It began as early as 1634 following an outbreak of plague.

In England there were gradual changes. The Latin words were replaced by the vernacular tongue. Like the serpent in the

Garden of Eden, the secular slowly slithered into the sacred, corrupting it with a jest, a guffaw, ribaldry, rough buffoonery until by the beginnings of the sixteenth century the original piously religious performances had become little more than popular street plays some of whose texts survive.

The coarse *Gammer Gurton's Needle* was a university farce by undergraduates. It was earthy, vulgar, violent, anarchical, it was 'all belly, bowels and blows'. Of better quality was *Ralph Roister Doister*, well-written, more comical with clowns like its braggart and its sponging parasite to amuse the audience. Such plays were performed from late afternoon onwards allowing the players to make comical mistakes of identification in the twilight but today they are only of academic interest. They were, however, the beginning of modern drama, acted by groups of wandering players.

By the beginning of the sixteenth century professional actors were performing on improvised stages in inn-yards. In London there were many such 'theatres' in the outskirts of the city. They were not allowed within the city walls for fear of a crowded audience causing an outbreak of plague. Instead, companies played in suburban inn-yards that had been adapted for the stage such as the *Saracen's Head* in Islington; the *Boar's Head* and the *Red Lion* in Whitechapel, the *Tabard* in Southwark and many others. Plays were popular. So popular that some of the 'temporary' adaptations became permanent conversions, among them the Whitechapel's *Boar's Head* and *Red Lion* with their well-constructed, fixed stages and seats for the better-off spectators.

In 1557 'a lewd play', *A Sackful of News*, was played at the *Boar's Head*, an inn that later became a theatre proper.[11] It only needed a perceptive entrepreneur to realise that a custom-built, full-time theatre would be even more profitable. By 1576 John Brayne with his partner, James Burbage, the father of Shakespeare's famous actor, Richard Burbage, had accumulated sufficient money to build London's first public playhouse, the *Theatre*, in Shoreditch. Its design followed the conventional plan of an enclosed inn-yard with upper galleries that provided access to private rooms. Stairways inside the theatre led from gallery to gallery. Those novel open-air places for plays had three levels of galleries like their bearbaiting forerunners that had been erected years earlier. The only addition for the new playhouse was a covered stage for the actors.

The baiting of bears, tied to a post, their teeth broken, and attacked by savage mastiffs had been a great attraction. The retired great actor, Edward Alleyn, had his own Bear Garden with its valuable collection of bears, bulls and vicious dogs. It was a profitable investment and a royal attraction. 'The Queen herself both watched and enjoyed such baitings'. Attempts to forbid performances on Sundays failed partly because of that royal interest. But actors were an even great threat as they attracted ever increasing audiences. 'The players cause great hurt to the game of bear-baiting and like pastimes maintained for the Queen's pleasure'. A century later in 1666 the diarist, Samuel Pepys, went there with his wife after a meal, 'where I have not been I think of many years, and saw some good sport of the bull's tossing of the dogs – one into the very boxes. But it is a very rude and nasty pleasure'.[12]

Bears, fencing, actors, there was a widening choice of entertainment but everything cost money:

> such as goe to Parisgarden, the *Bell Savage*, or *Theatre*, to beholde Beare baiting, Enterludes or Fence play, can account of any pleasant spectacle [if] they first pay one pennie at the gate, another at the entrie of the Scaffolde, and the thirde, for a quiet standing.[13]

Theatres could accommodate as many as 3,000 spectators, several hundred standing jostling and cramped in the pit, others, better-off, sitting on the expensive seating in the galleries.[14] Puritanical city fathers fulminated at the likelihood – near certainty – of misbehaviour and far worse depravities at these modern pits of sin where:

> greate multitudes of people, speicallye youthe, to plays, enterludes and shewes, namelye occasyon of ffrayes and

quarrelles, eavell practizes and incontinenge in greate Innes havinge chambers and secrete places adjoyninge to their open stagies and gallyries inveglynge and alluring of maides … to previe and unmete Contractes …[15]

And whenever they could, for any disturbance, suspicion of profanity, an outbreak of plague, the malodorous, dishonest, depraved theatres were closed. Within a hundred years during the Puritan government at the end of the Civil War every theatre was closed forever. Until the Restoration and its licentious playwrights.

In Shoreditch the *Theatre* of 1576 with the one-year-later *Curtain* were the forerunners of a rash of playhouses in London, the majority of them on Bankside south of the Thames where they were safely out of the jurisdiction of the censorious city fathers. Over the years there were many more custom-built playhouses: in 1580 there was *Newington Butts* in Surrey a mile south of London Bridge; in 1600 the *Fortune* in Cripplegate inside the north-west corner of the walled city; and, to the south along the popular and secure Bankside were the *Rose* of 1587; the *Swan*, 1595; the *Globe*, 1599; and, last of all, the *Hope* put up in 1614. The roofed Blackfriars theatre built at the beginning of the seventeenth century was for boy players.

Those Elizabethan playhouses were successful because their emergence coincided with the emergence of three other developments: good playwrights and good plays assisted by good acting companies. Such companies thrived because they were protected from prosecution by the patronage of a great man. They were his. Many such companies went on tours across England, and many visited Stratford in the 1580s, performing first in the Guildhall in front of the critical eyes of the town's officials and then, if approved, acted in the inns along Bridge Street or in the marketplace.

The Earl of Berkeley was one of those patrons. He had his own actors who occasionally played in the town. So did many other great men's troupes disproving the notion that Elizabethan Stratford was no more than a dirty village of idlers and oafs. To the contrary, there were constant visits and return visits by wandering troupes who found the town profitable. Surviving records show that in 1569 the Queen's Men and Earl of Worcester's Men played there; 1573 saw the Earl of Warwick's Men; then year by year: 1576, the actors of Leicester and Worcester; 1579, those of Lord Strange and also of the Countess of Essex; 1580, Derby's; 1581, Worcester and Berkeley; 1582, Worcester and Berkeley again; 1583, Berkeley and Lord Chandos; 1584, one after another the Earls of Oxford, Worcester, and Essex: 1585, unusually, no record; 1586, an anonymous company; and from Christmas that year to the next, 1587, no fewer than five separate groups, 'the best year for plays at Stratford during Elizabeth's reign'.[16]

Historically 1587 was an eventful year. It was the year of the execution of Mary, Queen of Scots. And for the theatre it was the beginning of greatness. Astonished audiences at Henlowe's *Rose* theatre on Bankside were transfixed by the sound of Christopher Marlowe's 'mighty lines' when his *Tamburlaine* was first played there. Within a year or two there came the dramatic astonishment of Thomas Kyd's *Spanish Tragedy*, a play of revenge with horrifying moments of the supernatural. They were years when the splendours and terrors and poetry of Elizabethan drama began. It was a good time for a hopeful writer of plays. It was also the time when slapstick comedy yielded place to drama. In the summer of 1588 Stratford audiences enjoyed the visit of the Queen's Men with its two great comic actors, Richard Tarlton and Will Kemp whose career was just beginning.

Tarlton had been a founder member of Queen's Company in 1583. At court he had amused Queen Elizabeth so much that, self-conscious, she commanded him to leave her presence. But eventually he went too far, insulting both Ralegh and Essex, her favourite courtiers. He was forbidden to return to court. He had been a fine fencer, and was famous for his merry jigs at the end of a play. Stocky, squint-eyed, with his flattened nose, buttoned cap, baggy trousers, big stick and small drum he had audiences roaring with laughter, falling over themselves.

He was a comedian. But in 1588 he died of a wrecked liver. Penniless.[17]

It was the beginning of years when people going to a theatre were beginning to prefer serious, well-written dramas to the long-known, now rather boring knockabout jesting. One of the greatest of Elizabethan playwrights, Christopher Marlowe, noticed the trend:

> From jigging veins of rhyming mother wits
> And such conceits as clownage keeps in pay
> We'll lead you to the stately tent of war …[18]

It is possible that in 1587 Shakespeare joined an acting company, the Earl of Leicester's Men. As usual, there is no evidence, only speculation. But Leicester's troupe was one of those that performed in Stratford that year and the prospect of finding a career among actors and playwrights would have appealed to a young, frustrated writer and poet anxious for an employment that would provide both money and satisfaction – even if in the beginning he were no more than an ill-paid novice.

Another Company known in Stratford was the Queen's. It was notorious for the violence of its actors. In the June of 1583 at Norwich, two of the players chased a playgoer who had not paid, and killed him. They even killed each other. Four years later on 13 June 1587, there was a death at Thame. Two players quarrelled. Enraged, William Knell, slashing with his sword, chased John Towne into White Hound Close. In desperate defence, 'fearing for his life', in panic Towne turned, thrust and his sword pierced Knell's throat, killing him. At the Inquest on 15 August Towne successfully pleaded self-defence and was granted the queen's pardon. Eventually he was released from prison.

In 1588 Knell's widow, the sixteen-year-old Rebecca Edwards, married an actor John Hemminges – or Hemming or Heminges, or even Hemming as his name was variously spelled in the list of actors in the First Folio of which he was the co-editor.[19] The outcome of Knell's death was that the Queen's Men arrived in

Stratford, two actors short, one of them dead, the other in gaol awaiting trial for murder. By coincidence, the Earl of Leicester died in the same year and his Company broke up. Some of its leading men, Kemp, Bryn and Pope, joined Lord Strange's Men. Others including Richard Burbage preferred the reconstituted Queen's group, by far the most prestigious of all the troupes, having been formed in 1583 by Edmund Tilney, the Queen's Master of Revels.

It is probable that Shakespeare also went there, filling the vacancy caused by the death of William Knell. By that time he was a known actor, the Company was short of a 'hired man' and its custom was to recruit from established players. Joining it in 1588 would have given him two full seasons to learn how to construct and write a play at a time when Marlowe and others were bringing dramatic life to the theatre.[20]

The story that he came unknown to London and held horses' heads outside the playhouse is a fiction of the mid-eighteenth century. Neither John Aubrey nor Nicholas Rowe later mentioned it but both did confidently state that he became a player, at first of only small parts. The horse-holding tale was yet one more improbability like the exaggerated story of deer-poaching. It was romance without fact, fiction. What did happen was that the imaginative Shakespeare was not content to be no more than a mediocre actor. His ambition was to become a dramatist and he began experimenting with the writing of plays, using the company's existing material and improving it. Around 1590 he rewrote the plodding 1584 text of *Felix and Philiomena* turning it into his own very successful light-hearted comedy, *The Two Gentlemen of Verona*.[21] His career as England's greatest playwright and man of genius was beginning. So was his association with the Dark Lady.

Some important events in Tudor history can be used as guideposts to the times when more trivial matters occurred, significant dates such as 1588 and the Spanish Armada; 1593 and the murder of Christopher Marlowe; 1597 and Shakespeare's purchase of New Place in Stratford-upon-Avon for £60; and 1605 and the Gunpowder Plot. Those years are essential as chronological landmarks. They can be used to show that the search for Shakespeare's Dark Lady was not a straightforward history from the first year to the last. Instead, they provide a stable background to a period when the same sequence of years provides eight entirely different, conflicting conclusions about William Shakespeare and the variety of women who have been 'identified' as the Dark Lady. Only one of the eight proposed was.

3

Jacqueline Field: The First of the Dark Ladies

I think we may safely follow Will's stranger steps to a Blackfriars houses near Ludgate. There Richard Field, son of his father's friend, Henry Field, tanner, of Stratford-upon-Avon, was settling in Thomas Vautrollier's great printing-house.

Charlotte Stopes, *Shakespeare's Sonnets*, 1904, xxi

By 1590 Shakespeare was in London, working with the Queen's Men, writing plays, and looking for somewhere to stay. History is not completely silent about him in his early years as a playwright. It is known what he looked like. There is a copperplate engraving of his appearance around 1600 made by a young and rather inexperienced Flemish painter, Martin Droeshout. He probably based that 'portrait' on a very competent miniature of William Shakespeare that had been made in the playwright's late thirties or early forties. It was Droeshout's engraving that was used for the portrait in the *First Folio*. Contemporaries considered it a fair likeness. Some twenty years later in the *First Folio's* 'To the Reader' Ben Jonson commended its accuracy:

Wherein the graver had a strife,
with Nature to out-doo the Life.

The hair is very like that of the bust in Stratford church. There is the same perpendicular forehead and the same expression of 'a self-satisfied pork butcher whose dull eyes and fat jowls seem to offer no clue as to what might be within …'[1] That judgement was not unfair. The bust probably did resemble Shakespeare in his final years. The surviving family who commissioned it made no objection. The carved head of the bust was fashioned by a Dutch stonemason, Gheerart Janssen, early in the seventeenth century. Patronised by an aristocratic clientele he had a thriving business in London's Southwark not far from the *Globe* theatre at the time when Shakespeare was still in London.

It was a Stratford associate, John Coombes a rich moneylender, who had sold land to Shakespeare, who had ordered the poet's bust to be made by a younger member of the Janssen family. He left £60 for its construction and it can be seen today in the chancel of Stratford's Holy Trinity church. It is set above head height, the half-length body, quill in hand, placed between two black pillars of Purbeck marble. Dover Wilson's disparaging description was not unjust. The bust is strangely vacuous of expression for a poet of genius.

That was in 1616. Around 1590 the young Shakespeare, although never an Adonis, was not as rotund of body nor as flabby of jowl. Not quite. As a young man he had been well-built, a euphemism for slightly overweight, not tall, but presentable in appearance, balding slightly in early manhood. He also had a slight but persistent limp. The limp seems to have been the result of an unknown accident. Two sonnets refer to it: 'So I, made lame by Fortune's dearest spite …' and 'Speak of my lameness, and I straight will halt …'. The word 'halt' meant that he limped.[2] And there was another physical defect – his hair. Semi-baldness seems to have affected him as a young man. He was self-conscious about it, referring to it three times in his early play, *The Comedy of Errors*. 'There's no time for a man to recover his hair that grows bald by nature'; and 'what he hath scanted men in hair, he hath given them in wit'; and 'There's many a man hath more hair than wit'.[3] But he was in London, he was acting with a fine Company, he was writing successful plays. Rapidly. And he was making enemies just as quickly.

He had had immediate success with the first plays he had written, three of them on the troublesome reign of Henry VI. They had an astonishing run of no fewer than fifteen performances between March and June in 1592. The delighted producer, Philip Henslowe, rubbed his hands. The plays had made money.[4] Others, such as the laughter in *The Two Gentlemen of Verona*, and the horrors of *Titus Andronicus*, had also been enthusiastically applauded and well-attended by paying customers. That an unknown writer, some sub-literate peasant from the countryside, had written them was resented by long-established playwrights known as the 'university wits'.

One of them was openly antagonistic to the ill-educated rural upstart. Robert Greene was a Cambridge graduate. Having written some semi-romantic novels he had turned to the theatre, writing plays of which his *Friar Bacon and Friar Bungay*, a mixture of comedy and calamity, was a success. Ironically, it had been performed by the Queen's Men. In his bitter *Groates-Worth of Wit* of 1592 written to be read by his fellow well-educated playwrights Greene denounced both Shakespeare and Christopher Marlowe, accusing Marlowe of atheism: 'Why should thy excellent wit, his gift, bee so blinded, that thou shouldst give no glorie to the giver: Is it pestilent Machivilian pollicy that thou hast studied: O peevish follie!'. Greene then derided Shakespeare for his effrontery, accusing him of plagiarism:

> Yes trust them not: for there is an upstart Crow, beautified with our feathers, that with his Tygers Hart wrapt in a Players hyde, supposes he is as well able to bombast out a blanke verse as the best of you: and being an absolute Johannes fac totum, is in his owne conceit the onely Shake-scene in a countrey.[5]

'Tygers Hart' was a resentful misquotation of a line in Shakespeare's *Henry VI, Part 3*, about the tyrannical Margaret of Anjou, 'O, tiger's heart wrapt in a woman's hide', words memorable enough to sink into Greene's angry memory.[6]

By the autumn of the same year Greene was ill. A surfeit of cheap wine and pickled herrings wrecked his impoverished and much abused body and he died penniless and neglected, on 3 September 1592. He was thirty-four years old, a poet dying in the home of a poor cobbler. He left a note to his wife that he had abandoned begging her, 'by the love of our youth and by my soul's rest that thou will see this man paid, for if he and his wife had not succoured me, I had died in the streets'. That lodger's wife, knowing that he had been a writer, crowned his head with a garland of bay leaves before he was buried in a new churchyard near the madhouse of Bedlam.

The *Groats-worth* sold well and was reprinted eight times from 1592 to 1637. It was edited by the printer, Henry Chettle, who also wrote plays for the Admiral's Men. In 1598 Francis Meres said Greene was 'among the best for comedy'. There is an irony. Both Marlowe and Shakespeare suspected that Chettle had written the profitable *Groats-worth* himself. Chettle denied it. He apologised to Shakespeare for the insult that Greene had written and that he had printed:

> I am as sory as if the originall fault had beene my fault, because my selfe hath seene his demeanour no lesse civill than he excellent in the qualitie he professes, besides divers of worship have reported his uprightness of dealing, which argues his honesty, and his facetious grace in writing that approves his art.

By that time Shakespeare was well-known. He had become an acclaimed dramatist. He was an actor with a good Company. He had written several popular plays that had filled a theatre-owner's purse. He was to compose long, elaborate poems for a young nobleman. And in London he would meet the Dark Lady.

When that time was is unclear. So is her 'darkness', whether it was of skin or of hair, eyes or, elusively, of spirit. She was his 'woman of the night' and she was to appear time and then time again in his plays whether those written early in pleasure or in others written in resentment years later. But who she was, when Shakespeare met her, or even whether she was no more than a demon stalking his poetical imagination, has been debated for as long as there has been Shakespearian scholarship. There have been many contenders of whom eight remain possibilities. One was Jacqueline Field, wife of the printer with whom Shakespeare is believed to have lodged during his early years in London. She was no more than one possibility of several, all of them known to Shakespeare within a few years of each other from no earlier than 1592 to no later than a year or two after 1600, years that created one of the greatest sequence of sonnets that the world has known.

Unaware that they were about to be made immortal, preserved in a set of poems that most of them never read, the contenders were, alphabetically: Jane Davenant; Penelope Devereux; Jacqueline Field; Mary Fitton; Mrs Florio; Amelia Lanier; Lucy Morgan, and Marie Mountjoy. Shakespeare's sonnet sequence was their memorial. An extremely doubtful candidate, admitted earlier on the principle of fair play to women, was Winifred Burbage. She has been added, debated and dismissed.

A sonnet sequence was not like a set of A–Z encyclopedias, from Volume I, 'Aardvark, a bush-pig', to the final entry in Volume XII, 'Zythum, a beer of ancient Egypt'. Shakespeare's sonnets were a series of anonymously personal poems written over the years from as early as 1582 to as late as the early 1600s. Nor were they evenly spread through time. Most were probably written within a few years of 1593. 'The Sonnets ... taken as a whole, exhibit an erotic life of tormented complexity and change, gesture at times towards the idea that love itself is timeless.'[7]

That assembly of 154 poems was not a true sequence. It was a collection of largely unconnected sonnets written over years about different subjects. Some were not even true sonnets. Number 99 had fifteen lines, number 126 was written in rhyming couplets. Some poems were as early as 1582 concerned with Anne Whateley and reluctant marriage. Sonnet 112 about the poet's complete indifference to personal criticism could be connected to Robert Greene's complaints in 1592, whereas the 'mortal moon' of Sonnet 107 either described the crescent-shaped formation of the Spanish Armada of 1588 or the death of Queen Elizabeth and accession of James I in 1603. Several others were also as late as the early 1600s.

The earliest sonnets in the sequence were almost impersonal, urging a young man to marry. They were succeeded by others writing about the same young man who had become a very close friend of the poet. Those 'young friend' sonnets were followed by others about another poet, perhaps Christopher Marlowe, who was an irritating rival for the favour of the young man. Sonnet 86 complained:

> Was it the proud sail of his great verse
> Bound for the prize of all-too-precious you ...
> Was it his spirit, by spirits taught to write
> Above a mortal pitch, that struck me dead?

There was occasional anxiety and panic in the long sonnet sequence but those worries were so isolated that they were almost hidden in the extensive collection. There were twenty or more about a dark lady. The title-page of the sonnets also mentioned a 'Mr. W. H.' but gave no details about him.

Sonnets 127 to 152 concerned the dark lady, less than a quarter of the 154. The series ended with two sonnets, 153 and 154, about a very unusual pair of cupids who were obsessed with finding a cure for the venereal disease, gonorrhoea, recommending 'a seething bath'. It was an unexpected way to end series of poems about love. Poets of genius can be unpredictable. They can also fail to impress. Not every reader has admired the sonnet sequence. Tolstoy considered the poems crude, immoral, vulgar 'and, even worse, 'senseless'. The English poet, Walter Savage Landor, dismissed them as worthless: 'The sonnets are hot and pothery, there is much condensation, little delicacy, like raspberry jam without the cream, without the crust, without bread'. He was not ambiguous. 'Pothery' is a choking smoke or dust, a fuss, a bother. But as a critic Landor was in a very tiny minority. Over the centuries the sonnets received increasing appreciation as Jones and Guy stressed,

> Mostly ignored by his contemporaries, they had a brief renaissance in the eighteenth century when used as a model by the Romantic poets such as William Wordsworth. Today they have been translated into almost every world language including Esperanto.[8]

They can be read as love-poems although they are love poems with a thunderstorm of emotions. They also have their own mysteries. Generally unremarked is the fact that the word 'rose' occurs about seventy times in the plays, and ten more in seven of the sonnets. Sonnet 130 in the Dark Lady sequence had:

> I have seen roses damasked, red and white,
> But no such roses see I in her cheeks …

yet:

> What's in a name? That which we call a rose
> By any other word would smell as sweet.[9]

Who or what the word 'rose' signified to Shakespeare has only partly been explained. Nor has it been discussed in detail. Roses fascinated him. He mentioned the flower in play after play from one as early as, *The Taming of the Shrew*, to one as late as *Antony and Cleopatra*. In *A Midsummer Night's Dream* he compared the flower to human lips and cheeks, wrote of morning dew on its petals, a dew that was distilled in the preparation of expensive cosmetics.

> Earthlier happy is the rose distilled
> Than that which, withering on the virgin thorn
> Grows, lives, and dies in single blessedness …[10]

In several sonnets the word 'rose' was a pun on the surname of the young Earl of Southampton, 'Wriothesley', which was pronounced 'rosely'. But, using poetical imagination, the rose could also be related to the Rosaline in *Romeo and Juliet* who was Romeo's first desire before he first saw Juliet. His friend, Benvolio, said it would be easy for Romeo to meet her:

> at this same ancient feast of Capulet's
> Sups the fair Rosaline whom thou so loves …

Romeo's other friend, Mercutio, also described her:

> I conjure thee by Rosaline's bright eyes,
> By her high forehead and her scarlet lip,
> By her fine foot, straight leg …

And there were other attractions that Mercutio specified and that groundlings in the theatre roared in laughter at:

> If love be blind, love cannot hit the mark.
> Now will he sit under a medlar tree,
> And wish his mistress were that kind of fruit
> As maids call medlars, when they laugh alone –
> O Romeo, that she were, O, that she were
> An open arse and thou a pop-rin pear!

It was crude humour and the audience loved it. A medlar was a fruit with a deep hollow at the top and its name was Elizabethan slang for a vagina. 'Pop'rin pear', from the Flemish town of Poperinghe, was a euphemism for the 'popped in' penis. Shakespeare was writing for his audience. There were very few Puritans amongst them.[11]

What neither actor speaking the lines would know was that 'Rosaline' was the fictitious name of the Dark Lady. Shakespeare had met her and he wrote about her, in love, in despair and in torment. He put her in *Romeo and Juliet* with its famous balcony scene but 'she' is not Juliet. She is 'Rosaline'.

Audiences know that those doomed lovers, Romeo Montague and Juliet Capulet, died in the tragedy's final death-scene. But very few remember that the play starts not with a Juliet but with Romeo infatuated with a long-forgotten Rosaline. In the play's early scenes she is everywhere. Mercutio mocked Romeo for his obsession for her dark beauty: 'Alas, poor Romeo, he is already dead, stabbed with a white wench's black eye, run through the ear with a love song …'.[12]

There is also a Rosaline in another early play of Shakespeare's, *Love's Labours Lost*. The description is not flattering:

> A whitely wanton with a velvet brow,
> With two pitch-balls stuck in her face for eyes;
> Ay, and by heaven, one that will do the deed,
> Though Argus were her eunuch and her guard …[13]

In legend Argus was the vigilant herdsman with 100 eyes, no more than two of them sleeping at any time. He was a fitting guardian for that lustful woman with dark eyes, dark brows and dark hair. The lines were the first public references to the Dark Lady but there were many others in private, not all of them flattering, in the sonnets. As well as Sonnet 144's 'a woman coloured ill' there were others about her. 'Black' occurs in five, sometimes admiringly: in Sonnet 127, 'in the old age black was not counted fair'. In 130, 'black wires grow on her head'. But in 131 is the unflattering 'in nothing art thou black save in thy deeds'. In 132, 'beauty herself is black'. And in Sonnet 147, 'who art as black as hell, as dark as night'. The Dark Lady sonnets are not conventional love poems.

That the woman also happened to play the virginal, more properly the 'virginals', invites the question of whether there was not also an intentionally sarcastic pun on 'virginal' in Sonnet 128. The virginals, a keyboard instrument contained in a box on a table, was more similar to the harpsichord than the later spinet and piano. Its quills or 'jacks' plucked rather than struck the strings. Shakespeare had watched her standing to play it and in Sonnet 128 praised the music:

How oft, when thou, my music, music play'st
Upon that blessèd wood whose motion sounds
With thy sweet fingers when thou gently sway'st
The wiry concord that mine ear confounds,
Do I envy those jacks that nimble leap
To kiss the tender inward of thy hand,
Whilst my poor lips, which should that harvest reap,
At the wood's boldness by thee blushing stand.
To be so tickled, they would change their state
And situation with those dancing chips
O'er whom thy fingers walk with gentle gait,
Making dead wood more blest than living lips.
Since saucy jacks so happy art in this,
Give them thy fingers, me thy lips to kiss.

The Italian translator, John Florio, to be mentioned frequently later in the book, described the virginals as one of several instruments that could provide private entertainment by a talented musician who skilfully 'plaies also upon the cittern, virginals, violins or flutes'. The queen, Elizabeth, had been taught to play both the lute and the virginals when she was still only a young girl and it partly explains the seemingly ambiguous name, 'virginals'. '*Parthenia*' was the title of the first music published for the instrument. The word meant 'maidens' songs', and the virginals were often played by young, unwed women entertaining their families.

But consorting with the 'Dark Lady' did not always provide pleasurable nights of indulgence. She was married. And she was her own person, selfish, inconstant in her whims of self-satisfaction. Her failings were resented by Shakespeare. Hypocritically, giving his own marital background, he accused her of adultery. She had cheated him and made promises to other men:

In loving thee thou know'st I am forsworn,
But thou art twice forsworn, to me love swearing:
In act thy bed-vow broke …

But admitted that he himself was unfaithful both to her and to his wife:

> But why of two oaths' breach do I accuse you
> When I break twenty? I am perjured most,
> For all my vows are oaths but to misuse thee
> And all my honest faith in thee is lost.

She had deceived him.

> For I have sworn thee fair, and thought thee bright
> Who art as black as hell, as dark as night.

But who she was, where she lived, her marriage, her background, that information is as elusive as Macbeth's dagger, dramatic but unobtainable:

> Come, let me clutch thee:
> I have thee not, and yet I see thee still.[14]

Shakespeare wanted her, needed her, wrote in torment about her, snarled, wept, shouted that she was a strumpet, a whore, giving herself to any man she fancied, she was the unguarded ship of Sonnet 137, open to all boarders '... anchored in the bay where all men ride ...'. He loathed her, wanted her, cursed her and longed for her. She was so desirable that in one of his coarsest sonnets, 151, the poet was sexually explicit about her effect on him:

> Love is too young to know what conscience is;
> Yet who knows not conscience is born of love?
> Then, gentle cheater, urge not my amiss,
> Lest guilty of my faults thy sweet self prove;
> For, thou betraying me, I do betray
> My nobler part to my gross body's treason;
> My soul doth tell my body that he may
> Triumph in love; flesh stays no farther reason;

But, rising at thy name, doth point out thee
As his triumphant prize. Proud of this pride,
He is contented thy poor drudge to be,
To stand in thy affairs, fall by thy side.
No want of conscience hold it that I call
Her 'love' for whose dear love I rise and fall.

There were no euphemisms in that sonnet about the desires of a lustful lover. It is, shudder the more puritanical of his critics, 'the most libidinous of sonnets', and over the centuries the poem been consistently condemned for its coarseness. As Rollins remarked: 'One might reply that the woman in question is represented as a prostitute, who presumably enjoyed grossness'.[15]

In 1854 an eminent American critic, Robert Grant White, observed:

> Again it is possible to think of Shakespeare in early youth writing such a sonnet as 151 for another, but impossible to admit that he would, in his own person, address to any woman, such gross *double entendres* as are contained in its last seven lines.

Others agreed. In 1924 Tucker dismissed Sonnet 151 as a poem that 'From the nature of its contents, might well be let to die'. Seventy years later the disapproval continued. Rex Gibson observed that 'This sonnet has been a source of great embarrassment to many readers, who feel uncomfortable about its explicit sexual references. Some have called it obscene and refused to believe that Shakespeare wrote it'. But he did.[16] Understandably the disgusting sonnet was excluded from books of popular poetry. In 1861 Francis Turner Palgrave omitted both it and Sonnet 20 with its filthy 'pricked thee out' from his best-selling anthology, *The Golden Treasury of English Lyrical Poetry*. It was not for Victorian family reading.

Three centuries earlier in Elizabethan times only the Puritans were as prudish. Most educated people knew and understood a Latin tag, '*Penis erectus non habet conscientiam*', 'an erect member has no conscience', a coarse pun on 'con' which was

French slang for the vagina, 'con' being emphasized by the 'conscience' occurring twice and 'contented' once in Sonnet 151. Underlying the venom was the inclusion of 'pride', another common expression for an erect penis that had risen proudly and lustfully at the thought of the woman.[17] That woman was the Dark Lady. She is known only through the sonnets. In them she is described as a woman of dark, possibly black hair, dark eyes, white-skinned, and talented. There is nothing more: no name, no home, no address, just a void. She is a woman of mystery.

Almost nothing is known about her appearance or her background. Her sonnets, 127 to 152, do say that she was married. Two sonnets, 142 and 152, write of others' beds. But of children there is ambiguity. Sonnet 153 includes the words 'babe', 'infant' and 'mother' but these are just as likely to be poetical similes as information about her maternity. Sonnets about her are secretive. She is a shape without substance. Like Anne Whateley she is a phantom in Shakespeare's life. She may even have been dark-skinned. In 1861 Wilhelm Jordan, a little-known German translator, thought that she was 'a seductress whose breasts were dark brown, whose hair was curly, and who may have been a mulatto or quadroon from the West Indies 'with African blood coursing through her veins, and the musical sense common to her rhythmic race'.[18]

It is more probable that she was a dark-haired woman whose clear, fair complexion contrasted attractively with the almost black of her hair. Her eyes also. Shakespeare had musical words for the sight of her in Sonnet 127:

Therefore my mistress' eyes are raven black,
Her eyes so suited, and they mourners seem,
At such who, not born fair, no beauty lack ...

And in his *Love's Labours Lost*:

O, if black my lady's brows be decked',
It mourns that painting and usurping hair

Should ravish doters with a false aspect;
And therefore is she born to make black fair.[19]

But her name, when Shakespeare met her, even whether she is no more than a demon stalking his poetical imagination, has been debated for as long as there has been Shakespearian scholarship. There have been many contenders of whom eight remain possibilities. One was Jacqueline Field, wife of the printer with whom Shakespeare may have lodged during his first years in London.

An American researcher, Charlotte Carmichael Stopes, somewhat mawkishly misnaming her 'Jacquinetta', suggested the Dark Lady 'was a Frenchwoman, therefore likely to have dark eyes, a sallow … complexion, and that indefinable charm so much alluded to'.[20] It was sentimentality and Schoenbaum ridiculed her. 'In a notably fatuous essay on the Sonnets Stopes proposes a new Dark Lady, Jacquinetta Field'. Quoting her he added; 'for charm read loose morals. Mrs Stopes' reasoning is not impeccable'.

It did not have to be. It is feasible that Jacqueline Field really was the woman known as the Dark Lady. After the death of her first husband she remarried and became the wife of Richard Field, a printer. He had been apprenticed to Thomas Vautrollier, a French Protestant from Troyes, whose business in the precinct of the old Blackfriars monastery had two printing-presses and six journeymen. Before her marriage his wife had been Jacqueline Dutwite, one of the many French Protestants in London. Vautrollier also had a business in Edinburgh. In his absences from London his wife looked after the Blackfriars press.[21]

Blackfriars was a wealthy district on the grounds of a former priory dissolved by Henry VIII, an area of foreign merchants, jewellers and goldsmiths. It was fashionable. Lord Hunsdon, later to be Lord Chamberlain, lived there. It was an aristocratic neighbourhood, partly owned by the Crown and included a hotel sufficiently luxurious to be visited by the Holy Roman Emperor.

Richard Field was a fellow townsman of Shakespeare, born in Stratford-on-Avon's Bridge Street, the son of Henry, a tanner and friend of John Shakespeare. By 1579 he was apprenticed to Vautrollier who died in 1587. Richard succeeded to his prospering business as a master-printer, using the same trade mark, *Anchora Spei*, 'The Anchor of Hope'.[22] In January the following year he married Vautrollier's widow. They had a child in 1590 – if it was Field's. Jacqueline Field was probably one of the first foreigners that Shakespeare had met. As Field and he had been schoolfellows in Stratford Shakespeare may have lodged with him and his young wife when arriving in London. Certainly the two men were well-acquainted.

The printer was able to give Shakespeare advice about London, offer him hospitality and provide the use of a library sufficient for all his needs. They included the foreign books that Field printed. For the Spanish volumes he translated his name as 'Ricardo del Campo' on the title-page. In 1593, 28 April, he printed Shakespeare's long poem, 'Venus & Adonis'. It was a considerable success.

On 12 June elderly Richard Stonley of Aldersgate, one of the tellers of the Exchange, methodically entered in his diary that he had purchased a copy, along with a work entitled the *Survey of France*. In three volumes, Stonley's diary was only rediscovered as recently as 1972, whereupon, with characteristic eagerness, it became acquired by the Folger Shakespeare Library, Washington. During a routine inspection of the new acquisition an astonished and delighted Folger curator, Laetitia Yeandle, spotted the lines: '12th June, 1593. For the Survey of Fraunce, with the Venus and Adonis pr Shakspere xii.d'.

She had found the first known original record of any purchase of one of Shakespeare's published works, and the earliest known notice of Shakespeare as a published author.

It cost six copper pence, half a silver shilling. A Bible was twelve times dearer.[23]

Jacqueline Field is one of the feasible candidates proposed as the Dark Lady in spite of Wilson's disparaging criticism, 'on the paper-thin grounds that, being French, she may have been dark-haired'. There was more to her than that. She had direct opportunities to entice Shakespeare, especially if her marriage to Field had been one of calculating commercial advantage. Few women thrived in business on their own in Elizabethan England. To prosper they married. A flirtation, or more serious, a love-affair, with an attractive actor and poet might have brought welcome relief from a boring existence. There is no proof. Secret lovers do not advertise. Despite Wilson's scepticism others have been less doubting. 'There were to be rumours later that Will had posted dexterously to her bed while Field was on one of his personal trips to Stratford'. And 'rumours would have it that Shakespeare himself performed Field's office 'twixt his sheets'.[24]

Whether Jacqueline Field was musical and played the virginals, is not known. The fact that she was French does not make her a musician. But there may be a hint in Sonnet 128 that praises the woman's 'sweet fingers' as they played the melody. In it there is an apparent significant repetition of 'jack' in line 5 and in the two final lines:

> Since saucy jacks so happy are in this,
> Give them thy fingers, me thy lips to kiss.

It was, perhaps, a personal, rather heavy 'in-joke' pun on her name, 'jack' for 'Jacqueline'. Shakespeare was fascinated by her. She was irresistible and he could not take his eyes off her. She was perfection, the way she walked, straight-backed, elegant, her delicate musical fingers, her changes of mood, the sudden smile, her quiet voice with its enchanting whispers of a French accent, he had loved her from the first days that they had met. During the years from 1589 to as late as 1596 Jacqueline Field may have been the elusive Dark Lady.

In the middle of those six or seven years London suffered another mortal outbreak of plague. The city was overcrowded with miserable standards of health. Stinking refuse fouled every street. Marauding rats and vermin lurked dirtily and dankly. Contamination was inevitable. And of those periodical outbreaks the worst since the Black Death was from 1592 to 1593. Theatres and public places were closed. The deaths continued. Children sang a nursery rhyme:

> Ring-a-ring of roses,
> A pocket full of posies,
> Atishoo, atishoo, we all fall down.

The roses, red blotches on the skin, were the first signs of infection. The posies were optimistic but ineffectual bunches of herbs to be carried and sniffed to prevent infection. But 'Atishoo ...', and the dead fell down.

Over the weeks there was a sudden increase. Nearly 10,000 died of the plague. The symptoms became well-known: fever, headaches, painful swellings, that erupted into scarlet-red blotches under the skin where blood was haemorrhaging. Sardonically the fatal signs became nicknamed the 'spotted death'. Of more than 20,000 London deaths that year over half were of plague. There were so many deaths that the constant clanging of church bells was forbidden. The dead were dumped in hastily dug pits. George Withers, soldier and poet, saw one:

> Lord! What a sight was there? And what strong smells
> Ascended from among *Death's* loathsome Cells?
> Yonn lay a heape of skulls; another there;
> Here, halfe unburied did a Corpse appeare,
> A locke of womans hayre; a dead mans face
> Uncover'd; and a ghastly sight it was.[25]

A contemporary of Shakespeare's, the writer Thomas Nashe, wrote a 'Liturgy in Time of Plague' of which the lines of the third of its six verses were some of the loveliest ever written about that horror:

> Beauty is but a flower
> Which wrinkles will devour;
> Brightness falls from the air,

Queens have died young and fair,
Dust hath closed Helen's eye.
I am sick, I must die.
Lord, have mercy on us![26]

The outbreak made no social distinctions. It writhed into the bodies of the poor and rich indifferently. In *Romeo and Juliet* both a Montagu and a Capulet could choke into the grave. 'A plague o' both the houses. I am sped', groaned Mercutio as he lay dying, killed in a duel.[27]

In London the theatres were closed. William Shakespeare continued to write but not only plays. He was composing a long narrative poem, 'Venus and Adonis'. It was printed by Field and published by John Harrison. After two sold-out editions Harrison obtained the copyright and had it reprinted six more times to his considerable profit. He repeated the money-making investment the following year with Shakespeare's 'The Rape of Lucrece'. Shakespeare must have been doubly pleased at the success. It brought him fame and money, and, punningly, it brought Jacqueline Field even closer to him. He wrote her a sonnet containing indecent *double entendres*:

So thou being rich in *Will* add to thy *Will*
One will of mine, to make thy large *Will* more.
Let no unkind, no fair beseechers kill;
Think all but one, and me in that one *Will*.[28]

The 'peasant' from Stratford had become a success as a playwright, as a writer of much admired long poems, and as a seducer. The few sonnets already written were unknown. The majority were to come.

Hoping to find a wealthy patron to whom 'Venus and Adonis' could be dedicated Shakespeare chose Henry Wriothesley, the youthful Earl of Southampton. He wrote a preface to the earl:

Right Honourable,
I know not how I shall offend in dedicating my unpolished lines

to your lordship, nor how the world will censure me for choosing so strong a prop to support so weak a burden. Only, if your honour seem but pleased, I account myself highly praised, and vow to take advantage of all idle hours till I have honoured you with some graver labour ...

It was calculated ingenuity. Those 'unpolished lines' of 'Venus and Adonis' were in reality part of an ingeniously devised erotic poem that Michael Wood described as:

> one that was likely to please an adolescent mind with the luscious topography of Venus's body' is obvious: fountains, hillocks and dales; the grass in the bottom of a valley, of course, is the most succulent; the brakes (thickets) are pubic hair. So the Bird of Venus and Cock of the Game sought to titillate students (and young lords like Southampton, who seems to have liked erotica).[29]

Through that admired and widely-read long poem of disappointed love and tragic death William Shakespeare was to meet both the Earl of Southampton – and one more candidate for the Dark Lady. According to Charlotte Stopes Shakespeare's Dark Lady was certain to have been Jacqueline Field. But it is no more than one possibility among seven others.

4

The Fair Youth of the Sonnets

'Adolescence' which is the first part of the young man's age: because I understand and perceive also that in this age Cupid and Venus were and would be very busy to trouble the quiet minds of young people.

Thomas Whythorne, *The Autobiography*, p. 12

That unexpected, viciously virulent outbreak of plague of 1592–3 forced the alarmed City authorities to close theatres and other places of public gatherings. For Shakespeare it was a period of enforced idleness. Some of it was passed writing his earliest plays: experimenting with one, *A Comedy of Errors*, in which everything happened in a single day. Another, the *Taming of the Shrew*, was performed at Gray's Inn at Christmas in 1594. Shakespeare also collaborated with Michael Drayton writing the script of *Edward III*. Alone, he wrote the popular and profitable tragedy of *Richard III*. But he was always struggling to match the genius of Christopher Marlowe's exhilarating, theatre-packing plays of *Tamburlaine* and *Doctor Faustus*. Worse, the contest between the two writers was not confined to plays and poetry. Both men were seeking the patronage of the young and very rich Earl of Southampton. Giroux wrote:

The one poet Shakespeare might have regarded as 'great' and 'a better spirit' than himself in 1592–3, and to whom he might have acknowledged himself to be 'inferior' was Christopher Marlowe. 'Hero and Leander' which Marlowe was busy composing at Scadbury in Kent in the early months of 1593, is also the one poem Shakespeare might have considered superior to 'Venus and Adonis'.[1]

Shakespeare began writing that long epic, 'Venus and Adonis', optimistically dedicating it to the earl, while perhaps still dallying with the delectable Jacqueline Field. The long 'Venus and Adonis', a narrative poem printed by the possibly cuckolded Richard Field, was a work of almost 200 verses. It was Shakespeare's 'first heir of his invention', based on Ovid's 'Metamorphoses', and it was exceptionally successful, reprinted no fewer than eight times. Shakespeare's version created a romantic comedy that turned darkly into a tragic ending. His dedication to the Earl of Southampton read:

> Right Honorable, I know not how I shall offend in dedicating my unpolisht lines to your Lordship, nor how the world will censure mee for choosing so strong a proppe to support so weake a burthen, onely if your Honour seeme but pleased, I counte myself highly praised.[2]

The earl's response was sufficiently encouraging for the suppliant poet to repeat the offering a year later with an entirely different poem. According to that ever-curious picker-up of snippets, John Aubrey, it was the time when Shakespeare was lodging in Shoreditch: 'at Hoglane within 6 dores of Folgate', a house down Hog Lane in Norton Folgate west of Spitalfields. It was conveniently close to Burbage's *Theatre*. The 'lane' had once been attractively lined with elm trees. Along it had been little bridges and 'easy stiles' allowing people to reach open fields but by Shakespeare's time it was gloomy with houses, cottage after grubby cottage, bowling alleys, yards with hooks for stretching cloth, and an atmosphere of resignation.

A visiting Spanish noblewoman, Luisa de Carvajal, was disgusted by her surroundings and her neighbours.

At times they grind me down with the noise that comes though the wall where I sleep. All you hear is the sound of meat being roasted and others cooking, eating, playing and drinking. On Friday it gets worse.

London was appalling. Death was a house-guest. There were about twenty-five hangings each month, some of the condemned being only children ten or eleven years old. There was no sanitation in the city and even more pestilence than in ancient Egypt. Luisa de Carvajal was appalled to see carrots loaded in carts that only the day before had carried suppurating victims of the plague. She did not like where she lived in London. Many actors lodged there and it was not a reputable area.[3]

It was 'known for 'wenches and soldiers' as well as a clutter of unlicensed barber-surgeons, procurers and beggars. The Privy Council distastefully noted that the area contained 'dissolute, loose and insolent' persons roistering in dicing-houses, brothels, taverns, and alehouses, but as well as those unpuritanical pleasures Burbage's men found the suburb convenient. Its cheapness made it popular with young actors, particularly as they were near the *Curtain* and *Theatre* playhouses just a couple of hundred yards apart. Audiences from the city could reach them beyond the city walls by passing through Bishopsgate over whose gates spikes held the impaled heads of traitors.

Shakespeare and Marlowe were competitors in their writings and in their search for a protector. For a time in the early 1590s both men were pursuing the same patron, the young and very rich Henry Wriothesley, pronounced 'rose-ly', Earl of Southampton, a follower of that rising courtier, the young Earl of Essex who was becoming a rival to the earlier favourite of the queen, Sir Walter Ralegh. Both Shakespeare and Marlowe, being no more than very ordinary supplicants, wrote obsequiously to the noble Earl of Southampton. But in themselves the two poets were quite different persons, most noticeably in their sexual tendencies. Marlowe was the freer spirit, one of Sir Walter Ralegh's associates in the so-called 'School of Night' whose members mocked established beliefs, an 'ungodly academy' of freethinking writers and philosophers.

They would meet at Ralegh's Durham House in the Strand, a princely riverside house in London, once the sumptuous home of Edward VI, then of the young Princess Elizabeth and, finally, of Lady Jane Grey. The building had been part of the Bishop of Durham's see until the queen gave it to Ralegh in the 1580s. Ralegh had long been a favourite of the queen. In 1587 he brought the astonishments of potatoes and tobacco from the newly-settled Americas. But five years later in 1592 he blundered. He fell in love with the beautiful Bess Throckmorton. She was an orphan, tall, fair-haired, blue-eyed, but she was also a maid-of-honour of Queen Elizabeth who was resentfully jealous of rivals. It was more than a blunder. It was a disaster. Ralegh had slighted his monarch. He was sent to the Tower and remained out of favour for the next five years. His wife was never forgiven. And as his fortunes declined so those of the young Earl of Essex ascended.

They were very different men. Essex was ambitious, a schemer, devious, but he was not a thinker except for personal advantage. Ralegh's critical mind welcomed free-thinkers like Thomas Hariot, scientist, philosopher and astronomer who 'burst from history into legend'. His sceptical mind was always welcome at Durham House. So was Dr John Dee, a scientist, inventor of the telescope, mapmaker and suspected magician who advised Queen Elizabeth on auspicious dates. He was popularly nicknamed 'the queen's conjurer'. Dee lived in the shadows of public life, suspected of dabbling in the dark arts – a practitioner of the dark arts. Fearing his magic a hysterical mob set fire to his satanical house in Mortlake and destroyed irreplaceable instruments, books and scientific implements.

Like Dee, any intellectual mind, scientist, mathematician, artist could be part of Ralegh's circle. George Chapman, whose first poem, 'Shadow of Night', was printed in 1594 was one of those sceptics, Christopher Marlowe among them, who were interested in extending science and philosophy beyond the limits of contemporary belief and good manners. The group was bound together by a common curiosity, suspected of being atheists and hence condemned by most of their fellows, but mocked by Shakespeare in his *Love's Labours Lost*:

> No face is fair that is not so full so black.
> O paradox! Black is the badge of hell,
> The hue of dungeons, and the school of night.[4]

After Marlowe's violent death one of his many enemies said that the poet had laughed that Moses had been a juggler, that Christ had been born out of wedlock, that Marlowe had blasphemously spelled God backward, and jeered that 'they that love not Tobacco and Boys were fools'.[5] It was a mixture of irreverence, mockery and devil-may-care defiance that would appeal to an immature, young man like the Earl of Southampton. As Shakespeare's rival for the affection of the earl Marlowe had advantages. He was the greater poet and he had an inclination to homosexuality that his poetic genius could make appealing to an adolescent. He seductively flattered Southampton in 'Hero and Leander', by comparing his appearance with Leander's beautiful, almost feminine body: 'His dangling tresses that were never shorn ...'; 'His body as straight as Circe's wand ...; and:

> How smooth his breast was, and how white his belly,
> And whose immortal fingers did imprint
> That heavenly path with many a curious dint,
> that runs along his back, ...
> Some swore he was a maid in man's attire
> For in his looks were all that men desire,
> A pleasant smiling cheek, a speaking eye,
> A brow for love to banquet royally;
> And such as knew he was a man would say,
> Leander, thou art made for amorous play:
> Why art thou not in love, and lov'd of all?
> Though thou be fair, yet be not thine own thrall.[6]

'Thou art made for amorous play'. It was direct and it may have ended in a successful seduction of a youth wanting to be seduced. Shakespeare could never have been so intimately flattering. It did not matter.

The rivalry between Marlowe and him ended on the evening of Wednesday 30 May 1593. Marlowe was stabbed to death in Dame Eleanor Bull's 'victualling house' on Deptford Strand after a supposedly drunken argument over the bill for food and wine. It may have been a violent quarrel that ended in tragedy. But it may have been a deliberate political assassination committed by one of Marlowe's three companions, Ingram Frizier. There were suspicions.[7] Within a month of the fatality Frizier was pardoned, having pleaded 'self-defence, and for the protection of his life'. Marlowe was buried by the north side of St Nicholas church tower, Deptford, in an unmarked grave. The tower survives. The grave does not.

Shakespeare mourned him in his Sonnet 86, a poem that contained a transition from the present tense to the past caused by Marlowe's sudden death. Shakespeare realised how close his rival had come to success in the pursuit of Southampton, that 'all too precious' prize:

> Was it the proud full sail of his great verse,
> Bound for the prize of all too precious you,
> That did my ripe thoughts in my brain inhearse,
> Making their tomb the womb wherein they grew?
> Was it his spirit, by spirits taught to write
> Above a mortal pitch, that struck me dead?
> No, neither he, nor his compeers by night ...

'Compeers' was a reference to Ralegh's almost notorious friends and followers, his School of Night, with their heretical attitude to Elizabethan religious beliefs.[8] Shakespeare also mourned Marlowe in a line of *As You Like It*: 'It strikes a man more dead than a great reckoning in a little room'.[9] It was one more intentional compliment to some of the dead playwright's own lines. 'Infinite riches in a little room' were words spoken at the very beginning of Marlowe's play *The Jew of Malta*.[10]

Where Shakespeare and Henry Wriothesley first met is unknown. It may have been in the earl's London home, Southampton House north of the walls beyond Holborn in open countryside. In the mid-twelfth century it had been the property of the Bishop of Lincoln before being acquired by the Earls of Southampton after the dissolution of the monasteries. It was one of the grand buildings of London. If that first meeting had not been at Southampton House then it would have been at the earl's Hampshire semi-palace, the converted Titchfield House on the south coast near Fareham, a building that had once been an abbey of the Norbertine or White Canons.

During Henry VIII's dissolution of the monasteries in the late 1530s Titchfield's religious buildings were sold in 1546 to the second Earl of Southampton and were converted into a family home with an imposing three-storeyed, crenellated gatehouse opening onto a paved, unroofed courtyard that once had been the monastic cloisters. Titchfield, originally meaning 'the pasture where young goats, kids, grazed', was near a small port on the Meon estuary. In the 1550s John Leland, 'king's antiquary' and topographer, saw the house on one of his itineraries:

> I left a praty lake on the lifte a little or I enterid into Tichefeld toun. Mr. Wriothesley hath buildid a right stately house embatelid, and having a goodely gate, and a conducte castelid in the middle of the court of it, yn the very same place wher the late monasterie of Premostratenses stoode caullyd Tichefelde ... There is also a parke, the ground wherof is sumwhat hethy and baren.[11]

At that time the house was newly-built. At their eviction the monastery's canons had already stealthily removed the church valuables and Southampton ordered the empty church to be pulled down and his luxurious house erected. It was to be built of the finest Caen stone imported from northern France.

It was palatial. To its cramped left at the far end of the courtyard were kitchens, pantries, stairs leading down to cellars and storerooms. To its spacious right were rooms for the house's owners and guests with stairs from the courtyard leading to the first floor and the luxuries of a banqueting room, a withdrawing room, a balcony overlooking the gardens and fountain, and bedrooms for family and visitors. It was 'a design intentionally very much along the lines of Florentine and northern Italian palaces. These were likewise mostly built around a square, with the principal rooms on the first floor, or *piano nobile*, approached by an ornate staircase. Given the contemporary fashion for things Italian, Shakespeare's host no doubt felt very proud of this aspect of his home. At Titchfield, therefore, Shakespeare would have felt he was walking into a mini-Italy.[12] Even earlier the original building had been a place of learning. In his book *Hampshire* Arthur Mee said:

> It had one of the finest monastic libraries in England with 224 volumes. The abbey was given by Henry the Eighth to Thomas Wriothesley, for the help he had given with the king's Great Business, which was the earl's polite name for Henry's abandonment of his faithful Catherine. He pulled the abbey down and built Place House with its stones. His house is now a magnificent ruin overlooking the great fishpond guarded by an ancient mighty oak. The square gatehouse stands across the vanished nave, lofty embattled turrets rise at the corners, and there are slender chimneys of delicate and intricate design. Still intact in the massive walls are deeply mullioned windows and the huge fireplaces lined with herringbone brickwork. We can clearly see the foundations of the great abbey church, the stone coffins in their places, and all reverent and in order. Here, we must believe, came Shakespeare to see his patron.[13]

Sic transit gloria mundi. Today Southampton's 'palace' is an imitation of a ruin, an emptiness of a façade of a bleak wall with no building, skeletons of windows, its history having shifted from a wilderness to an area where animals had grazed to a great church to a palatial house before reverting to abandonment, disintegration and extinction.

But Shakespeare had been there. He had stayed at Titchfield and he had been to St Peter's church, the burial-place of the Earls of Southampton. With its fine Norman tower and its multi-period mixture of Anglo-Saxon, Norman and later styles it is dignified and well-ordered, quiet. It also contains a whisper of a Shakespearian play. In its chancel a small tablet commemorates an Augustine Gobbo who had died in 1593. Being a writer Shakespeare remembered the amusing surname. A few years later around 1597 it reappeared in *The Merchant of Venice* as Launcelot Gobbo, Shylock's clownish servant.[14] It is at this stage of the Dark Lady story that the wisps and thin threads of information about her become both insecure and entangled. It starts with Southampton's mother.[15]

Lady Mary Browne, daughter of Viscount Montague, the head of a fervently Catholic family, was very lovely. She was also strong-willed. She had such determination that in 1566 in her early teens she defiantly married the second Earl of Southampton. He also was strong-willed and defiant. The marriage was sanctified 'without the consent of my lady, his mother'.[16] After the early deaths of two of their children a son, Henry Wriothesley, was born on Tuesday 6 October 1573. It was whispered that the baby was baptised by a Catholic priest. The boy, soon to have a sister, would become the third Earl of Southampton and, eventually, Shakespeare's patron.

Mary Browne's impetuous marriage was not a happy one. Her once-besotted husband turned against her, became neglectful, idle and, worse, had a preference for men, in particular his servant, Thomas Dymoke. The earl's son would develop similar homosexual inclinations. The young Southampton's father died early in 1581. Predictably and spitefully he left most of his possessions to Dymoke who took command of everything. As the widow wrote to her father, 'this house is not for them that will not honour Dymoke as a god'. There was worse.

The earl's vindictive last wishes directed that his young daughter should be looked after not by his widow, the child's mother, but by his sister, and that his son should be brought up away from his mother in the protective household of Lord Burghley, the Lord Chancellor, becoming a ward of court.[17] The separation was intentionally cruel. By its arrangement Mary was not to see her son for two years. In the autumn of 1585 Southampton became an undergraduate of St John's College in Cambridge. He was there for four years, quite unaware that he was the contemporary of great literary men. During that short time Christopher Marlowe interruptedly attended Corpus Christi College between 1580 and 1587. There were other fine writers there. Thomas Nashe and Robert Greene were at the same university.

In 1588, the year of the Spanish Armada, Southampton became a member of Gray's Inn. On 6 June 1589, by a special grant, he was awarded an MA on his sixteenth birthday. That summer with his mother he wrote to Burghley thanking him for his care and his guidance. But there was a problem, the question of his proposed marriage to Burghley's grand-daughter, Lady Elizabeth Vere, fifteen years old in 1590. Southampton agreed to the engagement, hesitated then asked for a deferment, 'a year's respite'. He had no wish to marry. He wanted glory. Burghley was furious to have been so slighted. Had he known, the Secretary of State would have been further angered to be informed that Robert Devereux, Earl of Essex, had secretly married Frances Walsingham, the widow of Sir Philip Sidney.

It was one of a thousand deceptions. The Elizabethan aristocratic court was a hall of distorting mirrors in which the only sounds were like whispers in an empty room. There were plots against the queen. There were religious doubts about the clean-living Puritans. There were official Protestant suspicions against unofficial Catholics whose Jesuit priests were smuggled into the country to be hidden in the homes of the nobility only to be sadistically tortured and executed whenever they were unearthed. In the early 1590s there were spies, informers, traitors and many ordinary men and women. They were the years of Shakespeare's first plays. And also of his Dark Lady whom he may have already met and who knew the young Earl of Southampton.

Lord Burghley, Chancellor of England, suspected that the Southampton household was inhabited by zealous and disloyal Catholics. To protect Protestant England from religious rebellion he placed a spy in the house, a man called John Florio. The young earl was not there. In France Henry of Navarre was desperate to defend his throne against the Catholic League and appealed to the English queen for help. Her favourite, the Earl of Essex, cajoled Elizabeth into giving him command of the expedition. In January 1591, the ardent, and typically impatient eighteen-year-old Earl of Southampton volunteered to join him and without permission impetuously crossed to Normandy. He did not wait for Essex. Predictably, he achieved nothing except frustration as Giroux noticed:

> It was observed in his lifetime that Southampton had two ardent passions: one for military glory, martial adventure, and renown, the second for that other glory, to shine as a patron of literature. Devotion to the sedate Lord Treasurer, a quiet life as his son-in-law, would achieve neither of these.[18]

Nothing came of the madcap venture in France although romantic minds did compare it with the exploits of Henry V at Agincourt. It was romance rather than reality. But it did happen in a year that may have inspired Shakespeare to write his trilogy of plays about those heroically, martial deeds of the English, his trilogy of *Henry VI, I, II* and *III*. It was the beginning of his fame as a playwright.

Despite his inexperience, impatience and arrogance Southampton did have one incomparable asset, his famous loveliness. 'A woman's face with Nature's own hand painted', rhapsodised Shakespeare enthusiastically.[19] The twenty-year-old earl was exceptionally attractive in his appearance. He had a refined, aristocratic, if somewhat feminine face, rather elongated and heart-shaped like his mother's. His features were regular with sensitively curved lips, finely arched eyebrows, and long dandified curling tresses of chestnut hair over his left shoulder. In appearance he closely resembled his mother in 'the lovely April of her prime'. 'Thou art thy mother's glass'.[20] Aware of his loveliness the young man added to it by his discriminating choice of elegant, dandified clothing. Park Honan stated:

> Southampton was becoming an exhibit. He enhanced a slender, lightly-built form with delicate fabrics, his clinging white doublet, dancing hat-feathers, and purple garters could be offset by a lovely tress of auburn hair falling to the breast.[21]

The earl had the attraction of his physical loveliness. He also had a defect – the seductive lure of homosexuality. He was attracted to both women and men. In those years homosexuality was not uncommon. Famous and infamous men, Francis Bacon, Christopher Marlowe and James I among them, were suspected of the vice. The Earl of Southampton was another. Years later in 1598, while he was campaigning in Ireland with the Earl of Essex, it was maliciously reported that the earl had slept in a tent with Piers Edmond, a brother officer, and they ate and drank at his table and 'the earle Sowthampton woule cole and huge [embrace and hug] him in his armes and play wantonly with him'.[22]

There were tongues in Elizabethan England and there was peril in their use. In 1593, six months after Shakespeare's 'Venus and Adonis', the writer Thomas Nashe dedicated his picaresque novel, *The Unfortunate Traveller or the Life of Jack Wilson*, to Southampton. He wrote: 'A dear lover and cherisher you are, as well as of the lovers of poets as of poets themselves'. It was ambiguous. A 'lover of poets' could be read as a 'man loving men', a catamite, the Italian *catamito*, 'a Ganymede', a man who liked to 'wantonly play with boys against nature'. In the popular book's second edition of the same year Nashe omitted the dangerous dedication.[23]

Derogatory rumours about Southampton had begun long before. As early as 1591 John Clapham, one of Lord Burghley's secretaries, Burghley being no lover of a former ward who had rejected a proposed wife, wrote a Latin poem entitled, 'Narcissus', the mythical youth in love with his own image. In the poem's sub-title Southampton was accused of 'Self Love' and urged to have an 'increase of manliness'.[24] And in courtly society Southampton became derisively nicknamed 'Ganymede', that lovely young cupbearer to the gods and, contemptibly, their plaything.

The erudite lexicographer and translator of Italian, John Florio, had been 'planted' in Titchfield by Lord Burghley to spy on the family's suspected Catholic activities. By the end of 1591 the distinguished scholar had acquired both the Earl of Southampton and the Earl of Pembroke as his patrons. Between 1592 and 1594 he was staying in Southampton's household, ostensibly as the young earl's language tutor but, in reality, as an agent put there to keep an eye both on the young man and on the others of that near-notorious Catholic family. Burghley had already used Florio on government business at the time of the Babington Plot in 1586.

Florio, born in London 1533, was a learned scholar who had published his *First Fruits* in 1578. He was to become famous for his translation of Montaigne's *Essays*. In London he lived at Shoe Lane just west of the malodorous and unhealthy Fleet River. In April, 1591 he published a second version of his book:

> Signor John Florio, that wrote the *First Fruits*, being an induction to the Italian tongue, thirteen years since, now perfecteth his *Second Fruits* in twelve chapters, both in the Italian tongue and the English. In these witty and familiar discourses many subjects are treated of, such as the set at tennis, games of cards or chess, fencing, the thirteen bodily parts of beauty in an woman; ending with a pleasant discourse of love and women. To this book is added *The Gardine of Recreation*, yielding six thousand Italian proverbs.[25]

He was not idle in business or pleasure. As well as acting as a spy for the English government by becoming a tutor to a family, the Southamptons, suspected of Roman Catholic sympathies, he also married an attractive young woman, possibly Shakespeare's 'Dark Lady', whose Christian name has been lost. Between espionage and private indulgence Florio retained sufficient mental energy to publish another book, a detailed dictionary in Italian and English called *A World of Words*. He dedicated it to three hoped-for benefactors, the Earl of Rutland, the Earl of Southampton and the Countess of Bedford. The Elizabethan world was a world of shadows and conspiracies. Scholar, translator, tutor, Florio was also a mole as Bate said:

> That Florio actually actively spied on Burghley's behalf is a strong inference, not a proven act. It is certainly the case that some years earlier Burghley's righthand man, Walsingham, had placed Florio in the French embassy, incurring the suspicion of the ambassador. The spy, 'Henry Fagot', Giordano Bruno, [an associate of Florio] reported to Walsingham a conversation in which the ambassador, Chateauneuf, said, 'What about Maitre Geoffroy, the doctor? In France they say he's a double agent, works both for the Huguenots and the Pope. They don't trust Laurent or Florio much either'.[26]

Florio would have been at Southampton's Titchfield home at the time when the earl's anxious mother, Mary, Countess of Southampton, already knew of Shakespeare both from his growing reputation as a poet and from his offering of 'Venus and Adonis' and then his second long poem, 'The Rape of Lucrece' to the earl. She had already met the poet who wrote of her beauty. The dedication of the 'Rape' was similar to that of 'Venus and Adonis' but it was warmer:

> The love I dedicate to your Lordship is without end: wherof this Pamphlet without beginning is but a superfluous moiety ... What I have done is yours, what I have to do is yours, being part in all I have, devoted yours.[27]

The Countess of Southampton was desperate that her son should not become a pattern of his homosexual father. There had already been danger from his youthful association with Marlowe. Knowing William Shakespeare from his dedications of long poems to the young earl she asked him to compose some sonnets urging her son to be aware of the need to marry and have the pleasure of children. Shakespeare agreed. He wrote seventeen.

An interpolation is necessary. There has never been a suggestion anywhere that Mary, Countess of Southampton, was the mysterious Dark Lady. High-spirited she was but she was not incestuous. She was not the woman to have a forbidden physical association with her own son. Whoever the Dark Lady was, Jacqueline Field or any other of the eight possible temptresses, she was not the Countess of Southampton who had been so callously treated by her husband years before.

To have been so abruptly separated from her son would have broken many women. Not the widowed Countess of Southampton. Being of independent mind she developed her own interests. She did not allow herself boredom. Widowhood or not the former Mary Browne was indefatigable, determined to live well, and after twelve years of widowhood married the elderly but wealthy Sir Thomas Heneage in 1594. It was a wedding cheerfully celebrated in Shakespeare's *A Midsummer Night's Dream*. Heneage died the following year. Undeterred, his rich widow married for the third time in 1598, becoming the wife of Sir William Hervey. She died in 1607 leaving many of her possessions to her husband. Shortly, Hervey remarried. He was to become one more shadow in Shakespeare's life.

Years before those events it may have been that publication of 'The Rape of Lucrece' in 1594, a poem about desecrated virtue and violent lust that had persuaded the countess to commission Shakespeare to write some virtuous sonnets for her son extolling the benefits of having a wife. They might persuade that wilful and reluctant young man of uncertain sexuality, to marry. Dutifully, and lucratively rewarded, Shakespeare wrote the poems. In quality the made-to-order sonnets were what they were, 'paid-by-the-line' poems extolling the benefits of marriage, the joy of having children, and the dangers and sadness of becoming old and childless.

The first of the sonnets described the pleasures of having children 'that thereby beauty's rose might never die', which was a rather heavy flattering pun on Wriothesley, 'Rosely'. The second sonnet described the horrors of growing old 'and dig deep trenches in thy beauty's field', becoming a 'tattered weed'. The third complimented the earl on his good looks, 'thou art thy mother's glass' but reminding him 'die single and thine image dies with thee'. It was clever, it was true but it was a vacuum. A conceited, handsome and well-to-do young man preferred to enjoy the moment. The future was a long way away.

They were good sonnets, worthy of Shakespeare, but there was an unexpected and unintended irony in them. The self-absorbed Henry Wriothesley, third Earl of Southampton, was not changed by them. But Shakespeare was by Wriothesley. The tone of the sonnets altered. The first group, some fourteen poems, had been ordered by Southampton's concerned mother. But the later sonnets, over a hundred of them are about a genuine friendship with its pleasures, disappointments and agonies between Shakespeare and the young earl. Sonnet 104 continued the theme of youth and age but it was an emotional poem:

To me, fair friend, you can never be old,
For as you were when first your eye I eyed,
Such seems your beauty still. Three winters cold
Have from the forests shook three summer's pride,
Three beauteous springs to yellow autumn turned
In process of the seasons have I seen,
Three April perfumes in three hot Junes burned
Since I first saw you fresh, which yet are green.
Ah, yet doth beauty, like a dial hand,
Steal from his figure, and no pace perceived,
So your sweet hue, which methinks still doth stand,
Hath motion, and mine eye may be deceived;

For fear of which, hear this, thou age unbred;
Ere you were born was beauty's summer dead.

'Three beauteous springs' does not have to mean thirty-six months. From the beginning of Spring 1592 to the onset of Spring in 1594 would have been no more than a day or more longer than two years: three winters, three springs, three April perfumes, two years from early 1592 to the blossoming trees of two years later.

Sonnet 104 was discreet. The poet and the young earl were friends, liking each other but a distance apart through separate worldly positions and through age. It was a respectful poem. Sonnet 20 was not. It suggested a different relationship between the two men, a physical one.

A woman's face, with Nature's own hand painted,
Hast thou, the master mistress of my passion,
A woman's gentle heart, but not acquainted
With shifting change, as is false woman's fashion;
An eye more bright than theirs, less false in rolling,
Gilding the object whereupon it gazeth;
A man in hue all hues in his controlling,
Which steals men's eyes and women's souls amazeth.
And for a woman wert thou first created,
Till Nature as she wrought thee fell a-doting,
And by addition me of thee defeated,
By adding one thing to my purpose nothing
But since she pricked thee out for women's pleasure,
Mine be thy love and thy love's use their treasure.

In today's order of the sonnet sequence Sonnet 20 comes very shortly after the 'made-to-measure' poems. It is an extraordinary work, a piece of 'nonchalant anti-feminism'. In it every line has a 'feminine' ending with a weak, unstressed syllable, and it is addressed to a man with an almost feminine appearance but with indisputable male organs. It was, wrote Paterson:

One of 126 love-poems dedicated to a bloke. (Let me also cite the recently unearthed portrait of Wriothesley which the Cobbe family – in whose possession it had been for 300 years – had assumed as of a female ancestor. Not only had Nature painted Wriothesley as a damn fine-looking woman, some unknown artist of the early 1590s had too, with rouge and lipstick).

Paterson added that the phrase 'for a woman' is ambiguous being capable of being understood as 'for the use of a woman' but also 'as a woman'.[28]

Years after its first printed publication in 1609 many editors recoiled, embarrassed, from the sonnet. In 1840 Richardson considered it 'one of the most painful and perplexing [poems] I ever read ... I could heartily wish that Shakespeare had never written it'. And almost a hundred years earlier George Steevens anticipated him: 'It is impossible to read this fulsome panegyrick, addressed to a male object, without an equal mixture of disgust and indignation'. In 1780, Malone, his contemporary, agreed but was more understanding of the differences between Elizabethan and Georgian moral standards: 'Such addresses to men, however indelicate, were customary in our author's time, and neither imported criminality, nor were esteemed indecorous'.[29]

Unarguably, Sonnet 20 was a homosexual poem, a statement of the androgynous nature of the relationship that was developing between the poet and the earl 'a love poem from one man to another, from a married yeoman father of three to one of the greatest nobles of the land'.[30] The young earl had every appearance of a lovely woman but with a man's body, 'a woman's gentle heart, but not acquainted'. It was a crude pun on the word quaint, 'being the old-fashioned predecessor for the female pudenda'. The Italian translator Florio knew it: '*Conno*, a woman's private parts, or quaint, as Chaucer calls it'.[31] Southampton being a man had been born with a penis, not a vagina, and there were clearly implied hopes of homosexuality in the final lines of the sonnet:

But since she pricked thee out for women's pleasure,
Mine be thy love and thy love's use their treasure.[32]

In *Romeo and Juliet*, a play written in those early years, Mercutio replies to an innocent enquiry about the time of day with a dirty joke about the word: 'Tis no less, I tell you, for the bawdy hand of the dial is now upon the prick of noon', 'hand', 'prick', the audience guffawed.[33] 'Treasure' was another ambiguity. It was the sexual delight of entering a woman's most precious and private organ, even raping her. Shakespeare used it in *Titus Andronicus*, a play written a year or two earlier than *Romeo and Juliet*:

… strike, brave boys, and take your turns,
There serve your lusts, shadowed from heaven's eye,
And revel in Lavinia's treasury.[34]

And for some years William Shakespeare and the third Earl of Southampton would revel in the medley of pleasures offered by Elizabethan London. One of them was an especial delight, the attentions of the 'Dark Lady'. Shakespeare was to write many words about her, her charms, her whims and her inconstancy.

Excluding his early sonnets of the 1580s the majority of them were written between 1590 and 1605. At some time during those years both Shakespeare and the Earl of Southampton were to meet their evasive mistress. Of the many women named as candidates in that period three can be excluded as either fictitious or impossible. Of the remainder eight could have been the witchlike seductress – any one of them from Jacqueline Field at the beginning to Jane Davenant at the end. They are all to be considered.

5

Titchfield: Treachery &
Another Dark Lady

I was thoroughly determined that, whatever came of it, I would
by God's grace never defile her wedlocked bed.

Thomas Whythorne, *The Autobiography*, p. 187.

Today Titchfield is a pleasantly small town of attractive Stuart
and Georgian houses only a few miles north of the Solent and
the English Channel. Not far away the ruin of Place House,
erected on the site of the deconsecrated Titchfield Abbey, is still
impressive with its surviving great gatehouse and embattled
turrets. Its owners had once possessed eleven manors and
lands of some 5,000 acres.

In the late sixteenth century the house was a busy place of
courtiers, servants and scholars. Royalty: Henry VIII, Edward
VI and Queen Elizabeth, had stayed there. On an old plan of
the rooms on the first floor is one labelled 'Playhouse room'. It
may have been the place where visiting acting companies such
as Shakespeare's rehearsed. One of Titchfield's lesser visitors
may have been the Dark Lady. She was in her early twenties,
married, and she was temperamental.

Living in a pleasant part of London she often went to
Titchfield. Who she was and how she comes into the story
of Shakespeare's Dark Lady is important. But first must
come an account of a woman, perhaps the same one, called
Avisa. According to a poem about her Avisa was a virgin, an

innkeeper's daughter. When she was almost thirty years old she became a faithful wife whose beauty and chastity teased and tormented many lustful admirers including both the naïve and susceptible young Earl of Southampton and his new, very close friend, 'the old player', William Shakespeare. Her 'story' was told in a long, tedious and enigmatic poem, *Willobie His Avisa* that described the woman's many disappointed suitors including the rejected earl who wept when she scorned his clumsy advances. The poem is another Elizabethan hall of mirrors, a *roman à clef*, a poem whose names were fictitious but intentionally no more than shallow disguises for the real men who pursued that unattainable woman hidden behind the cryptic name of 'Avisa'. Its author, 'Willobie' was a friend and defender of the disgraced Ralegh who had retired to his lovely home at Sherborne in Dorset. Willoughby lived only a few miles to the west at West Knoyle.

Ralegh had been charged of atheism but nothing came of the accusation except for some derision in Shakespeare's *Love's Labours Lost* to amuse his young and wealthy patron, the frivolously vacuous Earl of Southampton. 'Black is the badge of Hell and School of Night', mocked Shakespeare, going on to mock Ralegh in *Love's Labours Lost* as the 'magnificent Armado', 'a refined traveller ... a man in all the world's new fashions planted', deriding the discoveries of tobacco and potatoes that Ralegh had brought back from the New World. Ralegh was mocked as a pedant with pompous language.[1] One of his associates in that School of Night was John Florio.

In reply to the slanders 'Willobie' defended Ralegh by counter-attacking his enemies in a poem, *Willobie His Avisa*, a tedium of more than 3,000 plodding iambic pentameters in which 'HW', Henry Wriothesley, the Earl of Southampton, was assisted by 'WS', William Shakespeare. In succession, jeered Willobie, they had clumsily and vainly tried to seduce that innkeeper's virtuous daughter, Avisa. Her inn happened to be close to Sherborne and Ralegh. The chaste Avisa, of course, rejected her suitors. 'Your lawless lust I here defy'. She was also sufficiently educated in classical literature to justify her defiance by quoting lines in defence of virtue from the Roman poet, Catullus, in Cantos 30 and 42. A remarkable woman. But the amorously bisexual Catullus was perhaps not the perfect model.

The apparently anonymous 'Willobie' was Henry Willoughby of West Knoyle a few miles north-west of Sherborne. He was educated at Oxford first at St John's and then at Exeter College where he was granted his degree in 1595. By an ironical family coincidence he had an association with his opponent, William Shakespeare. Five years earlier his elder brother had married Eleanor Bampfield whose sister in the same month became the wife of Thomas Russell of Stratford, an old acquaintance of Shakespeare.

Willobie His Avisa was printed in 1594 and was reprinted in five more editions. At the beginning of the book was a poem of six verses praising *Willobie his Avisa*. Its authors were *Vigiliantius* and *Dormitamus*, a pair of giggling, adolescent punsters, two young Balliol undergraduates, one the vigilant Robert Wakeman, 'wide awake', the other, the dormitory-bound Edward Napper, 'fast asleep'.[2] The poem contained the first direct literary reference to Shakespeare, naming him and his poem, 'The Rape of Lucrece'. The second verse contained the lines:

Yet Tarquin plucked his glistering grape,
And Shake-speare paints poor Lucrece rape.

Which was a straightforward statement. The fifth verse was not so clear.

Then Avi-Susan join in one,
Let Lucres-Avis be thy name,
This English Eagle soars alone
And far surmounts all others fame,
Where nigh or low, where great or small,
This Briton-Bird out-flies them all.

The 'Briton-Bird' was Elizabeth Tudor, Queen of England. Her 'partner' in the poem, 'Avi-Susan' was Susanna, a rich wife in Babylon who had been accused of immorality by two rejected lecherous old men. Proved liars they were executed.[3] Elizabeth, the virgin queen, was equally free of guilt and virtuous. In the poem she was given the pseudonym of 'Avisa', the bird', and several royal birds appeared in the poem. The disguise was almost transparent. The queen's personal motto was *semper eadem*, 'always the same' and those words were repeated again and again to suitor after suitor in Avisa including the self-deluding youthful 'HW', Henry Wriothesley, 3rd Earl of Southampton.[4]

Willobie His Avisa was composed after Ralegh's fall from grace. While that expelled courtier sulked at Sherborne the author of *Willobie His Avisa* dipped his sharpened quill into a pot of poison to make derisory fun of the various suitors who had courted the queen over the years. The long comedy concluded with jibes at the vain-glorious self-centred, comical Wriothesley.

Elizabeth had been wooed, almost pestered, for almost twenty years since coming to the throne in November 1558 as a young twenty-five-year-old woman. The Spanish ambassador told the Duke of Feria:

> There are ten or twelve Ambassadors of us here, all competing for Her Majesty's hand, and they say the Duke of Holstein is coming next, as a suitor for the King of Denmark. The Duke of Finland, who is here for his brother, the King of Sweden, threatens to kill the Emperor's man; and the Queen fears they may cut each others' throats in her presence. ... As the months went by, the wooers were anything but 'merry as notes in a tune'. Discord was everywhere. 'Here is a great resort of wooers and controversy among lovers', wrote the harassed Sir William Cecil. 'Would to God the Queen had one, and the rest were honourably satisfied'. But there seemed little chance of that.[5]

Those would-be husbands and kings came from all parts of Europe: several from France; from Austria; even from as far away as Sweden whose unstable monarch also wooed Mary, Queen of Scots.[6] Ralegh had seen them all during his long years at court and from his sharp descriptions about their virtues and failings Willoughby was able to laugh at all of those luckless wooers of Avisa, the queen, including a nobleman wearing a lily who was old and rich with extensive lands. Then there was Caveileiro with his 'wannie cheekes', 'shaggy lockes', unluckily infected with the pox; there was 'D. B.' a Frenchman with a farm and enriched with a yearly income of an opulent forty pounds; and the absurd 'D. H.', Dydimus Harco, an Anglo-German who could provide the pleasures of occasional private sex for which he would pay. He did admit that, 'I am no saint ...', but he did give Avisa a ring.[7]

Willoughby derided them and turned each of them into a comical puppet even as his readers glimpsed the face behind the mask. Elizabethan readers of 'Willobie' recognised all of the targets, smiled, but laughed out loud at the poet's last target, Henrico Willobego, an Italian-Spaniard – which was a sharp thrust at Henry Wriothesley and his suspected Catholic beliefs. In Canto after tedious Canto from XLIV to LXXIV 'H. W.' wooed Avisa, pleaded with her, begged, wept. And in Canto after Canto Avisa rejected him. In LXIV she bade him stop his unmanly snivelling:

> If I do sometimes looke awrie
> As loth to see your blobered face,
> And loth to heare a young man crie,
> Correct for shame tis childish race,
> And though you weepe and waile to mee,
> Yet lete not all these follies see.

And in LXVIII:

> seeing the teares trill downe his cheeks, as halfe angry to see such passionate follie, in a man that should have government, with a frowning countenance turned from him.

In despair the unwanted Southampton turned to his newly-found friend, William Shakespeare, for advice and encouragement. In Canto XLVII the poet was prosaic and very down-to-earth:

> It is not hard to fynd reliefe,
> If thou wilt follow good advyse:
> She is no Saynt, She is no Nonne,
> I thinke in tyme she may be wonne.

But she was unwinnable. 'Avisa', the Queen of England, never did favour the immature earl. She respected grown men who were courteous and attentive, not egotistic, immature youngsters. After one of his childish outbreaks of temper, Elizabeth told Southampton to leave her Court. It happened during one of the last years when Sir Walter Ralegh was still a favoured courtier.

It was late one night. The queen had already retired. Three men, Southampton, Ralegh and a Mr Parker were gambling at *primero* late, a four-card game played for money. After a time the Squire of the Court, ironically yet one more Willoughby, albeit a 'young' one, but of no known connection to the author of 'Willobie', told them stop. They ignored him. He repeated the order saying that if he were to be disobeyed he would call the guard. Two of the players were sensible. Ralegh 'put up his money' and went. So did Parker. Characteristically, like a spoiled brat, Southampton argued, refused to go, lost his temper and hit Willoughby. In return he had his long, very carefully arranged hair painfully tugged and yanked. Next morning it was the gossip of a disdainful court. Even the queen had heard of the incident and of Southampton's stupid tantrums. A. L. Rowse wrote:

> The Queen gave Willoughby thanks for what he did in the Presence and told him he had done better if he had sent him to the porter's lodge to see who durst have fetched him out. The Queen followed this up by commanding the Earl to absent him from Court.[8]

Elizabeth had lost patience with Southampton over his semi-treasonable Catholicism, his conceited manners, and the rumours that he was linking himself too strongly with the enemies of Ralegh.[9]

The sleazy jibes about the earl in *Willobie His Avisa* had worsened his already questionable reputation. That satire also advertised Southampton's wilful courting of Elizabeth Vernon at the very time when he was openly rejecting Burghley's preference, Lady Elizabeth de Vere, a proposed match that had already been royally approved. As if those slurs were not sufficient the malevolent Willobie added hints and nudges about the earl's homosexuality, remarks that were not only embarrassing but, in Tudor years, very dangerous. Willobie was vicious. Sneers; slanders; stupid defiance of Burghley; unnatural tendencies; association with a common player. For Willoughby, a friend of the banished Ralegh, there was nothing that could be written that was too offensive against one of that knight's enemies. The immature 'I want my own way' Southampton was an easy target for any satirist as he sulked in the semi-banishment of his great house on the south coast. He would have been even more uneasy had he been aware that a man living there as his language tutor had been insinuated into Titchfield as a spy by his most powerful enemy, Lord Burghley. It was yet one more hall of mirrors in which the obvious was not the reality.

Giovanni Florio, once a language tutor at Oxford, was already well-known for his 1578 collection of Italian proverbs, *First Fruits*, a book that he was to expand into some 6,000 sayings in his *Second Fruits* of 1591. In that book, perhaps because he himself was an enthusiastic visitor of playhouses like the *Bull* and the *Theatre* to see their performances, 'he included under advice on how "to speak to a damsel" a sentence on how to invite her to go to the theatre to see a comedy'.[10] Living in Holborn near Gray's Inn, Florio had a choice of many theatres in London, converted old inn-yards like the *Saracen's Head* and the *Boar's Head* or the 'proper' playhouse of the *Bull* in Bishopsgate that the Queen's Men used as their winter quarters, or, much farther to the north in Shoreditch, the almost new *Curtain* and the *Theatre*. In Hackney today memorial plaques in Curtain Road and Hewett Street commemorate the existence of those playhouses. The first announces that 'William Shakespeare acted at the *Theatre*. Built by James Burbage. Plays by Shakespeare were performed here'. Florio would have known it well.

Whichever playhouse he chose to attend it is unlikely that Florio would have taken any friend to the *Red Bull*, former inn-yard in Clerkenwell with its reputation for violence and vulgarity and its audience of 'cutt-throats and other ill-disposed persons'. It was one of London's longest-lasting and rougher theatres. A large, rectangular building with the expected galleries it was one of the last inn theatres to be converted into a conventional theatre. There is a theatrical irony. That disreputable playhouse was bought years later in 1627 by Shakespeare's Company and 'was later the only one to keep them [Shakespeare's plays] on the stage'. The disreputable *Red Bull* was later owned by Charles II's favourite, Thomas Killigrew, and became 'the only open-air theatre to survive the theatrical holocaust of England's Commonwealth period'.[11] Even had Florio been disinclined to patronise such an unwholesome place there was no shortage of semi-respectable playhouses for anyone wanting to see an accomplished company of actors in a comedy or a tragedy.

Florio was an associate of the famous Danish astronomer, Tycho Brahe, who had an artificial nose made after his real one was badly mutilated in a duel. It was a conceit and an extravagance. Brahe had the replacement made of gold and silver and painted to appear a natural colour. It was whispered that he carried a phial of glue to keep the nose firmly in place.[12] Florio never mentioned it.

In London he lived for years with his wife in Shoe Lane just west of the Fleet River. It was a well-known street in Farringdon Ward stretching from Oldbourne down to the Fleet Street conduit. Children were born there. But by the early 1590s because of Florio's knowledge of foreign languages both Florio and his wife had been living on and off at Titchfield for some years. The identity of Florio's wife is one more mystery in the story of the Dark Lady.

As early as 1586 the queen's powerful Secretary of State, Henry Cecil, Lord Burghley, had used Florio as a secret agent during the government's secretive investigations into the treasonable Catholic Babington Plot. A year later Burghley was briefly in disgrace for having despatched the death warrant for the execution of Mary, Queen of Scots, without royal consent, but he was soon forgiven. He was trusted. 'My Spirit', Elizabeth nicknamed him. He was the spider of a web of secret activities. Giovanni Florio was one of his agents. Bate observed that in 1591 Burghley arranged that the essayist would be at Titchfield to spy on the Southampton family:

> That Florio actually actively spied on Burghley's behalf is a strong inference, not a proven act. It is certainly the case that some years earlier Burghley's right-hand man, [Francis] Walsingham, had placed Florio in the French embassy, incurring the suspicion of the ambassador.[13]

It might have been at Titchfield in 1594 that Florio and his wife first saw the playwright and the poet, William Shakespeare. And it may have been in Oxford that ten or more years earlier Florio met the Somerset poet, Samuel Daniel, an encounter that was to cause confusion, consternation, and frustration to researchers seeking the identity of the Dark Lady.

Born in London in 1553, by the 1590s the scholarly translator, Giovanni Florio, was physically unattractive with crooked shoulders and a hawkish nose. He was aging physically yet his mind was still obsessively preoccupied with his work. Intellectually he was incomparable even though he was as Yates noted:

> declining into the vale of years and, to judge from his prodigious literary productivity, devoting himself entirely to his work. At the time in question he as labouring not of love, but at the massive task of single-handedly compiling the first English-Italian dictionary.[14]

Florio was not only a spy and a scholar, he was a good, bi-lingual translator of Italian into English. For his 1598 dictionary, *A World of Words*, he was very matter-of-fact, using everyday language for his readers. It was a virtue that allowed him to interpret the Italian *schinchimurro* as the English, *'a skumming [defecating] of a dog ... a filthy great stinking turd'*. A very down-to-earth translation. There have been mistakes about him. One claimed that he was the father of 'Jennet' Sheppard, later Jane Davenant, wife of an Oxford tavern keeper, a woman who is another feasible candidate to be the Dark Lady. Shakespeare is known to have stayed at her husband's inn. But there is no credible evidence that she was Florio's daughter. Samuel Schoenbaum writes:

> Not until a century after Jennet's death do we encounter the remarkable claim that she was a daughter of John Florio, the writer, translator and Italian tutor of the Earl of Southampton.[15]

Florio enjoyed plays. Ben Jonson remembered that the translator frequently went to theatres, often asking friends 'Where shall we go? To a play at the *Bull*, or to some other place'. As early as 1583 the *Bull* theatre was being used by the Queen's Men and it is quite possible that Shakespeare first met Florio there in the early 1590s.[16] They certainly knew each other. It is believed, although not certain, that Shakespeare wrote the 'Phaeton' sonnet as an encomium at the beginning of Florio's 1591 book, *First Fruits*.

'Phaeton to his friend, Florio'
Sweet friend, whose name agrees with thy increase,
How fit a rival art thou of the spring!

And in the sonnet's seventh line the term, 'little birds', was to be used three years later in 'The Rape of Lucrece', confirming Shakespeare as the writer of the sonnet. He had made a joke about himself as a newly arrived writer. Phaeton had been a mythical youth who had rashly over-reached himself, failing to control the chariot of his father, the Sun, and tumbling to his death.[17] An amused young Shakespeare was comparing himself with that presumptuous daredevil, a newcomer brashly galloping his way into the private realms of the university wits. He seems to have liked the comparison so much that 'Phaeton' was mentioned time and again in his early plays, including twice in *Henry VI*, Pt III.[18]

Florio had spent many years teaching in Oxford and it was in that university city in the early 1580s that he met Samuel Daniel. That well-known Elizabethan poet had been born in 1562 near Taunton, possibly at the cloth-weaving village of Beckington near Frome. He was talented and as a young man in 1579 became a university undergraduate at Magdalen College in Oxford. It was a temperamental mistake. He quickly became bored with tedious pedantry, 'being more prone to easier and smoother studies, than in pecking and hewing at logic' and rote-learning and left after three years without a degree.[19]

Daniel's was an artistic family. His father, John, had been a music-master, one brother became a celebrated poet, and another was a highly-regarded musician and composer. If Daniel did have a sister in that tuneful family it is probable that she also was musically talented. That 'if' is central to the quest for Shakespeare's Dark Lady and it is a very large one. In Daniel's deathbed Will of 1619 there was a bequest to his sister, Susan Bowre. If there was another sister she was not mentioned perhaps because she had died some years earlier.

As always when the Dark Lady appears there is confusion. Charlotte Stopes believed that the mysterious woman had been Jacqueline Field. Jonathan Bate disagreed, preferring Samuel Daniel's sister as the mysterious woman who would become Florio's wife. In his *Athenae Oxoniensis* of 1691–2 the irascible chronicler of distinguished Oxford scholars, Anthony à Wood, included a reference to Daniel:

He was afterwards, for his merits, made gentleman extraordinary, and afterwards one of the grooms, of the privy-chamber to Anne, the queen consort of King James I. who being for the most part a favourer and encourager of his muse, (as she was of Jo. Florio, who married Sam. Daniel's sister).[20]

It was unequivocal. That sister could not have been the married Susan Bowre. In 1617 Giovanni Florio married his second wife, Rose Spicer. His first had been Daniel's elusive other sister whose Christian name is unknown. In various existing records she is more than 'Samuel Daniel's sister' or 'Giovanni Florio's wife'. Ironically, she has no existence in her own right, except perhaps as the nameless Dark Lady.

Bate considered that previous searchers for that elusive woman had consistently – almost obsessively – looked in the wrong direction, being convinced that she was to be discovered in the loose-living theatrical world of London. There were several persuasive candidates including Lucy Morgan, nicknamed 'Negro', a prostitute in Clerkenwell, and Emilia Lanier, mistress of Lord Hunsdon, patron of Shakespeare's Company. But, observed Bate, there was nothing to connect either of them with Shakespeare in the early to mid-1590s. Whereas:

> My Dark Lady, then, is John Florio's wife, who happens to have been the sister of Samuel Daniel, the sonneteer. It is a pleasing fancy that the Dark Lady sonnets might be addressed to the sister of a poet who wrote to a more conventionally fair mistress.

Rather than the self-employed madam of a London brothel or the kept mistress of a wealthy nobleman Bate believed that the mysterious Dark Lady had been an ordinary housewife:

> The 'profile' of the Dark Lady, as a criminal investigator would put it, therefore sounds as if it should be a married woman in or close to the household of Southampton ...

Knowing which people would have been visiting Titchfield in the early 1590s, he concluded that that unidentified woman was Mrs Florio:

My story is not a fantasy. To adapt what Oscar Wilde once said of Will Hughes, his candidate for the 'fair youth', you must believe in Mrs. Florio – I almost do myself. I began to work on the sonnets with a determination to adhere to an agnostic position ... but I have been unable to hold fast to my unbelief.[21]

Even her 'colour' in the sonnets would agree with this identity. Mrs Florio had almost certainly been dark as her husband would have preferred. Florio had already written that his conception of feminine beauty was that 'to be accounted fair' a woman should have 'black eyes, black brows, black hairs', and it is probable that his young wife was like that, a young woman of lovely darkness. Anthony Holden:

Better, even, to think of the Dark Lady in Shakespeare's own fictional terms – as that prototype of Shakespeare's many assertive women, Rosaline in *Love's Labours Lost*, the 'whitely wanton with a velvet brow', with dark 'pitchballs' for eyes.[22]

Daniel's sister probably married Florio around 1580. They had four children: Aurelia, Joane, Edward, and finally Elizabeth in 1589. It could only have been a year or two later when Edward and Elizabeth were still almost babies that Shakespeare was to meet that wife of Florio, the woman that some believe to be the Dark Lady. Shakespeare had been infatuated from the time when he first saw her. His eyes were drawn to her as she walked by him, rather quickly but with elegance. Usually, being a respectable married woman, she did not acknowledge him but sometimes she smiled, said a word or two before passing by. She was a mystery and she intrigued him. He pursued her. Perhaps flattered, perhaps as relief from boredom, she did not repulse him. There were empty rooms at Titchfield. There were beds and mattresses, and there were convenient times when the youngest children were sleeping.

They enjoyed their bodies even while Shakespeare's conscience disturbed him. Both of them were married and each of them had sworn to be faithful to their spouses. But opportunity, temptation and lust overpowered their consciences. In his Sonnet 152 at the very end of the long sequence he wrote:

In loving thee thou know'st I am forsworn,
But thou art twice forsworn, to me love swearing,
In act thy bed-vow broke, and new faith torn
In vowing new hate after new love bearing.
But why of two oaths' breach do I accuse thee,
When I break twenty? I am perjured most,
For all my vows are oaths but to misuse thee,
And all my honest faith in thee is lost;
For I have sworn deep oaths of thy deep kindness,
Oaths of thy love, thy truth, thy constancy;
And to enlighten thee, gave eyes to blindness,
Or made them swear against the thing they see;
For I have sworn thee fair; more perjured eye,
To swear against the truth so foul a lie.

Months later as her affection was fading Shakespeare remembered and in Sonnet 128 pleaded that he should not be abandoned:

... turn back to me
And play the mother's part, kiss me, be kind.
So will I pray that thou mayst have thy *Will*,
If thou turn back and my loud crying still.[23]

Selfishly she did not turn back to him. She had a better prize than an aging poet and paid actor. The youthful, aristocratic, wealthy Earl of Southampton had shown interest and her resistance was little more than a modest protest. What had been flattery from the poet and vanity from the nobleman became transmuted into resentment from the one and indifference and contempt from the other. Shakespeare had suffered double treachery. Bate:

The imagined relationship between the poet and the youth grows from routine flattery to intense love to bitter disillusionment and a sense of betrayal. The articulated relationship between the poet and the Dark Lady veers between mutual sexual use, regarded sometimes casually and sometimes guiltily, and bitterness stemming from the intervention of the fair youth. The element of guilt, and the sexual disgust that explodes in the single extraordinary sentence of Sonnet 129's anatomy of desire, may be caused by the fact that the union involves a breach by both parties of what Sonnet 152 calls the 'bed-vow', which in Elizabethan England strongly implies marriage vows.[24]

Jonathan Bate felt certain that the Dark Lady had been the wife of John Florio, and the sister of Samuel Daniel. 'Certainty' may be no more than belief. It is not certain to be fact.

6

Emilia Bassano/Lanier:
'A Devil Incarnate'

As for the Dark Lady, all was sheerest guesswork until Rowse produced a candidate who would not satisfy a court of law, but seems a splendidly likely choice.

Robin May, *Who was Shakespeare?*, 1974, p. 40.

There never was more than one Dark Lady but for centuries she was indistinguishable among her rivals, one among several others, just another woman that Shakespeare may have known. The beginning of the 1590s was not a time-warp in which individual men and women existed cocooned in solitary existences isolated from mankind. They lived among other people. Several of the suspected Dark Ladies were in London at the same time and they may have passed each other in the street, strangers unaware of the coincidence.

It has become accepted that the Dark Lady of Shakespeare's sonnets was one of eight known women but there is nothing tidy about the relationship between them. They do not stand in line abreast. Nor neatly in a queue. Or even in a cluster. They are like housewives shopping in a market, walking by each other around the stalls. Only time holds them together, the years around the end of the sixteenth century. In that short period six of those women were living in or just outside London's city walls. Marie Mountjoy's house was at the north-west corner in Cripplegate. Half a mile to the east at the far end of the city in Bishopsgate was Emilia Bassano. A quarter of a mile southwards by the north bank of the Thames Jane Davenant's husband was a wine merchant in the Vintry. Half a mile westwards Jacqueline Field's printing house thrived near St Paul's.

Not far outside the city's north-west wall were two more Dark Ladies: Lucy Morgan was amassing an immoral fortune as the madam of a Clerkenwell brothel. Mrs Florio was living with her Italian husband, the translator, John Florio, a quarter of a mile to Morgan's south, at Shoe Lane in Holborn. Exceptions to the London group were the well-bred maids of honour, Mary Fitton and Penelope Devereux. They were a long mile to the south-west enjoying the luxuries and indulgencies of court life at St James Palace in Westminster.

From 1591 to 1596 was a brief period. But those were the years of fame or notoriety for several of the candidates who have confidently been 'identified' as the mysterious woman who had been the poet's lover. And as late as 1600 there were two or three more. 'No man is an island', proclaimed John Donne. Nor was Shakespeare's mistress. She was one of many as Michael Wood has suggested:

> But if the sonnets are autobiographical and she was a real person, we probably do not have far to look to find her in the small world of theatrical and musical society in late 1590s London.[1]

At the end of Shakespeare's long sonnet sequence is the Dark Lady group of twenty-six poems numbers 127 to 152, verses that converted the medley of shadowy women into a tormenting mystery: a night-mare of Dark Ladies. One of them, Rowse's choice, was the married Emilia Lanier. She was no more than one of many possibilities. Jacqueline Field had been the first followed by Mrs Florio, and five other proposed Dark Ladies, all of them living in years overlapping those of their rivals. The daughter of an Italian musician, Emilia Bassano later to be Mrs Lanier, was no different. According to Rowse for several years before and after 1593, the year of the plague, she enticed Shakespeare. That elusive woman was proposed by Rowse as the only woman who ever could have been the enigmatic, theoretically undiscoverable Dark Lady. Without question, he stated:

> I did not think it likely that the Dark Lady would ever be discovered, still less discovered by me. And, indeed, I never set out to find her. All the attempts to put up some candidate by conjecture, and then seek to prove the case, were always so much waste of time – and pursuing a wrong method into the bargain ... She was waiting for me all the time, as she had been waiting for centuries in the Bodleian, in the manuscript case-books of Simon Forman, who knew almost everybody in Elizabethan London.[2]

Other scholars disagreed including Duncan-Jones:

> The search for the 'Lady' appears to have been driven by two motives. The first is a post-Romantic determination to conventionalize and familiarize *Shakespeare's Sonnets*, to attach the poems to that very courtly love tradition which ... Shakespeare was explicitly rejecting and debunking. Once identified, Shakespeare's *femme fatale* could supposedly join the ranks of other such ladies, from Petrarch's Laura to Keats's Fanny Brawne or W. B. Yeats' Maud Gonne, and as a consequence Shakespeare as a love poet could comfortably be assimilated into a great European tradition.[3]

Rowse, however, was certain that the elusive Dark Lady had been Emilia Bassano, half-Italian and, until 1592/3, the mistress of Shakespeare's theatrical company's patron, Henry Carey, Lord Hunsdon. From the tantalisingly fragmentary surviving evidence Emilia Lanier's life seems to have been an emotional turmoil of marriage, music, adultery and high-handedness, a self-centred female dominatrix with an inclination to a belief in the occult. According to Wilson she was 'a tantalisingly close socio-psychological profile to the Dark Lady of Shakespeare's Sonnets'.[4] Being of a musical family she would have been skilled in the playing of a spinet or virginals.

Yet there are doubts about her. Despite the popular acceptance that, being Hunsdon's mistress, she had to be the real Dark Lady surprisingly little is known about her. Even her precise names are not certain, Emilia, but sometimes Aemilia, surname first Bassano, then Lanier, the surname of her husband, but sometimes Lanyer. Born around 1570 she was the daughter of an Italian musician named Bassano. So little is known about her that it is not certain what she looked like, whether she was tall or short, slender or plump, lovely or plain as Ian Wilson has remarked:

> Indeed, the only missing piece of information about Emilia is anything regarding her physical appearance: whether or not she had the black hair and eyebrows so vividly described in Sonnet 127. Rowse thought he had found this in Forman's words, 'She was very brown in youth', but was swiftly corrected by critics spotting that Forman's actual word was 'brave' which in Elizabethan times could mean 'good-looking' or 'showy'. However, since Emilia's father, Battista Bassano, had both Italian and Jewish ancestry there has to be a reasonable likelihood that she herself was indeed black haired. If she was indeed the Dark Lady, Shakespeare and Southampton's involvement with her would seem to have been within a few months of her marriage on 18 October, 1592.[5]

Her family, coming from Venice to England, was of half Sepharic-Jewish, half Italian stock, a polyglot collection of skilled musicians who joined the English court late in Henry VIII's reign. Emilia was illegitimate, the daughter of her father and his common-law wife, the twenty-seven year old Margaret Johnson. With such a genealogical background it is possible that the colour of her skin was olive rather than white. Many unsettling things occurred during her childhood. Her father died when she was six, her mother ten years later bequeathing her daughter £100 sterling, that she was not to inherit it until she was twenty-one. There is no record that the girl ever received the money.

Through her father's connections with the court Emilia Bassano was brought up in the household of the Countess of

Kent, whom she remembered as 'the mistress of my youth, the noble guide of my ungoverned days'. As the countess's lady's maid, she regularly went to the royal court where the now aging queen, Elizabeth, 'danced six or seven galliards a morning, besides music and singing'. It was a tempting environment for a young woman who had only her talents to support and defend her in the dazzling but dangerous world of luxury, laughter and lascivious courtiers.

> Gorgeous ladies of the Court ... their eyes framed to move and bewitch [like] angels painted in church windows with glorious golden fronts beset with sunbeams ... their breasts they embusk up on high, and their round roseate buds immodestly lay forth to show there is fruit to be hoped. They show the swellings of their mind in the swellings and plumpings out of their apparel ...[6]

Around 1588 the far-sighted, coolly-calculating Emilia Bassano ensured her security. To her considerable advantage in her late teens she became the mistress of the elderly Henry Carey, Lord Hunsdon. Rich, handsome and a grand patrician he had been born around 1524, the illegitimate son of Mary Boleyn and Henry VIII. He was baptised 'Henry' after his royal father. Appointed Lord Chamberlain in 1583 he became the patron of Shakespeare's company, a group of actors that regularly played at court.[7]

Those are facts. What follows is speculation, persuasive but conjectural, that Emilia Bassano and William Shakespeare met in London, became lovers and that she was the woman who was adored, pleaded to and cursed in the sonnets. It was probably in the very early 1590s that the two first saw each other when the Lord Chamberlain visited the *Theatre* with her at his side. A play, perhaps by histrionic irony, *The Taming of the Shrew*, was being rehearsed. There was confusion, noise, clutter, the ordinary preparations for the afternoon's performance. Bustle everywhere. Actors strolled across the boards declaiming their parts, boy-players with women's roles fiddled with their wigs, stagehands lifted props down the long, projecting stage.

The City authorities considered playhouses were evil magnets that attracted idle vagabonds, thieves and whores who lingered around disreputable places like the *Theatre* in Shoreditch and the *Rose* far to the south on Bankside. Pickpockets thrived. A contemporary Elizabethan journal recorded:

> Wherefore the Lord Mayor petitioneth the Council for the suppressing of stage plays, declaring that they contain nothing but profane fables, lascivious matters, cozening devices, and other unseemly and scurrilous behaviours, which are so set forth that they move wholly to imitation. Moreover he verily thinketh them to be the chief cause of the late stir and mutinous attempt of those few apprentices and other servants, who no doubt drew their infection from these and like places, and also of many other disorders and lewd demeanours which appear of late in young people of all degrees.[8]

But the plays were popular and drew too much profitable income for their houses to be closed. In one, the *Theatre*, Shakespeare sat with his quill and ink deleting lines, adding others. Then he saw her. She was standing by Hunsdon, beautiful, hardly moving, twisting a ring around her finger. When she spoke to her lord it was quietly, with a smile. Shakespeare stared at her, wondering who she was, noticing how gracefully she moved, her slenderness, the delicacy of her hands, the murmur of her voice with its sensuous appeal of a faint foreign accent. He wanted to know her. Richard Dutton:

> Wood is, I think, the first to nominate Emilia Lanier as Dark Lady to Pembroke's 'fair youth'. What recommends him to her is her own poetic achievement, about which Rowse was at best equivocal; she is now 'accepted in her own right; her poetry is taught on university courses, published in modern editions'. He sees her unconventional accomplishments as befitting Shakespeare's attention, and argues that her Jewish ancestry might have influenced *The Merchant of Venice, c.* 1597. He also hints at a meaningful connection between the publication of her poems and that of the Sonnets: 'within a year, strangely enough,

Emilia Lanier registered her own religious poems, which would be prefaced with a cry from the heart about men's abuse of women'.[9]

As Shakespeare was one of the most important persons in the Lord Chamberlain's Men there were many opportunities for the two of them to meet. There was no need for subterfuge. Readers were told by Rowse: 'In regular Elizabethan fashion he [Shakespeare] got a social superior, his patron, to write to the Lady he desired access to'. No one then or since has seen or even heard of such a letter.[10] Physical attraction does not need written words. A look will be enough. There was a problem. She was pregnant.

Some years later when Emilia Lanier was a long-married woman with a young son she consulted Simon Forman, astrologer and medical doctor, who recorded what she had told him of the troubles of her former life:

> She hath had hard fortune in youth. Her father died when she was young; the wealth of her father failed before he died and he began to be miserable in his estate. She was paramour to my old Lord Hunsdon that was Lord Chamberlain and was maintained by him in great pride; then, being with child, she was for colour married to a minstrel.[11]

Because of the mishap she was conveniently given a husband. On 18 October at St Botolph's church in Bishopsgate she was married off to Alphonse Lanier, a court musician, one of a musical family from Rouen.

Hunsdon was generous. Emilia, now Mrs Lanier, was given an annual pension of £40 and allowed to keep much of the jewellery that had been given her. The young husband and wife went to live at Longditch in Westminster next to Canon Row, a fashionable area full of houses of grand merchants and haughty titled neighbours. There Emilia had a healthy son, Henry, and a daughter, Odilla who, as so often with infants in the unhealthy environment of Elizabethan London, died only nine months old.[12]

Alphonse Lanier was extravagant. By 1597 they were penniless. In the hope of gaining wealth from captured Spanish shipping he took service with the Earl of Essex to go to the Azores and to Ireland. By coincidence his fellow adventurers included the Countess of Southampton's third husband, Sir William Hervey, a man who is to reappear in this book when the sonnets' history is considered. Also in the company was a young Catholic poet, John Donne.[13]

Long before that enterprise Lanier's wife had become discontented and resentful of her enforced marriage. A self-centred woman she felt that she had been brought down in the world. Not many years before Lanier she had enjoyed the pleasures of the royal court. Then she had been courted and kept in luxury by a wealthy lord. But by 1592 she had been made to marry an unambitious, unsuccessful nobody. A thrifty domestic life was an ill companion to her restless character. Almost predictably she was attracted to the up-and-coming actor and playwright whom she had met at the *Theatre*. And Shakespeare was unlikely to repel a good-looking, available young woman. He had already enjoyed extra-marital affairs and written about them in a sonnet, 'Hung with the trophies of my lovers gone'.[14]

Many facts favour Emilia Lanier as the elusive Dark Lady. Shakespeare knew her. She had often been with Hunsdon when he visited the players. She was known to be dark 'with the looks of a Moor'. As Sonnet 130 joked: 'If snow be white her breasts are dun', teasing her about her light-brown skin. Historian Michael Wood:

> Indeed, she looks and sounds startlingly like the woman in the sonnets. Here we enter the realm of diverting speculation rather than of verifiable fact, but if she is that woman then Shakespeare's remarks on her skin colour and unconventional beauty take on a peculiar significance, as do the poet's references to her 'unworthiness', on which he took pity, and her unspecified foreignness.[15]

The evidence supports her as Shakespeare's female nightmare. She was lovely, dark, apparently a wanton, available though married, had a child, and was musical, artistically playing the virginals as Sonnet 128 proves:

> How oft, when thou, my music, music play'd
> Upon that blessèd wood whose motion sounds
> With thy sweet fingers ...

Whoever Shakespeare's Dark Lady was she was not dark only in appearance. She was also dark of soul, adulterous, demanding, inconstant and superstitious. What is known of Emilia Lanier provides 'a tantalisingly close socio-psychological profile to the Dark Lady of Shakespeare's Sonnets'. Vanity was a strong characteristic of hers. The playwright teased her in the playful Sonnet 130, telling her that there was nothing outstandingly remarkable about her appearance:

> My mistress' eyes are nothing like the sun;
> Coral is far more red than her lips' red;
> If snow be white, why then her breasts are dun;
> If hairs be wires, black wires grow on her head.
> I have seen roses damasked, red and white,
> But no such roses see I in her cheeks'
> And in some perfumes is there more delight
> Than in the breath that from my mistress reeks.
> I love to hear her speak, yet well I know
> That music has a far more pleasing sound.
> I grant I never saw a goddess go;
> My mistress, when she walks treads on the ground.
> And yet, by heaven, I think my love as rare
> As any she belied with false compare.

It was a poetical joke but his longing for her was not. He loved her, lusted after her, wanted his 'Will' in her 'Hell', Elizabethan slang for the act of sexual intercourse, 'Will' being used interchangeably for both the male and the female sexual organ. 'Hell' referred specifically to the female.[16] Shakespeare even made a pun of Will, his own name, his penis and her vagina to joke about the words:

So thou being rich in *Will* add to thy *Will*,
One will of mine to make thy large *Will* more.

The two lines came from what is probably the most explicitly crude of all his sonnets, Sonnet 135. It is filled with double-entendres about his desire to make love to Emilia Lanier. The poem is printed with *Will* in italics exactly as it was published in the 1609 edition of 'Shake-Speares Sonnets':

Who euer hath her wish, thou hast thy *Will*,
And *Will* too boote, and *Will* in ouer-plus,
More then enough am I that vexe thee still,
To thy sweet will making addition thus.
Wilt thou, whose will is large and spatious,
Not once vouchsafe to hide my will in thine,
Shall will in others seeme right gracious,
And in my will no faire acceptance shine:
The sea all water, yet receiues raine still,
And in aboundance addeth to his store,
So thou beeing rich in *Will* adde to thy *Will*,
One will of mine, to make thy large *Will* more.
Let no unkinde, no faire beseechers kill,
Thinke all but one, and me in that one *Will*.

But, entirely characteristically, Emilia Lanier gave less than she received.

1593 was an evil year. There was another outbreak of plague. In London, Christopher Marlowe was murdered. Sixty miles to the north three innocent people from the small village of Warboys in Huntingdonshire were hanged. There, four years earlier, a little girl, ten-year-old Jane Throckmorton, daughter of a well-to-do family, had a fever and started sneezing. Her seventy-six year old neighbour, Alice Samuel came to see her. Semi-delirious, in a panic, the girl shrieked: 'Look where the old witch sitteth'. It seemed nothing but a fevered mind but within two months her four sisters, aged nine to fifteen, and seven servants had similar fits. The following year in September a friend of the family, Lady Cromwell, the second wife of Cromwell's grandfather, called. Learning of the sicknesses and suspecting evil-doing she fiercely interrogated 'Mother' Samuel who exclaimed: 'Madam, why do you use me thus? I never did you harm as yet'. As yet! Lady Cromwell sickened and died in July 1592.

Suspected witches were always more in danger if accused by gentry. Alice, her husband, John, and her daughter, Agnes, were all held as prisoners, 'without legal sanction', in the Throckmortons' manor for several months. Accused of evil-doing they said the children's complaints were 'nothing but wantonness', a reply that did not please the family. Dissatisfied the Samuels were examined by the Bishop of Lincoln. 'Examined' did not mean gentle questioning. They were left in damp, dark cells, fed sparsely, and questioned fiercely and persistently. Exhausted by the endless interrogations the three gave up, admitted that they were guilty. Later they retracted. They were ignored.

On 5 April 1593, they were accused of witchcraft and tried in Huntingdon. The jury took five hours to come to a verdict. All three were found guilty and hanged on Mill Common two days later. Their naked bodies, the property of the jailor, were 'displayed for the edifice of the curious beholders'.[17] Belief in witchcraft persisted for centuries. Today's complacency about such superstitions is ill-founded. Many people still believe in long-range weather forecasts.

That same year, 1593, was a disaster for London. Plague spread, slaughtering the suburbs. Wealthy citizens fled. The poor stayed and died. Theatres closed. Shakespeare, although impatient for the long-promised physical pleasures of Emilia Lanier, reluctantly left London and went to Titchfield and the patronage of the Countess of Southampton as well as the increasing friendship between him and her son, the young earl. In the capital infection persisted. Deaths continued into April, into May and into late June when, in desperation, all public gatherings including fairs were cancelled. The Lord Mayor ordered fouled streets to be cleaned and kept sweet. 'No dung or filth to be laid in any of the highways'. Rats could not read. Infected houses were locked, painted with red crosses, guarded. Death coughed its untroubled way down the streets. 'There have died in London and the suburbs during this year 17,893 persons, whereof 10,675 were from the plague'.[18]

By 1594 it was over. Shakespeare returned to London. His young friend, Henry Wriothesley, came with him. And with him came disaster. That predatory and self-centred young earl found two ways into Emilia's desirable bedroom. The first was that he had the influence to procure a very profitable monopoly on the weighing of hay for her appreciative and very accommodating husband. The second way was even easier. He was an earl.[19] It was double infidelity. An earl was a better, more lucrative catch than an ordinary commoner and actor. Calculating advantage Emilia slept with the earl, betraying both the poet and her husband. The twice cheated Shakespeare raged:

> Love is my sin, and thy dear virtue hate,
> Hate of my sin, grounded on sinful living,
> O, but with mine compare thou thine own state,
> And thou shalt find it merits not reproving,
> Or if it do, not from those lips of thine,
> That have profaned their scarlet ornaments
> And sealed false bonds of love as oft as mine,
> Robbed others' beds revenues of their rents,
> Be it lawful I love thee as thou lov'st those
> Whom thine eyes woo as mine importune thee.
> Root pity in thy heart that, when it grows.
> Thy pity may deserve to pitied be.
> If thou dost seek to have what thou dost hide,
> By self-example mayst thou be denied.[20]

It meant nothing. He was thrown aside. Southampton casually enjoyed the bed of a lovely young woman who was also a wife and a mother. She enjoyed the passing attention of an earl. Then the two men and the woman went their separate ways.

In back-street slang she was a 'prick-teaser', promising everything, permitting very little, like that unlucky man who 'lay diverse tymes with a woman, who shew him all that he wished except the last act, which she would never agree unto'.[21] Emilia Lanier was the same, a cold, calculating woman who used her enticing body to advantage without risk of pregnancy. She permitted anything except sexual copulation. Despite this her life did not improve. Shakespeare turned from her, and in the next few years wrote several plays, perhaps significantly, *A Comedy of Errors*, *Love's Labours Lost*, and the tragedy of *Romeo and Juliet*.

The irresponsible, self-centred Earl of Southampton found other pleasures, dallying with the queen's lovely young lady-in-waiting, Elizabeth Vernon, who became pregnant:

> Some say that she hath taken a venue under the girdle [been seduced] and swells upon it. Yet she complains not of foul play but says the Earl of Southampton will justify it; and it is hinted, underhand, that he was lately here four days in great secret, of purpose to marry her, and effected it accordingly.[22]

She became the earl's wife in 1598, the year of another Elizabethan irony, the first performance of *The Merry Wives of Windsor*. Whether the new Countess of Southampton had a merry life is unrecorded. The later history of the dominating Emilia Lanier is recorded in a physician's notes in sadly declining detail. Abandoned by both Shakespeare and Southampton she had only her inadequate and unwanted husband for support. In desperation on 13 May 1597, she made her first visit to the physician and astrologer, Simon Forman, half doctor, half charlatan. His reputation has suffered because of his pretensions. 'Forman was the king of shysters and charlatans in Shakespeare's London, a quack, an astrologer, and perhaps an abortionist'. Ben Jonson mocked him and similar medical mountebanks in two plays, *Epicene, or the Silent Woman*, and *The Devil is an Ass*, jeering at the equipment in Forman's rooms.

They talked of Gresham and of Doctor Forman,
Franklin and Fisk and Savory ...
But here's not one of them that ever could
Yet show a man the Devil in true sort.
They have their crystals, I do know, and rings,
And virgin parchment and their dead men's skulls,
Their raven's wings, their lights, their pentacles
With characters: I have seen all these. But
Would I might see the Devil! ...[23]

It was mockery but it is probable that Forman's consulting room really was a litter of impressive alchemical equipment including thick medical books in Latin, glass globes, phials, tongs, multicoloured bottles of lotions, and a stuffed crocodile hanging from the ceiling. His patients were astonished and impressed.

Forman had been born near Wilton in Wiltshire at the end of 1552. His father died when he was eleven and he was apprenticed to a grocer whose stock included apothecary's drugs that the young man studied avidly. Over the years he taught himself astronomy, magic, philosophy. He was not unattractive, slightly below average height with reddish hair and a ginger beard. His face was freckled. Going to London he acquired a reputation for forecasting horoscopes, being

very judicious and fortunate, so also in sickness, which was indeed his masterpiece; and had good success in resolving questions about marriage, and in other questions very intricate. He was a person of indefatigable pains, and was always doing some thing relating to his profession.[24]

He was also a keen theatre-goer, particularly to the *Globe* theatre. Forman's notes are the earliest known accounts of seeing performances there of *Macbeth* in which he was impressed by Banquo's ghost; *Cymbeline*; and *A Winter's Tale* where the actor playing Autolycus amused him. There is a small mystery. He also claimed to have seen *Richard II* but his description does not match the structure of Shakespeare's tragedy. It may have been one of the many Elizabethan plays that have since been lost.[25]

As his medical and fortune-telling reputation grew he moved across the city to the Stone House on Philpot Lane, near Botolph's Wharf, just east of London Bridge. The house had once been the stone-built vestry of St Botolph's church on Thames Street, and it was prestigious enough to impress his gullible patients.[26] Immodestly, he claimed to be a proficient alchemist, an astrologer, and a practitioner of magic as well as a dispenser of reliable medicines. But by the standards of late Elizabethan London he was a good doctor, prescribing useful medicines.

When he met Emilia Lanier he first recorded her as 'a certain lady', one of many, but soon wrote her name. She consulted him because of his reputation as an astrologer, asking him about her husband's possible future knighthood and her own prospects. She was desperate for a change in her fortunes. To obtain Forman's forecasts she travelled right across London from her home in Westminster to see him at his address, just east of London Bridge. And saw him again and again: first on the 13th May, then on the 17th, then a fortnight later on the third of June, each time going by river.

For her it was some two miles from Westminster to his house near London Bridge, a dreary journey by foot to Charing Cross, then the Strand and Blackfriars, a dangerous walk along crowded, dirty streets, splattered by carts and horses in wet weather, always with the unpleasant possibility that the way would pass under a gateway with the remains of a rotting traitor's body decomposing and stinking on it. It was better by the river. At Westminster, Lanier's house was close to the Queen's 'bridge' where a set of short steps led down to the river and a ferry. The Thames was crowded with vessels of all sizes and there was always a risk of colliding, capsizing and drowning. But the danger was negligible and Emilia Lanier probably chose to travel by a 'nut', a small licensed boat for two people with a pair of experienced seamen rowing at the stern, passengers sheltered under an awning and resting comfortably on cushioned benches. It was not expensive. To go from Westminster to London Bridge cost only a few pence.[27]

On her second visit to Forman she asked for a prediction of her husband's fortunes after the disaster of the Earl of Essex's badly-organised expedition that had missed the Spanish treasure fleet because of the earl's incompetence. She also asked whether she would ever become a titled lady. Forman promised to make a prediction. Being an experienced lecher with a record of more than fifty 'conquests' of female patients he also recorded his impression of his latest client:

> She hath been favoured much of her Majesty and of many noblemen, hath had great gifts and been made much of – a nobleman that is dead hath loved her well and kept her. But her husband has dealt hardly with her, hath spent and consumed her goods. She is now very needy, in debt and it seems for lucre's sake will be a good fellow, for necessity doth compel. She hath a wart or mole in the pit of the throat or near it.[28]

Forman was attracted to her. It was mutual. The emotionally frustrated Emilia Lanier was also physically interested in him not only for the prospect of enjoyable sex but also for his predictions and his advice. And the sex could be controlled. On the tenth of September she invited Forman to enjoy a meal with her at Westminster house. He wrote in his notebook: 'If I go to Lanier this night or tomorrow ... shall I be welcome et halek?' 'Halek' was the Greek noun for a small fish. It was also a Greek verb for 'to grind', Elizabethan slang for sexual intercourse. The ambiguous halek was not a word for Victorian scholarship.[29] Judith Cook in her book *Dr Simon Forman*:

> The nineteenth academic, J. O. Halliwell Phillips – one of the first scholars to examine the Forman folios – had intended to publish the diary for the Camden Society but decided against it because 'the many "halek" notes rendered the material far too indelicate for conventional publication'. Instead he printed a mere handful of copies, marked 'For Private Circulation Only'.[30]

Forman did visit Mrs Lanier. They enjoyed an intimate supper, followed by pleasurable fondling, she tempting him, inviting him to spend the night with her. Expectations did not end in fulfilment. In bed although he 'felt all parts of her body ... she was familiar and friendly to [me] in all things, but only she would not halek'. That night and on every later occasion he never obtained his desire. 'She was an whore, and dealt evil with me after'. He tried to keep away despite her invitations, but she sent her maid, and optimistically he returned. Again, with no satisfaction. Forman wrote that she was a harlot who 'useth sodomy'. It was her coldly calculated choice, enjoying pleasure for the chosen parts of her body without any risk of pregnancy. She was, he shuddered, an incuba, a she-devil, a dark mare of the night, who drained men of sex while they slept, an Elizabethan cocotte who enjoyed her body but never succumbed to the need to go 'the whole way'.[31]

Almost in desperation he cast his own horoscope to find whether he would ever be able to trust her: 'why Mrs. Lanière sent for me; what will follow, and whether she intendeth any more villainy'.[32] It was his last entry about her. And she became a ghost. For eleven years Emilia Lanier vanished from history, tolerating her husband, existing, but resentful at the way in which men treated women, writing her indignant and angry condemnation of the humiliation. During that empty period she seems to have undergone a religious conversion. Rowse again:

> With her powerful temperament this is not surprising; she had plenty to be converted from – and, as might be expected, she throws herself passionately into her religious stance; with unmitigated advocacy, she goes the whole hog.[33]

She was bitterly resentful of men. All they had ever wanted from her was her body. Born illegitimate, a poor young woman deprived of her father's small bequest, frustrated by the death of her only patron, the patron who had forced her into an unwanted marriage because she was pregnant – by him! – thrown aside on a whim by Shakespeare, persistently pestered by Forman for sexual intercourse, and then left almost penniless and unwanted. It is unsurprising that she resented men. They had all disappointed her.

Almost ten years after she had broken from Forman the sonnets of William Shakespeare were published by Thomas Thorpe in 1609. They were bitterly critical of the treacherous Dark Lady who was, perhaps, Emilia Lanier : 'Thine eyes I love', Sonnet 132 began, but ended with:

> Then will I swear beauty herself is black,
> And all they foul that they complexion lack.

It may have been no more than a chronological coincidence but hardly more than a year after that illicit publication Emilia Lanier had her own book of poems printed, *Salve Deus Rex Judaeorum*, a long virtuous and heroic vindication of Biblical women. It was dedicated to:

> To the Vertuous Reader
> And this I have done, to make knowne to the world, that all women deserve not to be blamed though some forgetting that they are women themselves, and in danger to be condemned by the wordes of their own mouthes, fall into so great an errour, as to speak unadvisedly against the reste of their own sexe ... who, forgetting they were born of women, nourished of women, and that if it were not by the meanes of women, they would be quite extinguished out of the world ... do like Vipers deface the wombes wherein they were bred, onely to give way and utterance to their want of discretion and goodnesse.[34]

The poem was a long vindication of Biblical women from Eve to the Virgin Mary. It was published by Richard Bowen 'to be sold at his shop in St Pauls' Churchyard', and printed by Valentine Simms, the printer of some quarto editions of Shakespeare's plays.

In Elizabethan times it was early 'women's lib', defending defamed women like Eve 'whose fault was only too much love', and the book was dedicated to 'all virtuous Ladies in generall'. It acquired some very prestigious patronesses: Queen Anne, James I's wife, and the Countesses of Kent, Cumberland, Suffolk and Dorset. It was scholarly but pedestrian with its dozens of eight-line verses having a consistent theme defending some maligned Biblical women of the Bible: Eve and the apple; Sisera who killed Jael, the virtuous Judith who murdered the lustful Holofernes; wise Deborah , even the Queen of Sheba.[35]

There was a sad end to the final years of Emilia Lanier. Her pathetic and disappointing husband died in 1613 leaving her impoverished. In 1617 she opened a school for children but had trouble with her landlord over the payments for rent and repairs, and was arrested in 1619. By 1633 she was desperately pleading for sustenance for herself and two grandchildren. Perhaps through her former courtly connections she did obtain some kind of Crown pension.[36] She died on 3 April 1645, and was buried, ironically, in Clerkenwell which was to be the haunt of yet another Dark Lady, Lucy Morgan.

As the supposed Dark Lady, Emilia Lanier is no more than a name written by an optimistic quill, a possibility but not a certainty. According to Lanier's biographer, Susanne Woods, she:

> was open about her relationship was Lord Hunsdon, and there is no way to prove that she did not have other lovers. But it takes a leap far beyond common rules of evidence and logic to assert with uncompromising assurance that Lanyer was promiscuous. Yet even if Aemilia Lanyer had slept with half of London, it would not prove her to be the Dark Lady of the sonnets.[37]

7

Lucy Morgan: Royal Maid of Honour; Madam of Dishonour

> It is now generally agreed that textual hints in Sonnets 127-152 support Rowse's insistence 'that the woman coloured ill' was a well-known person of 'superior social standing'.
>
> A. W. L. Saunders, *The Sonnets*, 328, n. 661.

Candidates for Shakespeare's dark woman include an aristocratic Lady, a queen's maid of honour, and several respectable citizens' wives. Lucy Morgan was different. She was a 'fallen woman'. She was 'not even a bohemian member of the London middle-class but a well-known courtesan nicknamed 'Lucy Negro', celebrated for her dark complexion. 'Lucy' is an ironical Christian name for a lady of darkness: It is a diminutive of Lucia or Lucinda or Lucilla, and each one of them derives from the Latin, *lux*, 'light'.[1]

Lucy Morgan is one more wraith, a woman so insubstantial that she is a no one, a person entirely unmentioned in the majority of biographies of Shakespeare. In others she is given some reluctant, dismissive words before the writers turn with relief to the few certainties about Shakespeare's life. To Brown she was an 'Embarrassing Phantom. But still the ghost walks'.[2] Of all the dark ladies she is the darkest. In the 1590s on the backstreets of north London she was called 'Black Luce' because her maiden name was Lucilla.

How, where and when William Shakespeare met her is unknown. It may have been at a play in the theatre, or convivially in a tavern with her friends, even lustfully, and probably expensively, in a brothel. By that time, in the early 1590s when she was living an entirely different way of life in the shabby streets of London she had almost forgotten that she had once been a maid of honour to Queen Elizabeth. That unpaid 'maid of honour' had long been transformed into the very well-paid, 'made of dishonour'. It is another irony in the search for Shakespeare's dark lady that a prostitute should prove to be such a convincing candidate for the elusive Dark Lady.

Lucy Morgan had been a gentlewoman, a young lady from such a well-placed Welsh family that she became one of the queen's maids of honour at the royal court. George Bagshawe Harrison, author of three scholarly and prestigious journals of Elizabethan history, was the first to suggest that she had been the Dark Lady of the sonnets.

> The Black Woman ... as a courtesan, notorious to fashionable young gentlemen of the Inns of Court ... There have been several claimants to the dubious distinction of being the 'dark Lady'. The tone of Shakespeare's sonnets to her suggests that she was not a person of any position, and there is scattered evidence that in the 1590s one of the well-known courtesans was notoriously dark ... This 'Lucy Negro' I would tentatively identify as the Dark Lady.

Harrison went on to quote the Lancashire poet, John Weever's *Epigrams* to prove that dark-coloured women were commonplace in London:

> Is *Byrrna* browne? Who doth the question ask?
> Her face is pure as Ebonie is blacke,
> Its hard to know her face from her faire maske,
> Beautie in her seemes beautie still to lack.
> Nay, she's snow-white, but for that russet skin,
> Which like a vaile doth keepe her whitenes in.

To Harrison the Dark Lady was a black woman, a negress.[3] Some thirty years later Leslie Hotson disagreed. The lady had been fair-skinned.

To Professor G. B. Harrison belongs the credit of first suspecting the truth: 'This Lucy Negro (Abbess of Clerkenwell) I would very tentatively identify as the Dark Lady' – and also the discredit of believing Shakespeare's fair enslaver a blackamoor. Under so dark a misapprehension his 'very tentatively' is commendable, and he followed his negress no farther. Black Luce was of course no more an Ethiop than the Black Prince and Black Tom Wentworth (Lord Strafford) were, or a professional successor of Black Lucy's own across the Thames: 'Neer to black Madges in the Paris Garden'.[4]

In Elizabethan times 'black' was often a synonym for 'proud' and that may have been why Shakespeare referred to Lucy Morgan, as a 'proud' woman.

Some years before she enchanted and lured the poet she had charmed Queen Elizabeth. From March 1579 until June 1582 she had been a royal maid of honour, favoured by the queen for three reasons: her beauty, for her excellence in music whether singing or playing, and for her dancing. Born around 1560 she would have been nineteen years old in 1579 with the social background of any well-born sixteenth-century girl, literate, proficient in the playing of musical instruments, and in singing. By her adolescence she would have been accomplished in both music and dancing. It was an ideal upbringing for her to become a queen's gentlewoman, a maid of honour in the service of the queen.[5]

The later sixteenth century was a good time for lovers of music. In 1575 Thomas Tallis, 'the father of English cathedral music', and his pupil, William Byrd, had been granted a royal monopoly in the printing of music. Buying their scores enabled households to read, play, and sing music everywhere in the land. Families had a wide choice of instruments to buy such as virginals, trumpets and flutes. Outside the home there was a lute in every barber's shop to entertain customers as they waited their turn.

Most educated people could sight-read music and they often sang part-songs such as madrigals for several voices. And there were dances. For the elderly there was the slow pavane where the dancers' feet were never lifted from the floor. For the brisker there was the 'part-time' allemande, in which the dancers began quite slowly, stopped, restarted more quickly, stopped, then went from fast to very fast. For the even more enterprising there was the brisker galliard, or the cinquepas, or the coranto, even the volta, with the man's arm round the lady's waist, lifting her and spinning round and round as he did – although it was advisable for the man to remove his sword to avoid tripping over the sheath as he whirled his partner. In the less-informed country villages there were dances to the music of pipes and tabors, small drums.

The intimacy of dancing could lead to jealousy, arguments and bad behaviour. In his *The Anatomie of Abuses* of 1583 the puritan, Phillip Stubbes, condemned:

> the horrible vice of pestiferous dancing … what kissing and bussing, what smouching and slabbering of one another, what filthy gropings and unclean handling is not practised every where in these dances.

It was not only the indecency of dancing that disgusted Stubbes. He also condemned play-goers' behaviour, 'idleness, unthriftiness, whoredom, wantonness, drunkenness, and', exhausted of adjectives, 'what not'.[6] None of it would have disturbed the young Lucy Morgan. Her skilful playing of the virginals delighted Elizabeth as it would Shakespeare:

> How oft, when thou, my music, music play'd
> Upon that blessèd wood whose motion sounds
> With thy sweet fingers when thou gently sway'st …[7]

For three musical years she was one of the queen's favourites, playing musical instruments, singing and, always a delight, laughing. She was well-liked, so attractive that year after year Elizabeth gave her luxurious dresses. The Wardrobe accounts for 1579 listed 'Item for Eleven yards of silk grosgrain given

1. The *Swan*, the only contemporary sketch of the interior of an Elizabethan theatre. It was drawn by a Dutch visitor to London, Johannes de Witt.

Mr. WILLIAM
SHAKESPEARES
COMEDIES,
HISTORIES, &
TRAGEDIES.

Published according to the True Originall Copies.

LONDON
Printed by Isaac Iaggard, and Ed. Blount. 1623.

2. The title-page of the 1623 *First Folio* of Shakespeare's plays.
Opposite: 3. Claes Visscher's 1616 panorama of London showing St Paul's and the second *Globe* theatre.

S. PAVLES CHVRCH

Three Cranes

AMESIS

The Gally fuste

Bear Gardne

The Globe

Above: 4. John Norden's late 16th century drawing of London Bridge.
Left: 5. The *Swan* theatre on Bankside sketched by Visscher in 1616.

6. Today's recreated *Globe* theatre.

7. A memorial stone in Park Street recording where the *Globe* playhouse had stood.

Above: 8. A pen-and-ink view of London by Anthonis van de Wyngaerde showing St Paul's church with its steeple. The cramped streets of Southwark are in the foreground.

Left: 9. The second *Globe* theatre of 1616. The first had burned down in 1613.

10. Claes Visscher's 1616 drawing of the city from St Mary's church alongside London Bridge.

11. The crowded houses of Thames Street and Billingsgate in the mid-16th century. The Davenants lived just to the west by the river.

VENVS
AND ADONIS

Vilia miretur vulgus: mihi flauus Apollo
Pocula Castalia plena ministret aqua.

LONDON

Imprinted by Richard Field, and are to be fold at
the figne of the white Greyhound in
Paules Church-yard.

1593.

12. The title-page of 'Venus & Adonis', Shakespeare's first long poem.

Above left: 13. A contemporary sketch of the comedian Richard Tarleton with his drum. He had intended to dedicate his 'little book' to Mary Fitton.

Above right: 14. A drawing of Richard Burbage, the greatest actor of the Lord Chamberlain's Men.

Left: 15. Apprentices working in a printer's shop.

Above: 16. A game of cards, probably the popular four-card *Primero*.

Left: 17. The ruined gateway to Ralegh's home at Sherborne in Dorset.

Above: 18. The gaunt remains of the interior of the house.

19. Temple Grafton church where Anne Whateley had worshipped.

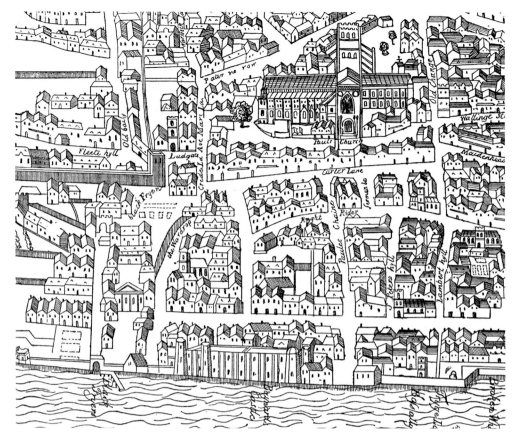

20. A mid-16th century sketch of London. In the left foreground is Blackfriars where Shakespeare bought his first city house. Jacqueline Field lived nearby.

21. The slab marking the site of St Olave's church. It had been in Silver Street where Marie Mountjoy's home stood.

Opulentius mercator Londinensis in Anglia.   Nobilis puella ornatus apud Londinenses.   Vulgarium feminarum in Anglia. vestitus gentilis.   Plebeij adolescentis in Anglia habitus.   19

Opposite: 22. A sketch of Elizabethan women shopping – and gossiping – in an open-air market.
Above: 23. Elizabethan dress. From left to right a merchant, a court lady, a London wife and a 'dashing' gallant.
Right: 24. Joris Hoefnagel's 1582 sketch of women's clothing: a spinster, two wives, and three noble ladies. Below are country women gutting freshly-caught fish.

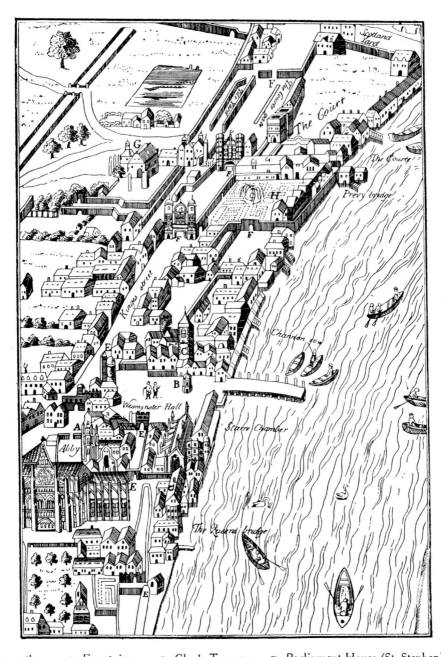

A, St. Margaret's;   B, Fountain;   C, Clock Tower;   D, Parliament House (St. Stephen's Chapel);
E, Palace Gates;   F, Gates;   G, Cockpit;   H, Queen's Garden.

25. Sketch of Westminster and Whitehall. Both Mary Fitton and Emilia Lanier knew the area well.

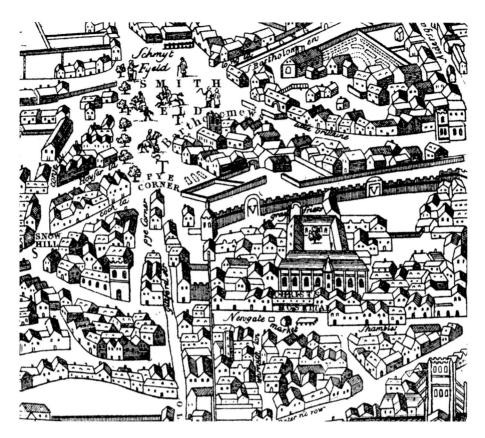

26. The area of Smithfield market. Bartholomew Fair was held nearby. So were public executions. Lucy Morgan's home was nearby in Shoreditch.

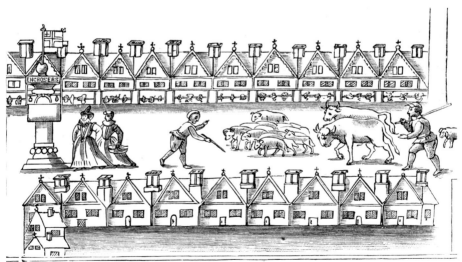

ESCHEAPE MARKET
from a very old Drawing. Vide D.r Combe.

27. Eastcheap butchers' market. Herds and flocks were herded to the stalls through London's narrow and fouled streets.

28. Titchfield. The elaborate gateway leading to today's ruined house. Mrs Florio frequently passed through it.

Above left: 29. In the garden of the former church of St Mary Aldermanbury is a memorial to Shakespeare and his colleagues Hemming and Condell who published the *First Folio*.

Above right: 30. In Southwark Cathedral by London Bridge is an elaborate memorial to William Shakespeare.

by our Commandment to Luce Morgan to make her a Gown of our great wardrobe'. Grosgrain, literally 'coarse-grained', was an expensive heavy corded fabric of silk and cotton often used decoratively by well-to-do ladies. It was a generous gift.[8]

On further occasions Lucy Morgan was given material for dresses by the queen. In 1580 she received three and a quarter yards of velvet 'to guard a gown for Luce Morgan'. At a price of more than a pound for a yard the velvet cost over four pounds sterling in the years when four copper pennies bought a pound of candles, the same price as a good meal of meat, cheese, bread and beer in an inn. Fourpence was a trivial sum, a paltry one-sixtieth of a pound sterling.[9] A long velvet gown was a luxury.

Lucy Morgan was obviously very well-liked. In March 1581 the gifts continued: 'Item for six yards russet Satin, and two yards of black velvet by us given to Luce Morgan'. 'The discerning eye will note how choicely russet satin trimmed with black velvet suited her black eyes and hair'.[10] Similar bequests continued up to New Year's Day, 1582 when even her own servant benefited: 'Mrs Morgan's servant' was given a ryal, a rose noble, a gold coin worth fifteen shillings, a fortune to a working-woman.

But the good years did not last. Early in 1582 Lucy Morgan was dismissed from the royal court. Theft has been suspected. More probably it was sex and susceptibility. Maids of honour to the queen were attractive young, nubile women, natural targets for lustful courtiers. Unwanted pregnancy was almost inevitable for many of the warm-minded maidens among the temptations of the Elizabethan court. Sir William Knollys, Comptroller of the Royal Household, deplored the continual danger from the predatory debauchers of the Court's beauties, lustful courtiers who preyed with 'wolfish cruelty and fox-like subtlety on the tame beasts', luring the impressionable girls into their own downfall.[11]

John Aubrey's anecdote of Sir Walter Ralegh, a maid of honour and a convenient tree was mentioned in the Introduction. Lucy Morgan may have been as easy to ensnare, seduced into an emotional carelessness that left her defenceless against the inevitable discovery, disgrace and dismissal.

Robert Greene in his *Coney-Catcher* described the many temptations that lured young girls to disgrace. One of them, he wrote, was sent to school, learned to read and write, to play the virginals, the lute and cittern, and sing prick-song. She was considered a lovely and well educated maiden. But her parents were over-indulgent and she was spoiled. As a young woman she encouraged the flattery of young men. She was naïve. One of her admirers converted flattery into seduction. Greene sighed. The innocent, over-trustful girl remembered that the deceitful 'admirer':

> was a brave young gentleman, and no less addicted to me, than I devoted to him, for daily he courted me with amorous sonnets and curious proud letters, and sent me jewels, and all that I might grace him with the name of my servant. I returned him as loving lines as well, and so contented his lusting desire, that secretly and unknown to all the rest, I made him sundry nights my bedfellow …

Soon, successful, sated, seeking fresher pleasures, he abandoned her.[12]

> The fraud of men was ever so,
> Since summer first was leafy
> Then sigh no more …[13]

And in the Spring of 1582 for an unknown offence, probably sexual, Lucy Morgan was dismissed from the royal court, ejected into the lonely streets of an unfriendly London. Disgraced, abandoned, too ashamed to return to her family in Wales, she had only her looks and the value of her brooches, rings and necklaces to keep her from starvation. She also had her body, Ivor Brown:

> She had no country home to which she could retire. She had her living to earn, her body to sell, and no reluctance to be a

'daughter of the game'. She first became a prostitute and then set up in business as a bawd in Clerkenwell, rivalling the notorious Elizabeth Holland who kept a well-known brothel in Islington.[14]

The year 1582 was not only a turning-point year for Lucy Morgan. It was one that affected people's lives all over the mainland of Europe. Over the centuries the old Julian calendar had become inaccurate and was systematically miscalculating the dates of holy days. To correct it the Catholic Church decreed that at midnight on 4 October 1582, ten days would be added to the date converting the following day into 14 October. Across the mainland of Europe there were riots, fears over when the crops would ripen, and religious hysteria about Christians dying ten days too early and finding the gates of Paradise closed to their doomed souls, losing the promise of everlasting bliss in heaven.

In Protestant England there was argument about the proposed change, less about the proposed change of date than of the precedent of following the decision of countries that were both foreign and Catholic. Arguments, almost quarrels, in favour and against were heard in court and in church. At last, in 1584, without enthusiasm, a Bill entitled, 'An Act giving her Majesty authority to alter and make new a Calendar according to the Calendar used in other countries' was put to Parliament on 16 March and maybe reread on the 18th. Religious prejudice prevailed and the Act vanished. English pride wanted no novelty contaminated by Catholicism. The calendar remained unchanged. It was not for almost two hundred years in 1752 that the Gregorian calendar was adopted and an alarmed population was shouting, 'Give us back our eleven days'.[15]

In that same turmoil of that year 1582, uncaring of problems over dates and years, unaware of the disgrace of a maid of honour whom he was to know well in years to come, there were unavoidable personal matters for Shakespeare. In Warwickshire's Stratford-upon-Avon the youthful tanner's son seduced Anne Hathaway that year, got her with child and entangled himself in an unwanted and unhappy marriage.

Twelve years later in London he was to have a much more enjoyable although emotionally disruptive association with Lucy Morgan. By that time, when the distant years in the royal court had become no more than a mist in her mind, Lucy was known to her chosen lovers as 'Old Lucilla' and to her lucrative clients as 'Black Luce'.

Her life was written in her name, 'Lucy'. It did not come from the virgin-martyr, St Lucy, persecuted and blinded at Syracuse in AD 304. Many churches in Europe were dedicated to her, but only two in England. She has no shrine there. With her emblem of eyes she is the patron saint of peasants and tailors. Lucy Morgan was neither virgin nor martyr. To the contrary, her Christian name, Lucy, or 'Lucilla', was derived from 'Lucy light', a phrase denoting the time of the year's fewest hours of daylight and the longest night of darkness. It was 13 December in the Old Calendar of 1582. In the revised calendar of 1752 the day became Christmas Eve.

> Tis the year's midnight, and it is the day's,
> Lucy's who scarce seven hours herself unmasks
> The Sun is spent, and now his flasks
> Send forth light squibs, no constant rays;
> The world's whole sap is sunk;
> The general balm th'hydroptic earth hath drunk
> Whither, as to the bed's feet, life is shrunk'
> Dead and interr'd; yet all these seem to laugh,
> Compar'd with me, who am their epitaph.
> John Donne, *A Nocturnall upon S. Lucies day, Being the shortest day.*

Lucy Morgan's epitaph was to be a sad one, a story of decline from royal maid of honour to seduction, disgrace, and a year or so of romance before metamorphosing into prostitution in a London brothel and a profitable but declining career as the years trudged by, life drooping slowly but inevitably into misery and impoverished death, a gradual sadness from Lucilla Morgan into Lucy Morgan to Black Luce to Shakespeare's Black Lady. William Shakespeare was to revel with and be revolted by her in the brief ripeness of better years for her around 1594.

Her life in London began in Clerkenwell outside the City walls. It was there that with her remaining money she set up a brothel in Turnmill Street just west of St John Street with herself as its 'madam'. She became known as Lucy Negro in London's dingy underworld, 'Black Lucy', 'black' being an Elizabethan colloquialism for 'lustful'.[16] She became sufficiently notorious for the Hereford poet, John Davies to mention her in his 'Scourge of Folly' of 1610:

> Such beginning, such an end. This not to applaud
> For Luce did like a whore begin, but ended like a bawd.[17]

Whores, bawds, prostitutes, London knew them all. Brothels, commonly known as 'stews', were everywhere in the suburbs and almost abundant in Clerkenwell.

Thomas Dekker was an Elizabethan playwright, and a contemporary of Shakespeare. His famous *Shoemaker's Holiday* was performed by the Lord Chamberlain's Men in 1601. Shakespeare may have acted in it. Dekker also wrote a curious piece, *Lanthorn and Candlelight*, in which a devil from hell stared at London's outlying, squalid districts and:

> saw the doors of notorious carted bawds like Hell gates stand night and day wide open, with a pair of harlots in taffeta gowns, like two painted posts, garnishing out those doors, being better to the house than a double sign.

Puritans shouted that every second house in Clerkenwell was a brothel and that there were harlots in Shoreditch, Southwark and were everywhere particularly in Clerkenwell's seedy Turnmill Street. Another writer, Thomas Nashe agreed, condemning 'our unclean sisters in Shoreditch, Southwark, Westminster and Turnmill Street'.[18] The street was just north of the Turnmill or Tremill Brook which eventually became a northern section of the Fleet river. In Lucy Morgan's time it was as neglected as the buildings around it. In 1598 John Stow regretted its neglect:

> This brook hath been divers times since cleansed, namely, and last of all, to any affect, in the year 1502 ... the whole course of Fleet Dike, then so called, was scoured, I say, down to the Thames, so that boats with fish and fuel were rowed to Fleet Bridge ... which was a great commodity to all the inhabitants of that part of the city.

It did not last. As in so many other parts of London where repairs were needed the stream was neglected. Almost £700 sterling, 1,000 marks, was raised in 1589 for a new scouring but

> so much money being therein spent, the effect failed, so that the brook, by means of continual encroachments upon the banks getting over the water and casting of soilage into the stream, is now become worse cloyed and choken than ever it was before.[19]

Lucy Morgan's new home in Turnmill Street was only a few yards from the polluted waters but by a geographical and cultural paradox her house was surrounded by fine buildings. Southampton House where Shakespeare had stayed with the young earl was only a quarter of a mile to the south-west. Grays Inn was the same distance to the west. Both St Mary's Nunnery and St John's Priory were about 200 yards to the north and the pleasant greenness of Ely Gardens was a short walking distance to the south-west. And immediately to the north of Lucy Morgan's house was the Priory of Clerkenwell, founded in AD 1000 for black nuns. On paper, except for the existence of the notorious *Red Bull* Inn a few grubby steps to the north the region was a delight. But in life it was not. The black nuns had long been expelled. In their place a 'black' woman had arrived.

Foreigners coming to London were impressed by the cleanness of the city, the great buildings, fine churches, the opulence of dazzling riches displayed along Goldsmiths' Row. What they did not see were the outlying suburbs, in particular the eight farthest to the north. They were neither white nor clean. There were no rows of fine shops lining wide roads. To the contrary there was a bewilderment of grubby lanes and alleyways and a stench of decay and neglect reeking the air. There was poverty. There was disease because there was little urban hygiene. Household rubbish mixed with urine and excrement stank in every street.

Even street names were misleading. Rose Alley was one. 'Rose Alleys' in old English towns nearly always had less to do with fragrant flowers than with the habit of 'plucking a rose' – an Elizabethan euphemism for 'making water', pissing in some convenient out-of-the-way alley. 'As for washing and bathing these were very much the exception rather than the rule; there is little doubt that most Elizabethans were dirty and smelly'.[20] As an aside, 'plucking a rose' also meant deflowering a virgin.

In London's convenient alleys there was not only human excrement but also human vice and because vice created money Lucy Morgan chose to make a living through it. Starting as a high-class courtesan with private patrons from the court she gradually transformed herself profitably into London's notorious 'Black Luce', 'black' referring not only to her eyes and hair but also a derogatory term for 'harlot'.

The house she converted into a successful brothel was just west of St John Street. Both geographically and for profit it was cleverly chosen. Lustful undergraduates from the law schools, away from home but with family money in their pockets, were ideal clients. They were plentiful and nearby. Turnmill Street's house of ill repute was no more than a quarter of a mile to the north-east of Gray's Inn across the Fleet River, an easy walking distance, just a few panting minutes, for eager young men to enjoy Lucy Morgan's agreeable harem. And to the south, not far from the Thames, was an abundance of other adolescent clients from Lincoln's Inn and Clements Inn.

Over the years Black Luce became sufficiently notorious

for Elizabethan writers not only to know but jest about her notoriety. George Chapman joked about her in his *An Humorous Day's Mirth*: 'Why, he was taken learning tricks at old Lucilla's house, the master-mistress of all the smock-tearers in Paris ... for she hath them all trained up before her'. Thomas Heywood's play, *Edward IV* nudged a knowing audience with: 'Commend me to Black Luce, bouncing Bess, & lusty Kate, and the other pretty morsels of mans flesh ...'[21]

Lucy Morgan, now 'Black Luce' prospered. But she had rivals, in particular the notorious Elizabeth Holland, a widow whose house of ill repute was not far to the north-east in the slums of Islington. It was not a pleasant area. John Norden, the queen's mapmaker, described it disparagingly:

> Although this place be as it were forsaken of all, and true men seldom frequent the same but upon divine occasions, yet it is visited and usually haunted of Rogues, vagabonds, harlots and thieves, who assemble not there to pray, but to wait for prey, and many fall into their hands clothed that are glad when they are escaped naked. Walk not there too late.[22]

It was a fitting area for Elizabeth Holland's notorious house of disrepute. Both hers and Black Luce's brothel prospered. There was no shortage of eager clients. But there was always a but. Being the madam of a whorehouse could mean having a profitable occupation. It could also be dangerously precarious. Puritans in particular were eager to catch and punish ungodly women like Mrs Holland.

In 1595 she was taken to the Court of the Queen's Bench accused of being in charge of a 'stew'. She pleaded not guilty and may have been acquitted. If so, her freedom did not last. The following year she was charged with the same offence, found guilty and condemned to be publicly shamed. Outside Newgate Prison she was put into an open cart with a large printed paper set on her shaven head. It proclaimed her foul way of life to the crowds of jeering spectators as the cart trundled through London suburb by suburb – including her own at Islington.

Then to Cornhill, Cheapside and Bridewell where there was more humiliation before returning to Newgate.

It was not over. She was fined £40, bound over for future good behaviour and compelled to provide guarantees that she would never return to her former, disgraceful way of life. Forty pounds sterling was an almost ruinous fine. One penny, of which a pound had 240, was the price for a spectator to stand in a theatre. A pair of workman's boots cost twelve pennies, a shilling. In the years when a luxurious cloak for the queen's favourite, the Earl of Leicester, cost only £20, a fine of £40 was exorbitant.[23]

Despite the punishment and the heavy fine Elizabeth Holland did not disappear. She prospered. Years earlier as a young woman she had been the mistress of a rich Italian. Then she sold herself to wealthy men. It was not enough. Independence rather than money alone was her intention. She had transformed herself from a prostitute to a madam. After Bridewell she did not regret and repent. She became the occupant of a richly appointed brothel at Paris Gardens Manor House. She bought a ruin and transformed it into a fort with a moat, a drawbridge and a well-barred gatehouse. It was well-chosen, profitably situated with theatres, bear and bull-rings and inns nearby. There is a Shakespearean irony. She had leased her 'house' from Lord Hunsdon, Lord Chamberlain and patron of the Queen's Men. A further irony was that Hunsdon had his own brothel, one of male prostitutes, in Hoxton.

Intentionally, Elizabeth Holland's place of business was a place of loveliness, lavishly but discriminatingly appointed with a fastidiously selected staff, some casual, some permanent, serving the wealthiest clients with every delight:

> Her wine, though more in measure, yet shall be drunk in less glasses: her music shall speak sharply, and just as sweetly, but not so loud: her wenches shall be fair and handsome, yet but few in number ... For when supplies are wanting she knows how to fetch them from places of fair reputation: her ordinary servants shall be comely and industrious ... and when extremity come

upon her, she shall have disguises to make them appear half-angels ...

Elizabeth Holland was discreetly rapacious. She fleeced her clients but it was done with style and with experienced, delightful girls. She endured and prospered for years. In 1631 there were some less than half-hearted attempt by troops to storm her 'castle'. They failed. Exceedingly wealthy and before there were further attempts to dislodge her Elizabeth Holland retired. Lucy Morgan did not.[24]

In Clerkenwell, unconcerned about the departure of her nearest rival, the former maid of honour turned courtesan, now madam of a house of strumpets, the adaptable Black Luce also prospered. Her house and her harem were widely known and visited. The privacy of her 'house' was her livelihood. And for her girls it was their protection. Historian of London vice, Fergus Linnane:

> Prostitutes who did not simply take their customers to a nearby alley for brief sex against a wall needed somewhere to entertain them. This was not a problem for the high-class courtesans, who would have houses of their own ... All other prostitutes found their lives and their working practices dominated by this problem.
>
> Girls who worked in brothels had a degree of security as long as they did not succumb to disease or drink. Women on the game aged quickly and might lose their looks by their late twenties, so their careers were usually short.[25]

Lucy Morgan had begun her new life in 1582 and that career was not short. Twelve years later, being both intelligent and selective in her choice of men and their pleasures, she was still attractive and had acquired some security when William Shakespeare met her. By that time he was already a known and rising playwright. Earlier triumphs such as his tragedy, *Titus Andronicus*, were rapidly being surpassed by the laughter of *A Comedy of Errors* and *Love's Labours Lost* with playgoers from all over London crowding to the *Rose* theatre day after day to see the performances.

The year 1594 had begun badly with fear of plague spreading across the city and as a precaution the royal court left Windsor. Returning to pick up more of the queen's possessions a carter saw her underclothes, not the still-to-be thought-of knickers but an ordinary linen smock, and the astonished man shouted: 'Now I see that the Queen is a woman as well as my wife!' Elizabeth heard him. 'What a villain is this,' she laughed, and sent him three gold angels for his impudence, each of them worth ten silver shillings.[26]

By that year the queen would have forgotten her long-departed maid of honour, Lucy Morgan who had matured from those early years in the royal court, still lovely, still with the poise of a true lady, and by 1594 with the maturity to make her a very desirable woman. Shakespeare saw her, met her, was drawn to her. To his emotional cost. She was lovely, she was physically desirable, but to him she had one unalterable disadvantage. She was a woman and women were changeable. And yet, whatever her mood, he could not stop hurrying to meet her, to look at her; her elegance, the way she walked, lissom, proud, distant, but with a sudden smile when she spoke quietly to him. The loveliness of her dark eyes entranced him. The poet wrote a mournfully 'black' sonnet to a lady of darkness:

Thine eyes I love, and they, as pitying me
Knowing thy heart torment me with disdain,
Have put on black and loving mourners be,
Looking with pretty ruth upon my pain.
And truly not the morning sun of heaven
Better becomes the grey cheeks of the east,
Nor that full star that ushers in the even
Doth half that glory to the sober west
As those two mourning eyes become thy face.
O let it then as well beseem thy heart
To mourn for me, since mourning doth thee grace,
And suit thy pity like in every part.
Then will I swear beauty herself is black,
And all they foul that thy complexion lack.[27]

In it there is much repetition of the sound 'mor': 'mourners', 'mourning', 'morning', which may have been puns on Lucy Morgan's surname, almost a pen-picture of her. There is something else. The word 'black' occurs twice in that sonnet, twice in sonnet 131, three times in sonnet 127 and once in several others whereas the word 'dark' is confined to just one, sonnet 147. Even there it is coupled with 'black' on the same line. Some writers have considered this as a hint that the Dark Lady may have been black-skinned, a negress. Wraight strongly disagreed with the prejudice:

> There is absolutely nothing remotely racist to be read into the sonnets that harp so constantly on the word, 'black'. The Dark Lady we are seeking to identify was, in fact, not black, and anyone seeking her in this ethnic sense is doomed to fail. She was apparently Welsh, although she had beautiful black eyes and black hair to match, no doubt, although her hair is not important to the Poet because he has no reference to her name, as we shall see.[28]

By 1594 Lucy Morgan from Wales was the madam of a harem of professional young ladies who were in such demand that the law-students of Gray's Inn invited them to their Christmas farce called the *Prince of Purpoole*, their Inn being on the place where the ancient manor of Portpool had stood. Lucy Morgan was delighted to accept. With her seemly choir of black-robed 'nuns' her arrival and her status were announced with due legal propriety:

> *Lucy Negro*, Abbess *de Clerkenwell*, holdeth the Nunnery of Clerkenwell, with the Lands and Privileges thereunto belonging, of the Prince of *Purpoole* by Night-Service in *Cauda*, and to find a Choir of Nuns with burning Lamps, to chaunt *Placebo* to the Gentlemen of the Prince's Privy-Chamber, on the day of His Excellency's Coronation.[29]

It was pompous and playful. It was the pornographic wit of educated young men. 'Cauda' was Latin for tail but it was also

Elizabethan slang for penis. 'Placebo' "I shall be pleasing", may have been the first word of *Placebo Domino*, the Vespers for the Dead, but for the living it was a promise that Lucy Morgan's 'nuns' would bring nothing but pleasure to the well-paying students of Gray's Inn.[30]

Lucy Morgan, nicknamed 'Black Luce' and 'Lucy Negro', had also at one time offered nothing but pleasure to William Shakespeare. It had been carnal abandonment and his eager body had rejoiced in it:

> Love is too young to know what conscience is;
> Yet who knows not conscience is born of love?
> Then, gentle cheater, urge not my amiss,
> Lest guilty of my faults thy sweet self prove;
> For, thou betraying me, I do betray
> My nobler part to my gross body's treason;
> My soul doth tell my body that he may
> Triumph in love; flesh stays no farther reason;
> But, rising at thy name, doth point out thee
> As his triumphant prize. Proud of this pride,
> He is contented thy poor drudge to be,
> To stand in thy affairs, fall by thy side.
> No want of conscience hold it that I call
> Her 'love' for whose dear love I rise and fall.

The sonnet was open in its bawdiness and description of sexual erection. Its fourfold repetition of 'con' was the French obscenity for 'cunt'. The poem is one of the most candid of all Shakespeare's verse in its description of physical love-making.[31] It was composed for Lucy Morgan and Shakespeare even named a character in one of his early plays after her. But not flatteringly. In his *A Comedy of Errors* of around 1594, a time when resentment against a rival may have replaced romance, that swarthy lady was described as 'swart, like my shoe, but her face nothing like so clean kept'.[32] It may have been after the time when his friend, the young Earl of Southampton, had replaced the playwright in her affections.

Two loves I have, of comfort and despair,
Which like two spirits do suggest me still;
The better angel is a man right fair,
The worser spirit a woman coloured ill.
To win me soon to hell, my female evil
Tempteth my better angel from my side,
And would corrupt my sail to be a devil,
Wooing his purity with her foul pride.
And whether that my angel be turned fiend
Suspect I may, yet not directly tell;
But being both from me, both to each friend,
I guess one angel in another's hell.
Yet this shall I ne'er know, but live in doubt,
Till my bad angel fire my good one out.[33]

The woman won. Southampton was lured to her. Always mercenary and opportunistic Lucy Morgan continually looked for the richest prize and when the young earl came into her life she readily deserted Shakespeare. Half-jokingly he pleaded with her to return. He even composed an amusing sonnet about her heartless departure in search of something more attractive:

Lo, as a careful housewife runs to catch
One of her feathered creatures broke away,
Sets down her babe ...

They were half-jokes. 'Housewife' would have been pronounced 'hussif', close enough in sound to 'hussy' to suggest the woman's sexual inclinations. As for 'feathered creatures', they were not clucking hens in a coop. They were well-to-do courtly popinjays, dandified fops like Southampton in their fashionable plumed hats looking for, and paying for an agreeable female body to 'play the mother's part', a euphemism for becoming a mistress. As for the 'babe', that was Shakespeare himself, a man abandoned but hoping for his lady to return. He could not resist the appeal of a pun:

So will I pray that thou mayst have thy *Will*,
If thou turn back and my loud crying still.

Nor could he resist the *double entendre* of 'have thy will', his name and her vagina. Even anxious and pleading he was still a writer.[34]

Lucy Morgan agreed to return to him. But there was an unexpected price for her favours. Both men had enjoyed her but her experienced and too-available body was vulnerable. By the year of Purpoole it had become diseased and destructive. Both men had used it and both of them contracted the pox. 'Till my bad angel fire my good one out', was the final line of the sonnet. It meant not only that the evil temptress had lured his faithful friend, but also 'until my friend contracts a venereal infection from my former woman'. He did. And Shakespeare already had. They had been sexually infected with the clap, probably the less dangerous gonorrhoea with its symptoms of aching bones, decaying flesh and loss of hair. The more dangerous syphilis had not yet become common in England.

Gonorrhoea was widespread and could be treated by squatting in a hot tub and washing the genitals in stinging vinegar or hot white wine, then enduring painful weeks of 'bad piss', wincingly urinating. In his final ironical pair of 'Cupid' sonnets, numbers 153 and 154, Shakespeare remembered the 'cure' and the unpleasantness of relieving his bladder:

... a seething bath, which yet men prove
Against strange maladies, a sovereign cure ...
I sick withal, the help of bath desired,
And thither hied, a sad distempered guest.

Growing a bath and healthful remedy
For men diseased ...[35]

Years later when he was writing his despairing tragedy of *King Lear*, Shakespeare could still remember the humiliating and very painful liquid outcome of making love to an enchanting but imperfect woman:

> Down from the waist they are centaurs, though women all above:
> But to the girdle do the gods inherit,
> Beneath is all the fiends:
> There's hell, there's darkness, there is the sulphurous pit: burning,
> scalding, stench, consumption. Fie, fie, fie! Pah, pah! Give me an
> ounce of civet, good apothecary, sweeten my imagination: there's
> money for thee.[36]

There was pox but there was also theatre for a writer. To provide a stage for a multitude of new plays by Shakespeare and his rivals another theatre was erected in London at Bankside. As always, there were complaints like this one from a contemporary Elizabethan journal:

> Hence plays are become the ordinary place of meeting for all
> vagrant persons and masterless men, that hang about the City,
> thieves, horse stealers, whoremongers, cozeners, coney-catching
> persons, practisers of reason and such like; there they consort and
> make their matches. Nor can the City be cleansed of this ungodly
> sort (the very sink and contagion not only of the city but of the
> whole realm) so long as plays of resort are by authority permitted.[37]

And in the final weeks of the year there were the revels at Gray's Inn where Lucy Morgan's troupe provided the unwholesome entertainments.

Towards the end of her declining career that former maid of honour is reputed to have married to an otherwise unknown husband although 'the fact that she was once indicted under the name of Parker in 1600 is not evidence that she had married a man of that name ten or more years earlier'.[38]

Once a proud young woman at the court of Queen Elizabeth 'Black Luce' had descended from maidenly honour to notoriety, poverty and shame. In 1595 she was accused of spreading pox. Five years later as the brothel-keeper of St John Street, Clerkenwell she was summoned to the Queen's Bench accused of evil living. By then with her shameful manner of life she was considered an infamous person and on 15 January she was committed to Bridewell. Convicted and imprisoned she was fortunate not to be sentenced to the degrading spectacle of being 'carted'. But:

> Whether Luce also was received at Bridewell with the usual cruel punishment of the four-lashed and knotted whip is not revealed. But without a doubt she laboured for a time dressed in the coarse blue gown and canvas coif, beating hemp with the delicate fingers which had so often played for Queen Elizabeth, and which Shakespeare had adored.[39]

She died at some time before 8 October 1610. No record was left of her life but 'Old Lucilla' was reputed to have died of syphilis. The Hereford poet, John Davies, gave her an epitaph:

> Such a beginning, such an end. This I'll not applaud
> For Luce did like a whore begin, but ended like a bawd.

This meant that she had started her unseemly life as a prostitute but had clambered upwards in the underworld to become a woman who employed other women to sell their bodies to men. She then kept some of their earnings in return for providing them with an income. She was a procuress.

According to George Bagshawe Harrison she had to be William Shakespeare's Dark Lady. It was a tentative conclusion. Lucy Morgan certainly was a possibility. Possibilities are not certainties.

8

Penelope Devereux, Lady Rich

Concerning Shakespeare's sonnets:
Perhaps these poems have to do with Sidney's Stella, Lady Rich, who aroused the jealousy of Elizabeth Vernon, Southampton's bride, and inspired a deep and desperate devotion on the part of Pembroke. Is her name not punned upon in Sonnet 146: 'Within be fed, without be rich no more?'

        Samuel Schoenbaum, *Shakespeare's Lives*, 1991, p. 328.

Dates are vital. The search for the elusive Dark Lady is not a straightforward history from the first year to the last. But, fortunately, times of important events provide a reliable background to a period of shadows in which the same sequence of years provides several completely different yet equally plausible stories about Shakespeare and his woman of the night.

There is a warning. Anyone attempting to decipher the enigmatic clues in Shakespeare's sonnets should accept that there is a possibility that Shakespeare's Dark Lady may never have been an actual person, no more than an ethereal wraith raised out of the fantasies of Shakespeare's imagination. Several pessimistic scholars have considered this probable. The present writer does not. This book has already reincarnated one 'wraith', Anne Whateley. The Dark Lady will not be another unbodied phantom. Like Anne Whateley, she lived.

Shakespeare was not writing a series of mechanical verses when he wrote the sonnets. Those poems are too full of pain, desire, despair, anger and bewilderment to be no more than impersonal made-to-measure exercises. There was a human Dark Lady, she did live, and with care she can be discovered amongst a confusion of candidates. 1595 was a disturbed year for several of those ladies. It was a restless, sometimes brutal year. The revelries at Gray's Inn continued raucously throughout January until the beginning of February. More decorously, in March actors of the Lord Chamberlain's Company were paid for their performance at court the previous Christmas. A few months later apprentices rioted in London. Three of their leaders were hanged, drawn and quartered. Catholics were persecuted. The Jesuit, Robert Southwell, was tortured by Topcliffe and executed at Tyburn. An English army went to Ireland and put down a rebellion. In July four Spanish galleys raided in Cornwall, burning Penzance. Next month there were rumours of a second Spanish armada. It ran aground in Spain.

Frances Drake and John Hawkins raided along the Panama isthmus. Sir Walter Ralegh returned from the Orinoco river in Venezuela telling astonished listeners that he had heard of a race of Amazon women who saw men only once a month yearly. If they bore a son they gave it to the father. They kept their daughters. He had also heard of a tribe whose heads were on their chests. In the same year audiences at the ageing *Theatre* playhouse saw the first productions of Shakespeare's *A Midsummer Night's Dream* as well as his *Richard II* and *Romeo and Juliet*.[1]

In 1595 Jacqueline Field was supervising a young printer's apprentice as he fumbled with tiny blocks of letters, trying to arrange them neatly. Less than half a mile to the north, just outside the walls of London, a bored Mrs Florio idled hours away at their home in Shoe Lane while her preoccupied husband was obsessed with his research into the relationships of words in Italian and English. A mile to the south of the Florios near St James' Palace and the River Thames Emilia Lanier fretted that her empty life had neither wealth, patronage nor pleasure because of the worthless, unadventurous husband she had been made to marry.

Lucy Morgan neither supervised, idled nor fretted. She slept contentedly in her Shoreditch brothel. The night's takings had been good and she still had her looks. Field, Florio, Lanier and Morgan were four of the eight women 'reliably identified' as the Dark Lady. There was a fifth.

In 1580, many years earlier than 1595, the well-born Penelope Devereux had been presented to the queen at court. Although there was no requirement for yet another maid of honour it was thought probable that the queen would somehow favour such a delightfully attractive girl. She did. Penelope stayed. At the time Elizabeth was being amused by a suitor, the young French Duc d'Anjou, short-legged, pock-marked but her 'dearest frog'. Eventually becoming a pest in his persistent wooing he was sent back to France with a gift of £10,000 and a consolation of vague promises.

In the court Penelope Devereux had become almost a legend for her beauty, charm and grace and delightfully modest manner. The pleasure lasted less than a year. She was one of life's butterflies, attractive but defenceless. Fifteen years later in 1595, unhappily married but with a lover, she may also have been Shakespeare's will-o'-the-wisp, his Dark Lady. Gerald Massey thought so. In his *Shakespeare's Sonnets Never Before Interpreted* of 1866 he was the first to claim that Penelope, Lady Rich, had been Shakespeare's secret lover. He repeated the claim in a second book twenty years later.[2]

Massey had been born in poverty in a hut at Gamble Wharf on the canal near Tring in Hertfordshire. When he was eight years old he was sent to work in a silk mill. Years later, determinedly self-taught and living comfortably in London, he was acknowledged as a fine poet by Tennyson and others. As a successful, self-educated man he deserved a better description a century later than Schoenbaum's uncharacteristically snobbish dismissal of a 'working-class poet, untutored mystic (often the worst kind) in his 600-page *Shakspeare's Sonnets Never Before Interpreted* ...' In 1888, Massey enlarged that book as *The Secret*

Drama of Shakspeare's Sonnets. Schoenbaum cruelly commented: 'That way madness lies'.[3]

Famous only briefly, Massey has disappeared from Shakespearian literature. Even the meticulous, alphabetical Index of the 2001 *Oxford Companion to Shakespeare* moves from 'masques' to 'Massinger' with no mention of him and almost every modern scholar searching the sonnets on the track of the Dark Lady has ignored him. Yet he may have been right. Penelope Devereux could have been Shakespeare's tormenting woman of darkness. Textual hints in the poet's sonnets 'appear to support Rowse's insistence that the Dark Lady was 'a well known person ... of superior social standing to Shakespeare'. This would enhance the claims of the dark-haired Penelope Rich, born Lady Penelope Devereux, sister of the Earl of Essex, and the 'Stella' of Sidney's sonnet cycle, *Astrophel and Stella*.[4]

She was born in 1563 at the newly-built, imposing Stoke Park Manor House at Stoke Poges in Buckinghamshire. Today only the west wing survives. The first daughter of the Earl of Essex Penelope had a sister, Dorothy, and a younger brother, Robert Devereux, later the ill-starred Earl of Essex who was to be favoured for years by the queen only finally to be condemned to death by her.

Both the manor and the church at the village of Stoke Poges are notable. Queen Elizabeth was entertained in the house. In the following century Charles I was imprisoned there. A hundred years later in 1749 the poet Thomas Gray wrote his famous elegy beginning, 'The curfew tolls the knell of parting day', in the churchyard of St Giles church. It was memorable poetry. 'I would rather be the author of that poem than take Quebec', the young General Wolfe is reported to have said in 1759 before his army stormed the heights of Abraham below Quebec. Both the French commander and Wolfe were killed in the battle.

Great poetry had been inspired almost two centuries earlier at Stoke Poges. The year 1576 had become a time of wonderment for the twenty-two year-old Sir Philip Sidney when he saw Penelope Devereux for the first time. For him it was a good time. He longed for her. He called her, 'Stella', his shining star. Her father hoped that Sidney would marry her a few years later. That golden-haired, black-eyed beauty, still only a child, was considered to be a suitable bride for the young knight. But it was a bad time. Her father had died too early for the match to be confirmed and the thirteen-year-old Penelope was adopted by her cousins, the calculating Hastings family, Lord and Lady Huntingdon. They had no interest in an unrich triviality like Sidney. They searched for a much more promising, much wealthier husband for their ward. And found one. Anthony Holden:

> At Court Lady Huntingdon soon picked up rumours that the very rich baron Rich of Leighs in Essex was dying and his young heir would be one of the leading landowners in the region. Quickly she passed on the news to her husband in Newcastle. On 27 February Lord Rich duly died, having signed his will two days earlier, and on 10 March the Earl of Huntingdon wrote to Lord Burghley to ask his help in fixing up the marriage ... Rich's son and heir was 'in years very fit for my Lady Penelope'. The marriage needed the queen's permission and Huntingdon wanted Burghley to persuade Elizabeth to give it. To be on the safe side he wrote to Walsingham with a similar request.[5]

In 1581 her guardian, the Earl of Huntingdon, having obtained Burghley's consent, had her married off to 'the rich Robert, Lord Rich', second Baron of Leigh. It was an unhappy match. The puritanical Rich was remote. He treated her as property, a female body that would provide a son for him. She was obedient, looked after their houses at Leigh near Chelmsford, several manors in Essex and their London home, the palatial Essex House on the Strand. She supervised the servants, bore children dutifully, but allowed herself to dream. It was a dream in a nightmare. Years later her second husband remembered that she was 'married against her will unto one, against whom she did protest at the very solemnity, and ever after'.[6]

Rich was a dour, probably sour man, humourless, the antithesis of his vivacious wife. He was also an extreme

Protestant, almost a Puritan whose ministers he favoured. His marriage to Penelope Devereux was a marital tragedy for her. Conversely, it was a good match for Lord Rich. He was of no well-born estate. She was of the gentry and she provided her husband with access to valuable social contacts. He also had her dowry of £2,000 sterling.

Sir Philip Sidney was ignored as an irrelevance. He could only admire his idol from a distance but from that distance he composed some of England's finest love-poems including *Arcadia* with its:

> When Nature made his chief work Stella's eyes
> In colour black why rapt she beams so bright
> Would she in beauty black, like painter wise
> From daintiest lustre, mixed of shades and light ...

He struggled to find the words that expressed his love. He found them: 'Fool,' said my Muse to me, 'look in thy heart, and write.'[7] But his poetry also included dismay at her fate, punning resentfully on her enforced husband's name:

> ... that rich fool who by blind Fortune's lot
> The richest gem of love and life enjoys.

And there were ironical parts of Sidney's sour sonnet about Stella's enforced imprisonment with a worthless man that she did not love, parts that were all the more futile because she herself was a direct descendant of a king's mistress, Mary Boleyn, a 'treasure of a royal heart'. Stella was rich in everything except for becoming a 'Rich'.

> Rich in all beauties which man's eye can see
> Beauties so far from reach of words that we
> Abase her praise saying she doeth excel;
> Rich in the treasures of deserved renown,
> Riches in treasures of a royal heart,
> Rich in those gifts which give the eternal crown;

Who, though most rich in these and every part
Which makes the patents of true worldly bliss,
Hath no misfortune but that Rich she is.

It was the most bitter of all his poems because of what she was suffering. Always enraptured by her, even when she was lost to him, he composed his long, music of words, *Astrophel and Stella*. Penelope, his golden-haired, black-eyed beauty, was 'Stella', the star. It was Sidney's masterpiece. Wraight again:

> This much admired Elizabethan soldier-poet and scholar, whose love for the Lady Penelope Devereux, the young sister of the Earl of Essex, had been thwarted by her marriage to the wealthy but hated Lord Rich, was later married himself, and happily, to Frances Walsingham, daughter of Queen Elizabeth's Secretary of State, Sir Francis Walsingham; but it was generally recognised that his early love for Penelope had been the inspiration for his Astrophel and Stella left in manuscript.
>
> Following the publication of this sonnet sequence in 1591, every scribbling poet had tried his hand at emulating Sidney's superb achievement in the genre, and sonneteering an imaginary lady, or eulogising a flesh-and-blood patroness disguised under another name in idealised form, became the most popular poetic pastime. No less than twenty-six sonnet sequences were published in quick succession within some six years, the most popular going into several editions.[8]

Sidney's sonnets were pirated in a crudely printed edition of 1591,

> but in April the following year Sidney's sister protected her brother's memory by arranging for the publication of a much superior, authorised version, which became exceedingly popular in the immediate months and years that followed.[9]

Four years later Sir Philip Sidney, still in love with her, fought in the Netherlands against the Spanish and was killed at

Zütphen in 1586. There is a popular story that, dying, he was offered water but refused it, telling the bearer to give it to a nearby common soldier 'for his need is greater than mine'.

It was in the summer of 1586 that Penelope's first son was born. She already had two daughters. The dutiful years trudged by. By 1595, just past her thirtieth birthday, she was drained with disappointment at her repetitive domestic life. There was some consolation. She had become famous not only for her looks but for her learning and her encouragement of the arts. She was multi-lingual, speaking and reading Spanish, French and Italian, having been taught by the linguist and scholar, John Florio who had been giving language lessons at Court in the early 1580s. She was unusual in that she could also write in those languages. Florio remembered her. Years later when he published his translation of Montaigne's *Essays*, he dedicated the second volume to Penelope Devereux, Lady Rich, and another noble woman.[10] She was already making a life for herself, a life of private self-indulgence. Peter Quennell:

> Many Elizabethan women – Leicester's second wife, for example, and her daughter Penelope who married Lord Rich – were as fiery and energetic as the men they loved. Usually, however, these dominant females were members of the ruling class, or married to rich London merchants.[11]

Penelope, Lady Rich, spent much of her time in London at Essex House in the Strand not far from, but unaware of, Emilia Lanier and it was not long before a cult developed of the beneficial Lady Rich. Poets and composers praised her for her encouragement, interest and reward. The first printed dedication to 'The right excellent and most beautiful lady, the Lady Penelope Rich', appeared in 1594 in Richard Barnfield's tale, *The Affectionate Shepheard* portraying her as 'the fair Queen Gwendolen' who loved a 'lusty youth, that now was dead', followed by many references to Sidney.[12]

He was the first of many writers and musicians hoping for patronage. The twenty-six year-old Robert Constable addressed his sonnet sequence to her. Many others dedicated poems and sonnets to the lovely Penelope Devereux, the unhappy Lady Rich. William Byrd, the greatest of Elizabethan composers, wrote songs about her. John Dowland, lute-player and songwriter, composed dances in her honour. Charles Tessier, the artistic French lutenist, dedicated his first book, the *Premier Livre du Chansons et Airs*, to her because she was both fluent in French and excellent musically, playing the virginals with delicacy.

Lady Penelope Rich passed her days and nights in apparent contentment with her husband at his Essex house at Leighs or in London. In those times of plague and disease she was fortunate. 'In April 1597 Lady Rich was attacked by smallpox, but recovered 'without any blemish to her lovely face'.[13] The unscathed Penelope Devereux, compulsory wife of Lord Rich, had a young family, a boring husband, she had followers and flatterers hoping for her patronage, she had a devoted admirer. None of them had captivated her. She wanted, even needed, more. Like the classical Penelope of Ithaca, warding off beseeching suitors, waiting for her husband to return from Troy, Penelope, Lady Rich of Elizabethan London, was a woman waiting for someone to entrance her.

> Essex, Penelope and Mountjoy had grown up in households that patronised private troupes of players; indeed the company that Shakespeare now joined, the Lord Chamberlain's Men, was backed by Penelope's great uncle Henry, Lord Hunsdon, and his son George Carey.
>
> Shakespeare was bent on writing topical dramas with political bite for the Chamberlain's Men and among the Devereux and their devotees he found themes and characters he could use ... For *Love's Labours Lost* he took the political background and French gossip from Essex's agenda, recreated the diplomatic deer hunts at Wanstead, and put Antonio Pérez on stage as Don Armado.[14]

Pérez was known to Lady Rich. On one of her occasional visits to court she had met that colourful, ageing foreigner, a dangerous criminal, who had fled Spain from the unpleasant attentions of the Inquisition. He was also wanted for theft and adultery. He arrived in England in 1593 by insinuating himself with the French embassy. The Earl of Essex befriended the plausible trickster. Posturing, flattering, the new arrival was not formally acknowledged by the queen but Elizabeth was entertained by his repertoire of risqué stories. And he amused Penelope Devereux.

Returning to England three years later Pérez was bewitched by her loveliness and entertained Lady Rich with lasciviously sexual word-play about gloves and dogs. In letters he signed himself, 'Your Ladyship's flayed dog' because dogs were famous for their obedience, adding, suggestively, that he had 'seen dogs in very favourite places of ladies', their laps. Despite his hopes of an 'affair' it did not develop. But it was through Pérez that Shakespeare met Penelope.[15]

In his newly-performed *Love's Labours Lost* Shakespeare mocked that notoriously conceited Spaniard as 'Don Adriano de Armado', a braggart in love with Jaquenetta, a dairy maid. Yet in the play, despite his boasting, the penniless upstart refused to fight a duel. He told his comrades that he could not because 'the naked truth of it is, I have no shirt'.[16] Shakespeare did have a shirt. He also had a reputation for fine words and he used them to ensnare the lovely Lady Rich, perceptively and coolly using her well-known liking for the poetry of the long-dead Sir Philip Sidney. As Sidney had done he praised her eyes. 'Thine eyes I love', he wrote:

> Nor that full star that ushers in the even,
> Doth half that glory to the sober west
> As those two mourning eyes become thy face ...
> The will I swear beauty herself is black,
> And all they foul that thy complexion lack.

Enthralled, obsessed with her; her unconcerned aristocracy, her assured manner, her distance, she was almost beyond desire. To entice her he wrote sonnets in Sidney's style. In his own poems he likened Penelope to Sidney's Stella, giving his hoped-for lover the same black hair and eyes as Stella. It was a poetical conceit because that was exactly what Lady Rich had been. His poems contained phrases echoing Sidney's sonnets. He even copied Sidney's comparison of black eyes being like signs of death by describing Penelope's dark eyes as:

> ... my mistress' eyes are raven black
> Her eyes so suited, and they mourners seem ...[17]

He was not Sidney. But it was rumoured that if Shakespeare was allowed an uninterrupted half an hour's talk with a woman she would be his. There was a problem. The unhappily married Lady Rich already had a lover, Sir Charles Blount. She denied it. Shakespeare knew she lied but, infatuated as he was, he was content simply to lie against her, making love, and share the deception.

> When my love swears that she is made of truth,
> I do believe her though I know she lies,
> That she might think me some untutored youth,
> Unlearnéd in the world's false subtilties.
> Thus vainly thinking that she thinks me young,
> Although she knows my days are past the best;
> Simply I credit her false speaking tongue;
> On both sides thus is simple truth supprest.
> But wherefore says she not she is unjust?
> And wherefore say not I that I am old?
> O love's best habit is in seeming trust,
> And age in love loves not t'have years told.
> Therefore I lie with her, and she with me,
> And in our faults by lies we flattered be.[18]

In the sonnet there was a preoccupation with age as though they were both in the withering stages of life. They were not. In 1595 he was thirty-one. She was a year older and perhaps at her loveliest. They were enjoying each other but there was a problem. Both of them were married. Shakespeare was the husband of the far-off, almost neglected Anne Hathaway. Lady Rich was the similarly neglected wife of the cold, often absent Lord Rich. By beginning an affair the poet and his paramour were committing adultery. To many Victorian editors of Shakespeare's works it was a marital sin that lurked uncomfortably behind the seemly editions. But one of their colleagues, Massey, thought them hypocrites:

> It is here they so triumphantly lift the vulturine nose and snuff the carrion that infests the dirt. They have no misgivings that the scent may be carried in their own nostrils.

They were not personal sonnets and there was nothing guilty in them. There was no wrongdoing on Shakespeare's part.

> The most searching investigation yet made will prove that there is not in the least foundation for the dark story to be told against our Poet save that which has been laid in the prurient imagination of those who have so wantonly sought to defile the memory of Shakespeare.[19]

Massey was deluding himself, ignoring evidence that was almost defiantly stated in the sonnets themselves. In them were three people, William Shakespeare, his Dark Lady, the notorious woman with eyes of black, Penelope, Lady Rich, and a third person, Charles Blount, 8th Lord Mountjoy, later the Earl of Devonshire.

At the beginning the association between the poet and the lady prospered. Her looks enthralled him. His words enchanted her. Physically it was more than a flirtation although too brief to be an affair. Always in the background was that third man, Blount. The association had a good beginning. In two bawdy sonnets Shakespeare punned indelicately on his name, 'Will'. It was crude backstreet innuendo. 'Will' could mean either the male, sometimes the female, sexual organ.[20]

In one sonnet he wrote: 'Whoever hath her wish, thou hast

thy *Will*' and continued through the poem with five more crude puns on the word, all of them explicit about sexual intercourse, such as the penultimate lines:

So thou being rich in *Will* add to thy *Will*,
One will of mine, to make thy large *Will* more ...

And in the following poem were the lines:

swear to thy blind soul that I was thy *Will*,
Make but my name thy love, and love that still,
And then thou lovest me for my name is *Will*.[21]

Yet she was always distant, a titled lady being occasionally entertained by an actor. She encouraged him – but casually – an interest but not a desire. Shakespeare was trapped in his desire for her. She was offhand, sometimes cruel:

For if I should despair, I should go mad,
And in my madness might speak ill of thee.
Now this ill-wresting world is grown so bad
Mad slanderers by mad ears believèd be.
That I may not be so, nor thou belied,
Bear thine eyes straight, though thy proud heart go wide.[22]

But it ended. Although Lady Rich could indulge herself in whims, casually using a poet and a player as a toy, it was Blount that she wanted as a partner in her life.

It was a bitter ending to Shakespeare's year. Elsewhere England was celebrating the thirty-ninth anniversary of the reign of Queen Elizabeth. There were joyful sermons, cannons, bonfires, feasts. The queen was lauded fulsomely. Modestly, she retired to bed. In the same year, 1595, Sir Thomas Heneage, second husband of the Countess of Southampton, died. And it was at the end of that year that *Romeo and Juliet* was first performed. The year is known because in the play Juliet's nurse remembered, 'Tis now eleven years, since the earthquake' and that was in 1584.[23] William Shakespeare was unconcerned about earthquakes. He was thinking of Penelope Devereux, Lady Rich. He wrote about her but not with tenderness.

His *Romeo and Juliet* was full of the woman, obsessed with her dark beauty, he himself 'stabbed with a white wench's black eye'. It was the first public mention of the Dark Lady. His sonnets were filled with bitter memories of that 'woman coloured ill', with the derogatory 'black' occurring three times in one sonnet, twice in two others. He was unforgiving of her treachery. She was his Dark Lady. 'In nothing art thou black save in thy deeds', an unfaithful harlot 'who art as black as hell, as dark as night'.[24]

Shakespeare's 'affair' with that fickle Dark Lady, Penelope Rich, was over. Sorry for himself he accepted her infidelity in one of his saddest sonnets, 146.

> Poor soul, the centre of my sinful earth,
> My sinful earth these rebel powers that thee array,
> Why dost thou pine within and suffer dearth,
> Painting thy outwards walls so costly gay?
> Why so large cost, having so short a lease,
> Dost thou upon thy fading mansion spread?
> Shall worms, inheritors of this excess,
> Eat up thy charge? Is this thy body's end?
> Then, soul, live thou upon thy servant's loss,
> And let that pine to aggravate thy store;
> Buy terms divine in selling hours of dross;
> Within be fed, without be *rich* no more:
> So shalt thou feed on Death, that feeds on men,
> And Death, once dead, there's no more dying them.
> Within be fed, without be *rich* no more.

In the same year, 1595, Mary Fitton came to the royal court as a maid of honour, and Charles Blount became Lady Rich's lover. A member of the powerful Essex clique he was often with Penelope at the time of the return of the disgraced Earl of Essex from Ireland. Mountjoy succeeded him as Lord Deputy in 1600.

By that time, Penelope, Lady Rich, still married, had become notorious as his mistress. She was 'a beautiful and wilful woman of the world, who had deserted her unsympathetic consort to live openly with a young and gallant lover, Charles Blount, Lord Mountjoy'.[25]

The years did not pass peaceably for Penelope Rich. In 1600 her brother, the Earl of Essex who had failed ignominiously to defeat the rebel, Tyrone, in Ireland, returned to England in disgrace. Fearing imprisonment, even execution, he attempted a rebellion. Trying to encourage the people to follow him his followers bribed the Lord Chamberlain's Company to perform Shakespeare's play *Richard II* about a popular rising against the crown. There was no rising. Elizabeth was reported to have said: 'I am Richard II, know ye not that?'

Essex had failed disastrously, was arrested and on 19 February 1601 was condemned to death.[26] Penelope Rich interceded on his behalf, writing to the queen defending her brother. Elizabeth was furious at the impertinence. Penelope was defiant. 'What I meant I wrote, and what I wrote I meant,' she declared. Despite her efforts her self-centred brother was unappreciative. In 1602, about to be beheaded, he accused those who had egged him to rebel and betrayed him:

> even his sister, Penelope, who did continually urge me on with telling me how all my friends and followers thought me a coward, and that I had lost all my valour; she must be looked to, for she hath a proud spirit.[27]

At Essex House early in 1601 Lady Penelope Rich was considered to have been engaged in her brother's conspiracy but not very deeply. After a brief house arrest she was cleared of blame. Sensibly she went into retirement until the queen's death in 1603. In 1605 Lord Rich divorced her. By a secret marriage conducted by his chaplain, William Laud, the future Archbishop, she married Charles Mountjoy now the Earl of Devonshire. It led to further disgrace because she was still considered too close to the traitor, Essex. Penelope

Devereux, perhaps Shakespeare's Dark Lady, had only empty years left. Blount died in 1606. She died the following year.

Seven years earlier, in May 1600, the young William Herbert, Earl of Pembroke, visited Lady Rich and Lady Southampton at Wilton House near Salisbury. The two ladies were dangerous company. Both had been involved in Essex's rebellion. But the immature boy was infatuated, almost obsessed with the notorious Lady Rich, that desirable woman of so many lovers. He did not win her. Ever changeable, the impressionable Herbert was later to be involved in the disgrace of Mary Fitton, yet another of the possible Dark Ladies.

9

Mary 'Mall' Fitton

Mary Fitton ... known as Mall ... was a real person about whom quite a lot is known. She was a maid of honour to the queen and at the end of 1600 very much in the news, the talk of the town, and soon to be disgraced. She had become a gift to the Sneerwells and Backbites in the Whitehall school for scandal. Shakespeare must have known her and did in fact mention her in his play of that year, *Twelfth Night*.

Ivor Brown, *The Women in Shakespeare's Life*, 1968, p. 174.

On 13 June in 1884 the top-hatted Thomas Tyler, a London scholar and a friend of George Bernard Shaw, pronounced that the identity of Shakespeare's Dark Lady had been a young Cheshire woman, Mary Fitton, a maid of honour to the queen. In his early years Tyler had concentrated on Biblical studies but by 1874 his interests were widening and he became a founder member of the New Shakespeare Society. By nature studious and scholarly he was often to be seen in the British Museum's Reading Room, unattractive in appearance, disfigured by an ugly goitre, a morbid swelling at the front of the throat stretching from his left ear down to his chin.[1]

On 30 May 1884, at a literary meeting in Gower Street he argued that Shakespeare's elusive 'Mr. W. H.' of the sonnets had been William Herbert, Earl of Pembroke. Bernard Shaw attended the meeting. So did Mrs Charlotte Stopes whose own painstaking research had led her to the conclusion that that mysterious dark woman in Shakespeare's life had been Jacqueline Field. But certainly not Mary Fitton! As she was leaving she said to Tyler: 'I hope I may live long enough to contradict you.' 'No you won't,' he replied, 'for my theory is going down in Time.'[2]

Two years later in 1886, in the facsimile edition of *Shakespeare's Sonnets, the first quarto, 1609,* that he was editing with the assistance of the Rev. W. A. Harrison of St Anne's church, Lambeth, he published the first claim that the Dark Lady had been Mary Fitton. It was an assertion he repeated and elaborated in his updated edition of the sonnets in 1890. The book identified Pembroke as 'the man right fair' and Fitton as the 'woman colour'd ill'. If he was correct then the association between that man and woman would have occurred in the years around 1597, a year of such unusual events that it confirmed the aphorism that 'the past is a foreign country'.

There was failure in 1597. Ralegh and Essex blundered in their attempt to capture the Spanish treasure fleet on its return from the Americas. There was literary success in the same year. Bacons's *Essays* were published. So was James VI's *Daemonologie,* that young Scottish king's semi-hysterical condemnation of witchcraft after some North Berwick women had been condemned to death for trying to cast a spell wrecking the royal ship bringing James's intended bride from Norway. And in 1597 there were events in the Elizabethan theatre. Ben Jonson's *Isle of Dogs* was performed at the *Swan* on Bankside. In the same year William Shakespeare was acting in his own new plays of *Henry VI, Parts I and II,* and drafting the first tentative lines of his forthcoming *Much Ado About Nothing.* In 1597 Mary Fitton had been a royal maid of honour for two years.

Almost 300 years later, towards the end of the nineteenth century, Tyler was so convinced about his identification of her as the Dark Lady that as an act of piety he travelled a tediously long 150 miles on a pilgrimage to the enchanting Cheshire village of Gawsworth near Macclesfield. There he went to the fifteenth-century church whose roof was extravagantly decorated with gargoyles. In the chancel was the impressively carved tomb of the Fitton family. The father, Edward, lay there proudly in his armour, his wife alongside him in a long gown, and below them, on the sides of the tomb, ten small statues of their children, seven of them daughters in hoods and ruffs. Tyler had reached the place where his Dark Lady of the sonnets rested.

Mary and her elder sister Anne had had their portraits painted when they were fifteen and eighteen. The picture showed Sidney Lee had been mistaken about the colour of Mary's hair. She was not fair. She was dark. There are two contemporary paintings of her, one of them at Arbury Hall in Warwickshire. Once believed to be a portrait of Mildred, Lady Maxey, it is now accepted as that of Mary Fitton and shows her to have grey eyes and brown hair rather than blonde. It is not hard evidence. Portrait paintings can be unreliable, sometimes intentionally to flatter the sitter. It is not always 'possible to ascertain the true hair colour of society women from portraits'. The colour of their eyes is more reliable.[3]

In 1886 Bernard Shaw reviewed Tyler's book on the sonnets. He had reservations about its Preface proclaiming Mary Fitton's 'darkness', and about the statement that the sonnets' 'Fair Youth' was the young Earl of Southampton, because Tyler's 'identification' of Mary Fitton as the Dark Lady did not agree with contemporary scholarship. There were doubts about her appearance.

> I am sorry for his [Tyler's] sake that Mary's portrait is fair, and that Mr. W. H. has veered round again from Pembroke to Southampton; but even so his work was not wasted: it is by exhausting all the hypotheses that we reach the verifiable one; and after all, the wrong road always leads somewhere.[4]

Tyler's conjectures were similarly contradicted by Sidney Lee in the *Fortnightly Review* of February 1898, and then in a book of the same year:

The theories that all the sonnets addressed to a woman were addressed to the 'dark lady' and that the 'dark lady' is identifiable with Mary Fitton, a mistress of the Earl of Pembroke, are baseless conjectures. The extant portraits of Mary Fitton prove her to be fair.[5]

But Shaw and Lee were mistaken. In her uneven book, *Gossip from a Muniment Room*, of 1897, Lady Newdigate-Newdegate, a direct descendant of Mary Fitton's sister, Anne, later to be the married Lady Newdigate, dismissed the idea that Fitton could ever have been the Dark Lady. She also:

> showed an odd sense of colour, and perhaps prejudice, when she wrote of 'the brunette described by Shakespeare' when the playwright's actual descriptions were of raven-black hair and pitch-black eyes.[6]

Mary Fitton could have been the Dark Lady. Neither her appearance nor her age nor the years late in the sixteenth century argue against it. Well-bred, born in 1578, by 1597 'Mall' Fitton had been a royal maid of honour at Queen Elizabeth's court for two years, having arrived there when she was seventeen. 'Fitton' was an unfortunate surname. Its derivation was from the Latin, *firmitas*, 'strength', but over the centuries it had corrupted into the mediaeval meaning of 'a liar, a deceitful man'.[7]

As with every one of the possible Dark Ladies of Shakespeare's sonnets there is no documentary evidence against Mary Fitton being that woman. Thomas Tyler's identification of Mary Fitton makes her as good a candidate as any of the others whether Jacqueline Field or Mrs Florio or Emilia Lanier or Lucy Morgan or Gerald Massey's Penelope Devereux.

Four hundred years after their deaths the search for the identity of the Dark Lady among those candidates rests entirely on evidence sifted from the often ambiguous evidence of the sonnets. And that evidence can be unpleasant, as unpleasant as the Dark Lady herself who was fickle, selfish and deceitful. She lured Shakespeare's friend, tempting 'my better angel from my side'. She deceived, 'put fair truth upon so foul a face'. It is all there in the emotion of the sonnets.[8]

> Some Victorian and Edwardian scholars, such as Gerald Massey and Thomas Tyler, devoted large parts of their lonely lives to the quest for 'the lady' ... Working before the twentieth-century critical cult of ambiguity and word-play, these writers seem to have been oblivious to the sheer nastiness of many of the 'dark lady' sonnets.[9]

Duncan-Jones criticism is too harsh. What evidence survives does support the possibility that Mary Fitton was Shakespeare's Dark Lady.

The year 1597 was a year of change in the theatre. The second Lord Hunsdon, Henry Carey, was appointed Lord Chamberlain and became the powerful patron of Burbage's and Shakespeare's company of actors. In England that year a privileged German visitor, Philip Hentzner, noticed how black Queen Elizabeth's teeth were, stained by the amount of sugar she took. Hentzner also wrote that smoking was commonplace even though tobacco cost a prohibitive three shillings an ounce. But men could afford to smoke because every inn, tavern and alehouse had a communal clay pipe that could be passed from customer to customer.[10]

In the same year of 1597 William Shakespeare became a property-owner. Disappointingly to bard-lovers he also showed himself to be a skinflint. By May he had enough money to pay sixty golden sovereigns for the prestigious but dilapidated New Place, the second largest house in Stratford-upon-Avon.[11] Built in 1475 by Sir Hugh Clopton it had been a grand building with ten fireplaces, two gardens and two orchards. But the 'Great House', as it was known locally, had been neglected. By 1596 it was both decrepit and haunted with a ghost of an owner's daughter who had been poisoned with arsenic. More misfortune followed. Shakespeare had bought the building from William Underhill. As the sale was proceeding Underhill was murdered by his son Fulke who was subsequently hanged at Warwick. Shakespeare had to prove that it had been from the father rather than the son that the purchase had been made. New Place was an uneasy house.[12]

Shakespeare returned to London and less unpleasantly disturbed accommodation. No longer an impoverished apprentice actor, he was living in a comfortable tenement in the well-to-do neighbourhood of St Helen's parish, a neighbour of Thomas Marley, a master musician. But Shakespeare, man of property, was also a man who treasured pennies. London bills were left unpaid, and sometimes quarrels over money developed in the aggressive, overcrowded streets of the city. There were disputes, daggers and swords. There was crime.

One of London's attractions was Bartholomew Fair in Smithfield with its entertaining fire-eaters, fencing-masters, stalls selling cure-all nostrums, cheap jewellery and gaudy ribbons. Visitors risked the attentions of pock-marked beggars, pickpockets and prostitutes. The Fair was delight and danger combined. Visiting its crowded jostle in 1598 Hentzner's companion had his pocket skilfully picked of its purse's nine silver crowns. He felt nothing.

On 29 November 1597 Shakespeare and more than thirty others in London were issued with Writs of Attachment to keep the peace. He was a niggard. By the end of the year he was reported for non-payment of a five-shilling tax. He was also summoned to pay the last instalment on some goods he had bought. Four more demands followed but as late as the middle of November he still had not paid the final one pound, three shillings and four pennies on a bill of five pounds. He was not only a genius. He was also a penny-pincher.[13] By a financial irony he was summoned for non-payment of the same city-rates as the medical charlatan and sooth-sayer, Simon Forman, living alongside the Thames.

Later that year Shakespeare's Company gave the first performance of his *The Merry Wives of Windsor* to the court at Windsor. As a maid of honour Mary Fitton would have seen the play and Shakespeare acting in it. The year 1597 was one more hall of mirrors, some with imperfect reflections.

Some scholars have tried to associate William Herbert with a hypothetical Dark Lady in Mary Fitton, one of the Queen's Maids of Honour, with whom he had a youthful love-affair that ended in mutual disgrace when she bore him an illegitimate child. She was dismissed from Court and William Herbert was cast into the Fleet to cool his ardour. The child died, and they did not consequently marry. Mary Fitton's two portraits show her to be brown-haired and grey-eyed., so that her eligibility as the raven-eyed beauty of the Sonnets is without substance, and the attempt to link the young William Herbert with Shakespeare as his 'Mr. W. H.' falls flat'.[14]

The writer, A. D. Wraight was correct about William Herbert and the enigmatic 'Mr. W. H'. He was wrong about Mary Fitton.

Through the influence of her father's friend, Sir William Knollys, an elderly Comptroller of Her Majesty's Household, in 1595 she became a maid of honour. Knollys helped because he was infatuated by her. To him the fact that he was an elderly husband was not a considerable disadvantage. When he was fifty years old he had married a wealthy but older widow, Lady Chandos. Now, some years later, he was Mary Fitton's unofficial guardian and would-be lover. The attractive young girl was seventeen years old. He was fifty-three. In clumsy overtures of love he offered to make her Lady Knollys when his present but aged and ailing wife died. Obsessed with his desire he wrote to her sister Anne about his infatuation.[15] Mary Fitton, engrossed with her pleasant life at Court, did little more than keep him satisfied with pleasant smiles. She was a maid with honour.

In June at Blackfriars her distant kinsman, Lord Herbert, married Anne Russell. Queen Elizabeth attended the wedding. For entertainment there was a masque of eight young ladies, sumptuously dressed in skirts of cloth of silver, silk waistcoats embroidered with gold, and mantles of rich-red carnation. Each of the ladies represented an emotion. Mary Fitton led, and when their decorous performance ended each of the eight chose eight more to be their partners. Characteristically bold, Mary Fitton asked the queen to dance. 'Whom did she represent?' asked Elizabeth. 'Affection,' Mary replied. 'Affection?' said the queen. 'Affection is false!' But she danced.[16]

There were other, innocent pleasures for a young woman with position and means such as going to see a play at one of London's prospering playhouses. They thrived. Plays were being performed on almost every weekday, usually in the afternoon, that time, wrote Thomas Nashe, 'being the best part of the day'. Hentzner knew how popular plays were and how they 'concluded with excellent music, variety of dances, and the excessive applause of those that are present'.

Mary Fitton would have gone to them in a private coach accompanied by an escort who paid the six pennies to permit the two of them to climb the stairs from the ground-floor to the first and then to the second gallery with its cushioned seats 'well-placed to see and be seen'. At the Lord Chamberlain's playhouse, the *Theatre* in Shoreditch, she would have seen and laughed at Will Kemp, the clown, playing the nurse's assistant in *Romeo and Juliet* and Dogberry, the incompetent constable, in *Much Ado About Nothing*.

Kemp was a favourite with audiences, bearded, always accompanied by his little, well-trained dog. Kemp could dance, sing, play an instrument and engage in repartee, often obscene, with the loudly laughing groundlings. They loved him. Although he had quitted the Company in a huff he was so fondly remembered that his name was placed fifth of the twenty-six 'principall actors' in the 1623 *First Folio* publication of Shakespeare's plays.[17] In 1600 accompanied by a drummer-boy, he went on a well-advertised 'dance' of 111 miles, his 'nine days' jig' from London to Norwich. The achievement, performed with sensible rests, lasted from 11 February to 11 March. He boasted about the exploit in his *Nine Daies Wonder*.

One of the many minor mysteries in any account of Shakespeare and the Dark Lady is why Kemp dedicated that book to Anne Fitton, a 'maid of honour'. Anne had never been part of the royal court. Mary had. As Kemp had gone on a continental tour immediately after his 'jig' it is arguable that the unlikely 'Anne' was a slipshod mistake for 'Mary'.[18] And there were other mistakes. Shakespeare benefitted.

In his diary of 13 March 1602, John Manningham, a barrister of the Middle Temple, wrote a well-known story about Shakespeare and his fellow actor, Richard Burbage. A woman at the theatre had seen Richard Burbage playing Richard III and was so enraptured that she made an assignation for him to visit her next day, telling him to announce himself as 'Richard the Third'. Shakespeare eavesdropped:

> Shakespear overhearing their conclusion went before, was intertained, and at his game ere Burbage came. Then message being brought that Rich. the 3rd was at the dore, Shakespeare caused returne to be made that William the Conqueror was before Rich. the 3. Shakespeare's name was William.[19]

That there was a Dark Lady in Shakespeare's life is certain. There is considerable evidence to support Mary Fitton as that woman. The sonnets evoked by her fascination and her transferred affections describe a love-hate relationship between the poet and the woman that he loved. Two of the sonnets actually name with delicate puns on her name with 127's 'or if it were' and the entire Sonnet 136 in which both Mary Fitton and William Shakespeare are named:

> If thy soul check thee that I come so near,
> Swear to thy blind soul that I was thy *Will*,
> And will, thy soul knows, is admitted there;
> Thus far for love my love-suit, sweet, ful*fil*,
> *Will* ful*fil* the treasure of thy love,
> Ay, *fill it* full with wills, and my will one.
> In things of great receipt with ease we prove
> Among a number one is reckoned none.
> Then in the number let me pass untold,
> Though in thy store's account I one must be;

For nothing hold me, so it please thee hold
That nothing me, so it please thee hold
That nothing me, a something, sweet, to thee.
Make but my name thy love, and love that still
And then thou lovest me for my name is *Will*.

The sonnets are full of her, her loveliness, her pride, her fickleness. Almost all of them contain accusations of tyranny, infidelity, lies, pride, and darkness; black as hell, dark as night. Shakespeare knew that she was a wanton, 'one that will do the deed, though Argus were her eunuch and her guard'.[20]

They had met in the playhouse and they had dared to make love there. But for Mary Fitton a visit to the theatre was just one of many pleasures at Court. There were also dangers in the Court itself. Sir William Knollys was responsible for the behaviour of the young maids there. Shakespeare mocked him in *Twelfth Night*, portraying him as the besotted Malvolio, in a series of puns beginning with *Mala-voglia* into 'Mal-voglio' with its meaning of 'I want Mall', 'I wish for Mall' into 'I will have Mall'. Shakespeare jeered at Malvolio because he himself already had had Mall.

The pathetic Knollys was 'a Malvolio on a grander scale', someone unkindly described him. He was besotted by Mary. He was also aware that there were many young courtiers who lusted for her lissom young body. He wrote to her father, assuring him of his care:

I will no fayle to fulfille you desire in playing the Good Sheperd
& will to my power dffend the innocent lamb from the Wolvyshe
crueltye & fox-like subtlety of the tame bests off this place ...

Like the majority of guardians he discovered that his wards were not always appreciative of his watchfulness. Irritated by the girls' persistent noisy behaviour, he tricked them in an episode recorded by Sir Nicholas L'Estrange:

The Lord Knolls, in Queen Elizabeths time, had his lodging at
Court, where some of the Ladyes and Maydes of Honour us'd to

friske and hey abut in the next roome, to his extreame disquiete a nights, though he often warned them of it; at last he gets one to bolt their own backe doore, when they were all in one night at their revels, stripps off to his shirt, and so with a payre of spectacles on his nose, and Aretine in his hand, comes marching in at a posterne doore of his owne chamber, reading very gravely, full upon the faces of them. Now let the reader judge what a sadd spectacle and pitiful sight these poor creatures endur'd, for he fac'd them and often trafverst the roome in this posture above an houre.

He worried. When Mary Fitton was suffering from a nervous condition known as the 'mothers', a young woman's malady of melancholy home-sickness with spasms of hysteria and insomnia she had to be sent from the court and her absence almost caused Knollys to have a breakdown himself.

Elderly but pathetically attempting to appear youthful Knollys dyed his 'party' beard in the popular vari-coloured style of a yellow moustache above a chin fringed with brown hair darkening into an almost black dangling beard above legs covered in yellow cross-garters.[21] The result was laughable. People laughed. The laughter turned to scorn. A year or two later when William Shakespeare and Mary Fitton were still enjoying their brief affair Knollys was mocked cruelly by Shakespeare in *Twelfth Night* because Knollys could not have Mall.[22] But that practised young seducer, William Herbert, soon to be third Earl of Pembroke, could. And did.

Because of his initials some researchers have believed Herbert to have been the mysterious 'Mr. W. H.' of Shakespeare's sonnets. He was nothing as worthy. He was a self-centred rake. Years before inheriting the earldom in 1600, he was systematically copulating with any available young woman whether commoner or well-born. As long as they were female they were satisfactory. He had no intention of marriage. He was a selfish seducer. Among his many upper-class victims were Elizabeth Carey, the daughter of Sir George Carey; and Bridget Vere, Lord Burleigh's grand-daughter; as well as the niece of the Earl of Nottingham. There were others.

Waspishly a contemporary sniffed: 'I do not find any disposition at all in this gallant young Lord to marry', adding that Herbert was 'immoderately given up to women'. And the women gave him what he desired.[23] He had already met the lovely Mary Fitton at the wedding of his cousin to Lady Anne Russell.

The year 1597 was an historical hall of mirrors. In his late teens the self-centred William Herbert was physically attractive with an aristocratically haughty face, sensitive lips, fine eyebrows, hair dangling in long tresses. He looked very like his mother, Mary, Countess of Pembroke. But he worried her. She knew that he was wild, impetuous and immoral. She already was aware of Shakespeare's reputation as a poet and playwright. In despair, she requested him to write some sonnets to encourage her son to take a wife, to persuade that wilful and rampantly immoral young man to marry. She was yet another remarkable Elizabethan woman. Some years after her death that cheerful purveyor of gossip, John Aubrey, smilingly wrote a note about her:

> She was a beautifull Ladie and had an excellent witt, and had the best breeding that that age could afford. Shee had a pretty sharpe-ovall face. Her haire was of a reddish yellowe.
>
> She was very salacious, and she had a Contrivance that in the Spring of the yeare, when the Stallions were to leape the Mares, they were to be brought before such a part of the house, where she had a *vidette* (a hole to peepe out at) to looke on them and please herselfe with their Sport; and then she would act the like sport herselfe with *her* stallions. One of her great Gallants was Crooke-back't Cecill, Earl of Salisbury.
>
> In her time, Wilton House was like a College, there were so many learned and ingeniose persons, She was the greatest Patronesses of witt and learning of any Lady in her time.[24]

But in 1600 her son was to be intimate with a suspected Dark Lady, a maid of honour to the queen, an attractive nubile young woman, a natural target for courtiers to seduce. Mary Fitton welcomed Herbert's dishonourable courtship. Sir Robert Cecil noted:

> In that tyme when that Mistress Fytton was in great fauour, and one of her Majestie's maids of honour, and during the time yt the Earle of Pembrooke fauord her she would put off her head tire and tucke upp her clothes and take a large white cloake and marche as though she had bene a man to meete the said Earle out of the Courte.[25]

The 'head tire' was a wig, probably fashionably almost black to conceal her naturally brown hair. For those secret trysts with Herbert she did actually transform herself into the Dark Lady.

That carefree recklessness with William Herbert was socially disastrous for her. She conceived. Seven or eight months later in February or March, lying in the care of Lady Hawkins, she prematurely gave birth to an illegitimate and sadly short-lived son. The father remained unconcerned and unwed. In his indifference Pembroke was unlike Sir Walter Ralegh who fathered a child on a maid of honour but 'I doubt not but this Hero tooke care of them both, as also that the Product was more than an ordinary mortal'.[26]

But at the court of Queen Elizabeth the outcome was predictable. Mary Fitton was instantly banished. Persisting in his refusal to accept responsibility for her or for any of the women he had seduced the shallow and self-centred Herbert was sent to the unpleasant Fleet prison and banned from further appearance at the queen's court. In his history he was little more than a thin shadow. 'For his person he was not effectual', criticised Sir Francis Bacon. He was a cad.

Across London there was gossip, giggle and disgrace. In January 1601, Shakespeare mocked the scandal in *Twelfth Night* because everyone knew that the unwed Mary Fitton was pregnant.[27] She left London becoming the jest of the heartless town, a ridiculed victim of the satirists who wrote acidic ballads on any current scandal, selling the pamphlets in the streets. As expected, there were insulting verses about her, Knollys and Herbert:

Party beard, party beard ...
the white hind was crossed:
Brave Pembroke struck her down
And took her from the clown
Like a good woodsman.

Everyone knew the identities of the beard, the hind and the woodman. Knollys was the 'party beard' and the 'clown'. Mary Fitton was the 'white hind', an innocent doe who had been 'crossed', seduced by the good 'woodman', Herbert. 'Woodman' was Elizabethan slang for a 'wencher'. In Shakespeare's popular *Measure for Measure* the Duke was described as 'a better woodman than you tak'st him for', a more successful hunter and deflowerer of women. So was William Herbert, the practised lecher.[28]

Shakespeare, resentful that Mary Fitton had abandoned him in favour of the shallow William Herbert, took his revenge. He mocked her. In a passage of coarse jokes about women in *Twelfth Night* Sir Andrew Aguecheek bragged about his 'cutting a caper', meaning having sex, and his companion, Sir Toby Belch shrugged: 'Wherefore are these things hid? Wherefore have these gifts a curtain before them? Are they like to take dust like Mistress Mall's picture?'

It was cruel. Mary Fitton's reputation had been exposed to the gaping world like an uncurtained portrait, neglected, uncleaned and ruined.[29] Years later she became the mistress of Vice-Admiral Sir Richard Leveson. He died in 1605. She then married one of his captains, William Polwhele, but was widowed in 1610. She remarried, and died in obscurity in 1647, another forgotten Dark Lady.

10

Mrs Marie Mountjoy

> Shakespeare's cryptic Dark Lady has been confidently but differently identified as Jacqueline Field by Charlotte Stopes; as Mrs. Florio by Jonathan Bate; Emilia Bassano by A. L. Rowse; Lucy Morgan by G. B. Harrison; Penelope Devereux by Gerald Massey; Mary Fitton by Frank Harris; and as Jane Davenant by Arthur Acheson.
>
> I do not intend to add Marie Mountjoy to this list (the 'Dark Landlady') though her credentials are no worse than any of these.
>
> Charles Nicholl, *The Lodger*, 2007, p. 339

Charles Nicholl could have been mistaken. At the end of the sixteenth century Marie Mountjoy was living at Silver Street in London's Cripplegate ward. William Shakespeare was to be a lodger with her. She became yet another woman, the seventh, to be suspected of being Shakespeare's Dark Lady. Six of those metamorphoses have already been confidently identified as that elusive temptress. The eighth would follow.

When Marie Mountjoy appeared all but one of them were still alive. The exception had been Mrs Florio who had died some years earlier, perhaps shortly after the birth of her fourth child. Of the others Jacqueline Field had moved from her printer's house to a more comfortable home in Wood Street not far from Marie Mountjoy. Emilia Lanier was beginning to write the opening lines of her long, sacred poem, *Salve Deus Rex*

Judaeorum. Lucy Morgan was imprisoned in the Bridewell, a prison 'for the strumpet and idle person'. In his play, *The Dutch Courtesan*, the satirist, John Marston, punningly summarised her former home and her final gaol as: 'tis most certain they must needs both love well and die well, since most commonly they live in Clerkenwell and die in Bridewell'.[1]

In the same years Penelope Devereux, wife of Lord Rich, was enjoying the warm attentions of her lover, Lord Mountjoy. She was also pleading with an implacable Queen Elizabeth to spare the life of Penelope's rebellious brother, the Earl of Essex. In the fading years of the sixteenth century Mary Fitton had danced with the queen. But only a few years later she was in disgrace, expelled from the royal court for having born the bastard child of her seducer, the complacent and disgraceful William Herbert. There was to be one more Dark Lady, the last and eighth, Mrs Jane Davenant. In the years around 1600 she was in London, childless, with her husband, a vintner. She had not yet moved to Oxford where she would meet William Shakespeare.

For some twenty years Shakespeare would almost always be a lodger in London until he finally returned to Stratford-upon-Avon. In the late 1580s when he first arrived in the city he had lodged with his Stratford friends, the Fields. But he was restless, moving, renting, then moving again. By 1597 he had rooms in Bishopsgate. Two years later he had gone across the river to Southwark to be near the new *Globe* playhouse. He did not stay. Instead, he was renting yet one more room, this time in Silver Street. It was not until March 1613 that he bought his first house, a fine one in Blackfriars near Puddle Dock.

The move to Silver Street had taken Shakespeare away from the raffish atmosphere of Southwark and the Bankside playhouses to a respectable area near some of his theatrical colleagues and fellow actors, John Hemming and Henry Condell, the future editors of the *First Folio*. They lived in the parish of St Mary Aldermanbury. Condell was a churchwarden there. Hemming was a sidesman in the same church. In his Will of 1616 Shakespeare left each of them money to buy a commemorative ring.[2] Silver Street was in an aristocratic neighbourhood of north-west London. It was a district of handsome houses and Shakespeare went there to lodge with a French family, the Mountjoys.

More than twenty years earlier Christopher Mountjoy and his wife Marie had been among the hundreds of Huguenots who had fled from France after the Catholic religious massacre of St Bartholomew's Day in 1572. They had lived for years as aliens in Cripplegate's parish of St Olave until they finally became naturalised citizens. Christophe Montjoie anglicised his name into Christopher Mountjoy. Marie remained Marie. Almost thirty years after leaving France Mountjoy was prospering in London as a maker of fine, and very expensive, headdresses, 'tires', for women.

His home at the north-west corner of London's City Wall stood at the west end of Silver Street with a short extension to the west round the corner on Monkswell, or 'Muggle', Street. It was close to the little parish church of St Olave in Hart Street, an insignificant place containing no noteworthy monuments but to become Samuel Pepys' parish church. Both he and his wife were buried there. Nearby there were almshouses.

Mountjoy's house was an impressive L-shaped building, well-built, twin-gabled, three-and-a-half storeys high with projecting upper floors. Downstairs its lengthy imposing frontage contained its 'wig-maker's' shop. In the house there was space enough upstairs for a room for a lodger. In the workroom of the ground-floor shop women and long-trained apprentices, sewed and delicately stitched the costly and elaborate 'tires', hair-pieces composed of silk, Venetian gold, silver thread and tiny jewels. Benches were neatly draped with the almost priceless cloth of gold, a 'tissue' of gold woven into a light silk base. Luxury for the affluent.[3]

The Mountjoys had an only child, their daughter, Mary. The parents taught her the intricacies of manipulating the thin threads of silver wire. She also learned how to use a twisting-wheel to link the fragile wires and she was soon as proficient in the skills of creating fashionable headdresses as her father and mother. She was what a French dictionary defined as a *perruquière*, 'a woman who makes periwigs or tires'.

Some sixty years later the house was burnt down in the Great Fire of London in 1666, then rebuilt only to be demolished in the blitz of the Second World War. In the post-war development the empty site became part of the central carriageway to the London Wall.

Through persistence, some good fortune and his own natural skill Christopher Mountjoy had turned himself into the finest 'tire-maker' in London. A tire, like a tiara, was a head-ornament, an intricate medley of precious gems, and in fashioning them Mountjoy was more a jeweller than a wig-maker, creating elaborate hair-pieces, fantastic creations of gold and silver thread enriched with pearls and jewels. Queen Elizabeth had one. The rather foolish and frivolous Queen Anne, wife of James I, was extravagant, casually ordered another one and owed Marie Mountjoy £59, an enormous sum in the seventeenth century, the equivalent of several thousands of pounds today.[4]

Tires were almost commonplace in Tudor times. The historian, Edward Hall, in his *Chronicle* wrote of 'ladyes ... with marvuelous riche & straunge tiers on their heades'. The 'wigs' were not a novelty. Powerful women, good or bad, had been extravagantly ornamenting their hair with them for centuries. In the ninth century BC Jezebel, Phoenician Queen of Israel who was hated by the prophet Elijah, 'painted her face, and tired her head ...'.[5] Head-tires quite frequently included human hair. Blond hair was much valued and was sometimes taken from dead bodies, the 'crispèd snaky golden locks' stolen 'to be the dowry of a second head'. Fair hair could be sold.

> Before the golden tresses of the dead
> the right of sepulchres, were shorn away
> To live a second time on second head,
> Ere beauty's dead fleece made another gay ...[6]

Christopher Mountjoy had no compunction about using the hair. He bought it, used it, sold it, searched and haggled for more. Thomas Dekker, the playwright, joked about the selling of blonde wigs in his *The Shoemaker's Holiday*:

> Margery: 'Can'st thou tell me where I may buy a good hair?'
> Hodge: 'Yes, forsooth, at the poulterers in Gracious street.'
> Margery: 'Thou art an ungracious wag, perdy, I mean a false hair for my periwig.'[7]

Mountjoy had an apprentice, Stephen Belott, who had just completed his seven year service. In 1604, having just returned from a visit to Spain, it was clear that he liked the Mountjoys' daughter, Mary, and the parents approved the match. With an adolescent daughter and an eligible young bachelor who was knowledgeable in the trade the proposed marriage would ensure the continuation of the business as the parents aged. In the arrangements Marie Mountjoy had asked for the assistance of her lodger, William Shakespeare. In Elizabethan times a marriage agreement was a serious matter. It involved a property settlement and Shakespeare would have had the responsibility of creating a dowry that was acceptable both to the parents and to their daughter and her fiancé. Mountjoy promised a dowry of £60.

Other people were involved. Two friends of Stephen Belott went several times to Shakespeare to discuss and confirm the amount of the marriage portion that Christopher Mountjoy had offered. Several years later Shakespeare himself stated that there were 'many conferences' between them. A servant of the Mountjoys, Joan Johnson, also remembered how 'one Shakespeare' had made the arrangements for the forthcoming wedding and on 19 May 1604, Stephen and Mary were married in St Olave's undistinguished church. They went back to Silver Street to live.

It was in the middle of the Christmas season at Whitehall. Nineteen days earlier the King's Men had performed *Othello*. Shakespeare may have written the play in Mountjoy's house.

Matrimonial happiness and paternal generosity did not endure. In Easter 1612 Shakespeare became involved in a

Mountjoy quarrel and lawsuit. Mary's marriage to Belott was in difficulties because her miserly father was refusing to pay his promised marriage portion of £60. Worse, he publicly announced that he would leave his daughter nothing in his will despite his promise to give her £200 on his death. And, even worse, he would not have his son-in-law 'at his table'. Mountjoy did not pay the promised marriage dowry. Exasperated Belott brought suit in the Court of Requests to force his father-in-law to pay what was owed. A long line of witnesses testified to a variety of problems, some important, some trivialities such as to whether Mountjoy had given Belott money to go to the barber when the young man was an apprentice – and whether he had paid for Belott's stockings at that time!

William Shakespeare, gentleman, was given a list of five questions to answer. He was called only once. He testified that he had known both men for about ten years, that Stephen Belott had been a good and faithful apprentice, that Mrs Marie Mountjoy had asked him to see to the marriage arrangements. He said that Belott had been living with the Mountjoys at the time but he did not know the exact terms of the marriage settlement and he knew nothing of what Mountjoy may have promised.

Finally the court decided that the case was not in its jurisdiction and referred it to the London Huguenot court of which both the tire-maker and his former apprentice were members. Mountjoy was ordered to pay Belott twenty nobles. He refused. He was twice summoned to the church elders, failed to appear and in the end he was suspended from the church with a request that its members pray for his soul.[8] Prayers were needed. Mountjoy was prosperous but too mean to fulfil his obligations. Worse, he had a mistress. It was scandalous, it was dissipated, '*tous deux père et gendre debauchés*' 'both the father and the son-in-law were degenerate' observed the disapproving religious elders. They were not to know that Mountjoy's wife, Marie, also was enjoying an affair with a neighbour and was to have a second one, an involvement with London's best-known playwright.

The attractive and somewhat bored Marie Mountjoy, 'damsel, beauty and gentlewoman', had been born around 1566 and married by 1582 when she was about sixteen. She would have been in her mid-thirties when she became entangled with Shakespeare. In 1597 she was already having a sexual involvement with a near-neighbour. For some time she had been 'strongly inclined' towards a Mr Henry Wood, a general trader living in the insignificant Swan Alley off Coleman Street nearby, 'a fair and large street, on both sides builded with divers fair houses besides alleys, with small tenements in great number'. It was close to Mountjoy's business in Silver Street, and to Marie. Not completely by coincidence both husband and wife were independently to ask the advice of Simon Forman who had already advised Emilia Lanier. London was a village of gossip and worry.

The married Henry Wood, Marie's 'other man', was a cloth merchant and a trader in foreign goods. He was also a worrier. In 1596 he was selling material to Amsterdam. At the beginning of 1598 he was wondering whether it would be profitable to buy salt. Three months later he was fretting that some of his business acquaintances might not be reliable. At the end of the year he was hesitating about investing in coal and whether he could sell Dutch cloth to France at a profit.[9] He also fretted about his adulterous affair with Marie Mountjoy and whether her affection for him was cooling. Being neurotic it is not surprising that he went for advice to London's source of guidance, Simon Forman who noted in one of his casebooks:

Mr Wood p Mari M
Vtrum quid Amor erit
alterd noc 1598 the
20 March.[10]

Concerning Marie Mountjoy Mr. Wood asked whether her love for him will remain constant, 'whether her love will be altered?' [In a hasty scrawl Forman noted] 'Mary alained'.

The word [alained] is hard to read because it is written in an oddly, narrow, squashed up script, and because much of it is a series of minims almost impossible to differentiate. In my view, what Forman wrote after Marie Mountjoy's name is not the tantalising but non-existent 'alained', but something rather more prosaic – her address. The word is 'olaive', referring to her parish of St Olave.[11]

History brings irony with it. Unknown to Wood, Marie Mountjoy had already been to see Forman. But with an acquisitive husband too mean to pay for hired transport Marie had a long, often unpleasant walk through London's swarming streets. As it had been for Emilia Lanier some years earlier it was a tiring, sometimes distasteful trudge to the Stone House through busy crowds. She went to the corner of Silver Street, turned the corner and walked all the way down long Wood Street past its sidestreets with their markets, Honey Lane, Bread Street and Milk Street, then, at the end turned the corner into Cheapside. It was the city's main market and its widest street, properly paved, boasted a beautiful frontage of well-to-do houses four and five storeys high. Visitors to London gaped. On the south side was Goldsmiths' Row with ten houses and fourteen shops, some of them butchers. Sir Thomas More had been born nearby in Milk Street. There is a commemorative plaque.

Keeping away from splashes of mud from passing carts Marie Mountjoy went on into Lombard Street, a street of wealth with businesses of rich Lombard bankers, moneylenders and other mercenary merchants. Horses were tethered at the doorways. Their droppings fouled the road. She turned right into Gracechurch, formerly 'Grass', Street, where there was shop after shop of poulterers. There was bustle. There was noise. There were crowds, customers with baskets, deliverymen's carts, passers-by, it was jostle and noise. Marie Mountjoy muttered softly to herself in French.

There were the inns of the *Bell* and the *Cross Keys* that in the early days of theatres had been used as playhouses. Another, the *Boar's Head* at the corner, was an inn well known enough for Shakespeare to use it for Mistress Quickly's tavern in *Henry*

IV. Daytime drinkers sprawled contentedly outside. The street led towards the Thames at the end of New Fish Street and the banks of the river. Just before that a side-lane led to Forman's home. For Marie it had been a long and tedious three-quarters of a mile trudging through the crowds and noise of London.

It had been on 22 November 1597, that Forman recorded that he had been consulted by Mrs Marie Mountjoy of Silver Street asking him to find where her purse was. It had been lost weeks before, on 16 September, probably in Silver Street. In it had been her gold ring, a hoop ring and a French crown. At the end of the month she saw Forman again, this time because she was unwell with pains in her head, her side and stomach, and her legs were weak, Forman diagnosed that she was pregnant but might suffer a miscarriage within a few weeks. She did.[12]

It is possible that Marie's intended child was illegitimate and 'this is the second such whisper suggestive of a certain sexual looseness in the Mountjoys' marriage'. Mountjoy had already been brought before a magistrate for his 'lewd acts and adulteries, *paillardises & adultères*', accused '*d,avoir eu 2 bastardes de sa servante*'. It was tittle-tattle, gossip. But it could contain truth. The pair, husband and wife were, after all, French![13] And it was through the French church in Threadneedle Street that Marie may have met the French, twice-married Jacqueline Field, Mademoiselle Dutwite by birth, who had moved from Blackfriars in 1600 to live nearby in Wood Street. It was another twist in a tortuous story, two Dark Ladies almost becoming neighbours![14]

As a maker of elegant tires the acquisitive Christopher Mountjoy was an artistic and financial success. As an employer he was a miser and an immoral disgrace. It was rumoured that he had fathered two bastards by his servants. It is also probable that he had had sex earlier with another servant, Margaret Browne. She dreaded that she was pregnant. She went to Forman who recorded: 'A tall wentch freckled face … She hath much gravell in her Reins & heat of the back, pains stomach, she supposeth herself with child'.[15] She was over-apprehensive. Three years later she was happily married to her fiancé. By that time Christopher Mountjoy was no more than a murky unpleasantness of her past life.

By the ending of the sixteenth century Shakespeare was a famous and prosperous actor and playwright. He was so successful financially that he was able to become one of the shareholders in the purchase of land for the new *Globe* theatre. He also invested money in Stratford-upon-Avon, buying eighty bushels of corn and malt to be resold at a profit. But turn the coin over. He also remained a tightwad, leaving taxes and debts unpaid, a few shillings here, a few more there, by October 1600 still owing thirteen shillings and fourpence, two thirds of a pound sterling, unpaid in Surrey. But he did pay his rent at the Mountjoys. And he had other speculations. He eyed Marie.

So did Henry Wood. By nature timid and a worrier, he went to Simon Forman to ask 'whether the love she bears him will be altered or not?' Forman replied equivocally. The episode was like a third-rate bedroom farce. At the same time that Wood fretted about Marie Mountjoy she herself was proposing to go into business with his wife. For reassurance about the venture she consulted Forman who informed her ambiguously that, 'they may join, but take heed they trust not their wares much so they will have loss'. Commerce and carnality combined. Marie and Wood continued enjoying their adultery. And Marie and Mrs Wood prospered as Mrs Mountjoy brought her husband's clients to see the wares on offer at the shop of her lover's wife.[16]

'Man proposes, God disposes'. There was to be a disruption to that comfortable conjunction of three lives. There was to be a fourth, William Shakespeare. As a lodger in Silver Street he often gossiped with Marie Mountjoy as she threaded pearls and twisted the coils of gold wire. Over the long, empty weeks he developed a liking for her and teased her about her French accent. The memory of those laughing conversations was so strong that he recreated it in a scene of comedy in his latest play, *Henry V*.

Shakespeare may even have taken Marie to see it performed at the recently erected *Globe* theatre on Bankside where a modern plaque in Park Street commemorates its site. It was there that *Henry V* was to be 'sundry times played by the Right Honorable the Lord Chamberlain his servants'. In *Henry V* the English king gently mocked the dauphin's daughter about her imperfect English. The girl had already worried about the English words for 'hand' and 'finger' but groaned that she would never remember 'd'elbow, de 'nick', et de 'sin'. Now she had to meet and converse in English with the King of England.

> Katherine: Your majesty shall mock at me: I cannot speak your England.
> Henry: O fair Katherine, if you will love me soundly with your French heart, I will be glad to hear you confess it brokenly with your English tongue. Do you like me, Kate?
> Katherine: Pardonnez-moi. I cannot tell vat is, 'like me'.
> Henry: An angel is like you, Kate, and you are like an angel.
> Katherine: Que dit-il? Que je suis sembable à les anges?
> Her maid: Oui, vraiment, sauf votre grace ainsi dit-il.
> Henry: I said so, dear Katherine, and I must blush to affirm it.
> Katherine: O bon Dieu! Les langues des hommes sont pleines de tromperies.
> Henry: What says she, fair one? That the tongues of men are full of deceits?
> Katherine: Sauf votre honneur, me understand very well.[17]

It was the most gentle of mockery and Marie Mountjoy laughed at it. And the laughter turned to affection and the affection turned to desire. They became lovers.

William Shakespeare was a paradox. He was a sensitive poet and an imaginative playwright. He was also mean, miserly, watchful of opportunities to make money. It may have been the result of memories of his youth when he had nothing and few prospects of improvement that compelled him to keep whatever money he could. Even when he was famous he never forgot those early, empty, hopeless years.

There is an irony. Marie Mountjoy also was a paradox.

Her husband was successful but she was neglected. She was lovely but not virtuous. She was emotional but not faithful. Any affair between the poet and the inconstant woman could have no stability. His sonnets said so. There would always be a conflict between the fair and the dark, the contrast between her naturally almost black hair and the near-golden 'tire' that covered it. Shakespeare wrote a punning sonnet teasing his dark-haired mistress about her struggle between her natural hair and the pretence of a fashionably fair wig:

> In the old age black was not counted fair,
> Or, if it were, it bore not beauty's name.
> But now is black beauty's successive heir,
> And beauty slandered with a bastard shame;
> For since each hand hath put on nature's power,
> Fairing the foul with art's false borrowed face,
> Sweet beauty hath no name, no holy bower,
> But is profaned, if lives not in disgrace.
> Therefore my mistress' eyes are raven black,
> Her eyes so suited, and they mourners seem,
> At such who, not born fair, no beauty lack,
> Sland'ring creation with a false esteem:
> Yet so they mourn, becoming of their woe,
> That every tongue says beauty should look so.[18]

It was an amusement but their life together was not always amusing. She was completely her own dark woman, dark of hair and dark of inclination. When he described her he was not always flattering:

> A whitely wanton with a velvet brow,
> With two pitch-balls stuck in her face for eyes;
> Ay, and by heaven, one that will do the deed,
> Though Argus were her eunuch and her guard ...

The unsleeping Argus was an ideal watchman for a straying woman with dark eyes, dark brows, dark hair and dark inclinations.[19] That 'black' description of the temptress occurred in no fewer than a fifth of the Dark Lady sonnets, sometimes admiringly: 'in the old age black was not counted fair'; and 'black wires grow on her head', but in others uncomplimentary, 'in nothing art thou black save in thy deeds'; and 'beauty herself is black'; and, worse, 'who art as black as hell, as dark as night'. The Dark Lady 'black' sonnets are unconventional love poems.[20]

Consorting with Marie did not always provide pleasurable moments. She was married, she was her own mistress, she was constant only in her inconstancy. Self-satisfaction was her way of life. Whether it was Henry Wood or William Shakespeare or, quite independently, the possible availability of one of her husband's acquaintances, it would always be Marie Mountjoy who made a decision. And Shakespeare resented her calculated availability. Being married himself it was hypocritical to accuse her of adultery. But she had cheated by making promises to other men, Wood in particular. Shakespeare raged: 'In loving thee thou know'st I am forsworn.'She had deceived him. He wanted her, needed her, pleaded, wrote poems of love and of hate about her, snarled that she was a strumpet, a whore. He loathed her, wanted her, cursed her and begged for her.

Marie Mountjoy was the Dark Lady. She is visible in the sonnets as a woman of black hair, dark eyes but white of skin. In the poems there is no name, no place, just a woman in a void. She is a woman of mystery. She is a shape and yet she is nothing. Today, like the long-ago Anne Whateley, she is a phantom in Shakespeare's life. That elusive wraith's name, when Shakespeare met her, whether she was no more than a demon stalking his imagination, has been debated for as long as there have been Shakespearian scholars. The mystery is over. The Dark Lady was Marie Mountjoy. Perhaps.

Marie Mountjoy died in late October 1606, a plague year. She was still quite a young woman, little more than forty years old. For a time Shakespeare remained a lodger in Silver Street. From there it was less than a quarter mile to the *Mermaid*, a casual stroll south down Wood Street to Cheapside, across to

Bread Street and the tavern in an area where 'divers fair inns be there'.[21] It was not far east of St Paul's. Shakespeare knew it and other taverns well. A plaque in Fleet Street commemorates his association with the *Mitre* where more than a century later Samuel Johnson was to befriend James Boswell. Shakespeare and Ben Jonson also drank convivially there. Shakespearian actor and writer Robert Speaight:

> We can picture him going the rounds of the taverns, the *Dagger* in Holborn, where the ale was strong and the company doubtful, the *Mitre* and the *Mermaid* in Cheapside; the *Boar's Head* in Cheapside, the *Devil* at Temple Bar. The great days of the *Mermaid* did not come until 1603, but Jonson, it seems, had already been frequenting it, and who knows but that Shakespeare might have met him there before either of them reached the meridian of their fame?[22]

The *Mermaid* was well run, famous for its fish dinners and its excellent wine that cost two pence more a quart than other taverns. It was worth it. Entertaining at home, Ben Jonson sent to the tavern for wine and food when 'Inviting a Friend to Supper', listing the proposed menu:

> Yet you shall have, to rectify your palate,
> An olive, capers, or some better salad ...
> Digestive cheese, and fruit there sure will be,
> But that which most doth take my Muse, and me
> Is a pure cup of rich Canary wine
> Which is the Mermaid's now, but shall be mine;
> Of which had Horace or Anacreon tasted,
> Their lives, as do their lines, till now had lasted.[23]

The famous 'Mermaid Club' was founded at that old but fashionable inn by Sir Walter Ralegh in 1603. The building was destroyed in the Great Fire of 1666. The popular tavern was only a couple of hundred yards west of the Vintry wharf and the home of the wine importer, Jane Davenport's husband.

11

Mrs Jane Davenant

There is the lady too, dwelling in the house 'where hangs the badge of England's Saint'. Shall we then knock on the door of an inn called the George or the St George in Oxford, and then inquire after the Dark Lady in the guise of the landlord's beautiful wife? So several, most notably Arthur Acheson, have done.

Samuel Schoenbaum, *William Shakespeare* ..., 1987, pp. 181-2.

According to Arthur Acheson, a latecomer among the many sleuths on the trail of the Dark Lady, the identity of that beautiful woman was Jane Davenant, the wife of a wine merchant in Oxford.[1] Having already published a verbose book, *Shakespeare and Rival Poet*, proving that that poet had been George Chapman Acheson turned to the problem of identifying the nameless woman of the sonnets. He searched. But, like a badly-trained red Indian scout, he followed every false trail and ignored every helpful clue.

In his later just as ill-written, book *Mistress Davenant, the Dark Lady of Shakespeare's Sonnets*, he confidently wrote that he was, 'Demonstrating the identity of the Dark Lady of the Sonnets and the authorship and satirical intention of 'Willobie his Avisa ...' The inclusion of 'Willobie', a book published in 1594 and discussed in an earlier chapter here, showed that like that imaginary tracker he was following the wrong path at the wrong time. 'Avisa' may have been the Mrs Florio of Chapter

Five but she was not Jane Davenant. Acheson's scholarship was dubious and his writing was worse, every paragraph verbose and repetitive.

He believed that the Dark Lady affair had begun in 1592, the year when Queen Elizabeth visited Oxford. William Shakespeare and his friend, the young Earl of Southampton, had been in the company accompanying her. The city was so crowded that Shakespeare had been compelled to stay at the nondescript *George Inn* in Cornmarket Street. For Acheson's 'nondescript' it is more accurate to write 'non-existent' for Shakespearian studies. The name of the inn was not the *George*.

It was Acheson's belief that it was at Oxford in 1592 that the poet first met Jane Davenant. Bernard Shaw praised him for his discovery. For his short play about Shakespeare's mysterious woman he much preferred Jane Davenant to Mary Fitton as the unidentified Dark Lady. But there were problems in Acheson's story. The year 1592 was wrong by at least a decade. Nor did Shakespeare go to Oxford that year with Southampton or anyone else as part of the queen's entourage. He never went there in 1592. That was only a year or two after he had arrived in London as a young man desperately escaping from the matrimonial trap of Stratford-upon-Avon. And the inn in Oxford was wrong. It was not the *George*. It was the *Golden Cross*.[2]

Acheson was not discouraged by such trivial criticisms, however justified, of his 'discovery'. In yet another book, *Shakespeare's Sonnet Story* of 1922, he put forward even more far-fetched whimsies. Today he has been relegated to the backwaters of Shakespearean scholarship, seldom mentioned anywhere in book after well-informed book in which the Dark Lady is mentioned. He is ignored, even in an index. But even the longest manuscript of mistakes can contain one or two ink-drops of truth. Jane Davenant was one. And Shakespeare did meet her.

In the early years of the seventeenth century on their enforced tours away from London to escape from another outbreak of plague, the Lord Chamberlain's King's Men frequently visited

Oxford. One of the regular overnight places for a visitor was not the *George* but the *Golden Cross*. It stood against the so-called 'taverne' whose landlord, John Davenant, and his wife, Shakespeare had known for some time. Almost every year on his dutiful visit to Stratford as Anne Hathaway's long-married, usually absentee, husband he broke the tedious journey from London by staying at the Oxford wine-house. Those brief but regular visits led to idle but malicious tongues as Schoenbaum explains:

> She had less discretion than her husband, though, if there is truth in the salacious gossip that began making the rounds late in the seventeenth century. This held that Mistress Davenant shared her bed with the poet who had extricated himself from the meshes of the Dark lady.[3]

The Davenants had been living in Oxford since 1601 having escaped, almost in desperation, from the cramped confines and incessant outbreaks of infection of London. Every one of their children had died early there.

In the late sixteenth century that crowded and unhealthy city was a very different place from Oxford. It was noisy, dirty and crowded, catering for every whim and vice. The reality of life there was quite unlike Sir Thomas More's imaginary state of *Utopia* in which 'There be neither wine-taverns, nor ale-houses, nor stews [brothels] nor any occasion of vice or wickedness, no lurking corners, no places of wicked counsels or unlawful assemblies'. London had them all.[4]

The Davenants had been living there alongside the Thames by Venours Wharf that led to Three Cranes Lane in Vintry ward just west of the subterranean Walbrook stream. The *Cranes* was a well-known tavern there, famed for its good wines.

The Davenants house was near the church of St James Garlickhithe, a 'hithe' being a haven or landing-place where garlic had been sold years earlier. The house was no more than a few minutes stroll from Simon Forman's 'dispensary' that Jane Davenant was to visit in desperation. The Davenants were in an area of London with a distinguished medieval history:

Then is the parish church of St. James, called at Garlick Hithe, or Garlick Hive; for that of old time, on the bank of the river of Thames, near to this church garlick was usually sold ... Monuments there ... Richard Lions, a famous merchant of wines and a lapidary, sometime one of the sheriffs, beheaded in Cheap by Wat Tyler and other rebels in the year 1381. His picture on his grave-stone very fair and large, is with his hair rounded by his ears, and curled: a little beard forked; a gown, girt to him down to his feet.[5]

The Vintry, near Vintners' Hall, was a prospering area of wine-sellers. The Davenant's house, almost opposite the *Globe* theatre across the Thames, was about a quarter of a mile west of London Bridge. From the windows of her home in Maiden Lane Jane Davenant could see ships unloading the tuns of wine for her husband's winery.

On the Garlickhithe wharf were the Vintners' Company's three timber cranes used for lifting the heavy barrels of French wine from the boats, the single-decked hoys that had carried them from France. They were laden with barrels of ordinary wines for the inexpensive ale-houses and the finer vintages of red St Émilion and Pomerol, and white Sauvignon Blanc and the sharper Muscadet that better taverns and inns demanded. The creaking of the three robust cranes signified the wines' arrival and their images were painted on the sign of the local tavern.

Shakespeare knew about the imported wine and laughed about it in his plays. Doll Tearsheet was a woman 'active between the streets', the warm-hearted, hard-drinking hostess of the *Boar's Head* tavern a quarter of a mile north-east of the Vintry. She mocked at the sight of her lover, the drunken, grossly overweight Sir John Falstaff slumped on a bench:

Can a weak empty vessel bear such a huge full hogshead? There'
a whole merchant's venture of Bordeaux stuff in him. You have
not seen a hulk better stuffed in the hold.[6]

Two hundred years later John Davenant was another of those merchants of wines. His wife, Jane, affectionately known as 'Jennet', was four years younger than Shakespeare. She had been baptised at St Margaret's church in Westminster at the beginning of November in 1568. She came from a good family. Two of her three brothers, Thomas and Richard Sheppard, were sufficiently qualified to be court glovers and perfumers. The third brother catered for the royal court.

Around 1585 Jane had married John Davenant, a London merchant and wine importer. By 1600 they had had six children but they had all died very early, either stillborn or in infancy. In desperation early in 1598 she went to Simon Forman the 'notorious astrological physician of London' but he could offer her little more than sympathy.

William Shakespeare was to offer her more comfort. Living as they were in the Vintry on the north bank of the Thames the Davenants could see the *Globe* playhouse across the river and were in hearing-distance of the theatre's trumpets as they announced the presentation of a play. John Davenant would cross the river to the theatre because he was 'an admirer and lover of plays and play-makers, especially Shakespeare'. But the man and his childless wife were to leave the city. Honan again:

> Nothing compensated her husband for those human losses. To escape the plague-ridden city and its memories he abandoned his prosperous London life. Around 1601 Davenant moved to Oxford to become the landlord of a tavern.[7]

It was a four-storey high drinking place known locally simply as the 'taverne'. Many years later it became the *Crown* inn that had stood near today's *Golden Cross*.

A tavern was a social level above and much larger than a common ale-house. It sold wine as well as beer. Frequently its customers were entertained by a harper or a ballad-singer. And over their tankards and glasses drinkers could play at shove-penny, cards or dice. Not all taverns were as respectable as John Davenant's. Some landlords acted as money-lenders

– exorbitant ones. Some were 'fences' accepting stolen goods. And although taverns did not have overnight accommodation there were exceptions with some very private rooms let 'by the hour'. That was not true of Davenant's respectable 'taverne' that was used as a Common Room by university dons. It was also, very occasionally, a playhouse. The King's Men had played *Hamlet* there in 1603, the actors usually lodging at the galleried *King's Head* in Cornmarket, almost opposite Davenant's tavern where they staged 'their plays in the inn yard'.

Next door to the tavern was the coaching-inn of the *Golden Cross* standing in a courtyard where the King's Men performed 'as they did at a similar courtyard of the *King's Head* tavern'. Standing as it did just inside the old City walls Davenant's tavern would have been one of the first inns a traveller from London would have come to. As an ordinary wine-house it had no bedrooms or stables for overnight guests but both were available at the neighbouring *Golden Cross* which was the oldest inn in Oxford, having 'served without a break for some eight hundred years. For many years it had been known more simply as the *Cross*, probably because for centuries it had been owned by the Bishop of Winchester. Why it became golden is unknown.

Alongside it Davenant's tavern was a large and busy place. Very occasionally a specially favoured overnight guest could sleep upstairs in one of its many rooms or, even rest downstairs by a large log fire. Unknown to its landlord his house also contained an artistic surprise. Early twentieth-century alterations on the second floor of the inn exposed a beautifully decorated room known as 'the bedding room'. Concealed behind its later panelling were some very well-preserved wall-paintings of interlacing vines and flowers done at some time between 1560 and 1580. On a frieze above them were the pious words:

… In the morning early
Serve God devoutly;
Fear God above all thing,
And [honour Him] and the King.

The walls of the room had been wainscoted before Davenant's arrival and there was nothing remarkable to be seen. But redecorating in November 1927 uncovered the paintings and they were restored and preserved. The chamber is shown to visitors, the keyholder describing it as the Painted Room.[8]

The move from London to Oxford changed the fortunes of the Davenant family. Jane had five more children and they all lived. One of them, the second, William, christened on 3 March 1606, became a well-known Restoration poet and dramatist. John Aubrey wrote about him in his *Brief Lives*:

> Sir William Davenant, knight, Poet Laureate, was borne in the city of Oxford, at the Crowne Taverne. He went to schoole at Oxon to Mr.Sylvester, but I feare he was drawne from schoole before he was ripe enough.
>
> His father was John Davenant, a Vintner there, a very grave and discreet Citizen; his mother was a very beautifull woman and of a very good witt, and of conversation extremely agreeable.[9]

Anthony á Wood, using John Aubrey's notes, wrote a short account of the playwright. It included some notes about his father, John Davenant:

> He was 'a sufficient vintner, kept the tavern now known by the name of the Crown (wherein our poet was born) and was mayor of the said city [Oxford] in the year 1621. His mother was a very beautiful woman of a good wit and conversation, in which she was imitated by none of her children but by this William. The father, who was a very grave and discreet citizen (yet an admirer and lover of plays and play-makers, especially Shakespeare, who frequented his house in his journies between Warwickshire and London) was of an melancholic disposition, and was seldom or never seen to laugh, in which he was imitated by none of his children ...'[10]

William Davenant was either Shakespeare's son or his godson. It is known that Shakespeare did have a godson, the seven-year-old William Walker, son of Alderman Henry Walker, to whom he bequeathed a legacy of 'xx shillings in gold'. But William Davenant was left nothing. It suggests that he was either Shakespeare's bastard or a man entirely unrelated by blood to the playwright.

There is the thinnest of clues about his parentage in *King Lear*, a play written and performed probably in the year that Davenant was born. In it, just once, is the word 'godson', a word that is never used in any other of Shakespeare's plays. Rene Weis:

> For it to occur in a play written at just the time when William Davenant was born, the only person on record as having passed himself off as Shakespeare's godson – someone who occasionally claimed to be his actual son – would be a most remarkable coincidence. At the very least, the claim that the dramatist Davenant was the godson of the playwright William Shakespeare must be seriously considered.

Years later there was much gossip. It was tittle-tattle. The eighteenth-century antiquarian and biographer William Oldys in his *Memoirs* repeated what Alexander Pope had heard from the actor Thomas Betterton that one day the young Davenant, rushing home from school, was asked by a clergyman why he was in such haste: 'O sir, my godfather is come to town, and I am going to ask his blessing.' To which the divine replied, 'Hold, child, you must not take the name of God in vain.'[11]

The story is apocryphal. Had it been true then the year would have been around 1612 or 1613 when Davenant was six or seven years old and Shakespeare almost fifty, an elderly, well-to-do stockholder, actor and an important member of the Lord Chamberlain's King's Men. Within a year or two he would be leaving London for ever. It is more likely that the story came from Davenant himself to glorify his connection with Shakespeare. That it happened to insult his mother was an unfortunate incidental.

Whether that connection existed is debatable. What is not is that Shakespeare undoubtedly did have a family. Each year, perhaps reluctantly, there was a visit to Stratford-upon-Avon and his wife. It was probably taken in the summer when the hours of daylight were longer and the chance of the weather being better. On horseback it was not an arduous journey, a hundred miles or so, quite different from that long, lonely, icily cold ride to Worcester so many years earlier when his only thought was to obtain a licence to marry Anne Whateley. In that year it was love. Years later, it was duty, going to see his wife and their daughters.

A horse could be hired for a week or so, two shillings for the first day, then a shilling or one shilling and sixpence for each following day, the rider being responsible for fodder and stabling for the mount. Fifty or sixty miles a day could be a comfortable ride with breaks for rest and food.

To reach Stratford-upon-Avon from London there were two choices. With wayside inns plentiful a rider from London could go through Uxbridge and head northwards through Amersham, Aylesbury, Bicester and Banbury before the few miles to Stratford. The alternative was the road to High Wycombe, Oxford and Chipping Norton. Shakespeare seems to have preferred the Oxford journey, perhaps because of Jane Davenant. His putative godson, William Davenant, talked about the visits to his friends:

> Mr. William Shakespeare was wont to goe to into Warwickshire once a yeare, and did commonly in his journey lye at this house in Oxon, where he was exceedingly respected ... Now Sir William would sometimes, when he was pleasant over a glasse of wine with his most intimate friends ... say, that it seemed to him that he writt with the very spirit that did Shakespeare, and seemed contented enough to be thought his Son. He would tell them the story as above, in which way his mother had a very light report, whereby she was called a Whore.

Whether William Davenant was Shakespeare's illegitimate son is little more than a triviality of Shakespearean history. That, just for a good story and self-gratification, Davenant was prepared to term his mother little better than a common harlot, tells the reader even 300 years later that Davenant himself was a contemptible egotist. But that his mother was undoubtedly Jane Davenant is a dagger-thrust in the search for the Dark Lady.[12]

She was known to be cheerful, amusing and attractive, a taverner's wife enjoying the tavern's companionable drinkers while her sombre husband worked at his accounts in a back room. She was, in Shakespeare's own words, 'my hostess of the tavern, a most sweet wench'.[13] There were street-corner whispers that the lovely, vivacious but neglected 'Jennet' had found comfort with Shakespeare and that witty, beautiful woman had given birth to an illegitimate son. Gossips giggled that of Jane's children William, the second, born in 1606, was Shakespeare's bastard. That boy, later the playwright, Sir William Davenant, when he was tipsy, encouraged the rumours. It has already been noted that Bernard Shaw believed that it was Jane Davenant who was the woman most likely to have been Shakespeare's Dark Lady.

She had been born in 1568. If there had been an 'affair' between her and the poet shortly after her move to Oxford around 1602 or 1603 then she would have been in her mid-thirties. Anthony Holden:

> Shaw is not alone in naming Jeanette as his candidate for the Dark Lady ... Given the date of her son William's birth – and the possibility that he was the product of an extended liaison, more than merely a one-night stand – Jeanette may in fact have been a spur to the creation of Shakespeare's Desdemona, moving him to Othello-like agonies as he rode on to Stratford or London next morning, leaving her to return to her husband's bed.[14]

Vulgarly known as a 'one night stand' it may have been all that was possible during those infrequent and brief visits to Oxford. But that night was pleasure both for the wife and the poet. There were plenty of discreet rooms in the tavern for their secretive enjoyment while her husband attended to his accounts and tapsters attended to thirsty customers. Shakespeare wrote her a laughingly vulgar sonnet about his name and their shared pleasure:

> If thy soul check thee that I come so near,
> Swear to thy blind soul that I was thy *Will*,
> And will, thy soul knows, is admitted there;
> Thus far for love my love-suit, sweet, fulfil,
> *Will* fulfil the treasure of thy love,
> Ay, fill it full with wills, and my will one.
> In things of great receipt with ease we prove
> Among a number one is reckoned none.
> Then in the number let me pass untold,
> Though in thy store's account I one must be;
> For nothing hold me, so it please thee hold
> That nothing me, a something, sweet, to thee.
> Make but my name thy love, and love that still
> And then thou lovest me for my name is *Will*.[15]

It was vulgar but to two people enjoying sex together it was amusing. 'Will' was a sixteenth-century euphemism for both the male and the female sexual organs. Shakespeare had already teased her about it in another sonnet of which the final four lines read:

> So thou being rich in Will, add to thy Will
> One will of mine to make thy large Will more.
> Let no unkind no fair beseecher kill:
> Think all but one, and me in that one Will.[16]

It was a love that could not last and did not last. Shakespeare could never stay at the tavern for more than a night or two at most, without raising questions, or worse, suspicions, in Davenant's mind. And for the two lovers it was a luxury for them to enjoy uninterrupted love-making. Jane had an infant, a daughter who could not be neglected, a little child entirely unaware of her mother's other concern, a careful housewife who:

Sets down her babe, and makes all swift despatch
In pursuit of the thing she would have stay;
Whilst her neglected child holds her in chase,
Cries to catch her whose busy care is bent
To follow that which flies before her face,
Not prizing her poor infant's discontent ...[17]

It was a doomed love-match, a thing of one or two nights over three or four years until William Davenant was born. Too many infants, too little time. The affair faded and, over the years, was almost forgotten.

By 1605 it had ended. It was a bad year for Shakespeare and Jane Davenant but it did see the first performance of his *Timon of Athens* in which the bitterness and misanthropy was perhaps a reflective memory of the disappointments of Oxford. It was a bad year for another playwright. Ben Jonson and his fellow writer, George Chapman, were imprisoned because of the anti-Scottish sentiments they had written in their *Eastward Ho!*

There was a more serious anti-Scottish event. In November Guy Fawkes was arrested in the cellars of the Palace of Westminster where he had been arranging barrels of gunpowder in readiness for the next day's opening of Parliament by James I. He and most of fellow conspirators were agonisingly executed the following January.

1605 was also the year when there were 'late eclipses of the sun and moon' in September and October. Some months later Shakespeare mentioned those events in *King Lear*. There were better things for him. In May 1605, Augustus Phillips, his fellow actor, bequeathed him a thirty shilling piece of gold, 'to my fellow William Shakespeare'. That same 'fellow' was not only an average actor and great dramatist, he was also a mercenary investor. In July he bought the lease of half the tithes in Stratford, Old Stratford, Welcombe and Bishopston. All that occurred in 1605. Four years later in 1609 George Eld printed a pirated edition of *SHAKE-SPEARES SONNETS, Never before Imprinted*.

Jane Davenant died early in April 1622. Her husband died a fortnight later. She has been the eighth and the latest of the possible Dark Ladies. They are all feasible and they all have had eager, often persuasive supporters. Only one can be the true woman. The identity of that mysterious woman can be discovered by considering the reliable evidence, all of it, not sifting and rejecting what is unsuitable for a particular theory. That evidence has been completely presented in this book.

12

The Elusive 'Mr. W. H.'

Who the dark-haired woman was God knows; her husband was named Will. There has been no small speculation about the identity of the friend, 'Mr. W. H.' to whom the 1609 printer dedicated the sonnets as their 'onlie begetter'. That he was not, but Thorpe was willing enough to keep the woman out of sight.

John Haffenden, *Berryman's Shakespeare*, London, 2001, p. 43.

Shakespeare received no money when those sonnets were published. In 1609 his poems were printed without permission and without payment. They had been sent to a printer by a thief known to Shakespearian studies as 'Mr. W. H.'. He was the mysterious person whose initials appear on the title-page of the illicit 1609 edition of Shakespeare's sonnets. The meaningless full-stop-punctuation of the Dedication of the edition read:

> TO. THE. ONLIE. BEGETTER. OF.
> THESE. INSUING. SONNETS.
> Mr. W.H. ALL. HAPPINESSE.
> AND. THAT. ETERNITIE.
> PROMISED.
> BY.
> OUR. EVER-LIVING. POET.
> WISHETH.

THE. WELL-WISHING.
ADVENTURER. IN.
SETTING.
T. T.

'T.T.' were the initials of the printer, Thomas Thorpe. Usually, he only signed his initials if the writer of the piece was dead or away from London. In the case of the sonnets there was a different reason. It meant that 'Mr. W. H.' did not wish to be identified. The cryptic dedication was probably deliberately obscure to avoid any trouble for the printer if the book caused a legal problem. Thorpe was just trying to keep out of trouble.

What a 'begetter' of the sonnets meant has been argued over for centuries, whether the man who wrote them, or the thief who stole the hand-written sheets, or the person who had them printed. And why? 'Begetter' has puzzled scholars for years.

So has the identity of 'Mr. W. H.' One possibility was an obvious one. The 'W. H.' stood for William Herbert, the Earl of Pembroke. Another was more subtle, the inverted name of Henry Wriothesley, the Earl of Southampton. Ingenious writers added a queue of commoners to that pair of peers. Oscar Wilde proposed a William Hughes. Leslie Hotson preferred a William Hatcliffe. And there was a bran-tub of alternatives. One enthusiast suggested that 'Mr. W. H.' had to have been a man called William Hall. There were other identifications, all of them eagerly argued: a William Hart; a William Hathaway; a William Hole; or a William Houghton who was perhaps a 'Haughton'.

In addition to the names of real people there was the dispiriting possibility that 'W. H.' was a printer's mistake for 'W. S.'. Finally, dejectedly, there was also the realisation that the truth might be beyond discovery, or, even worse, something so mundane, that the two letters stood for nothing more than 'William Himself'. To some, there was no need for concern. The question of 'Mr. W. H.' was of no consequence, no more than the unimportant fact that Thorpe, the publisher, had dedicated his printed quarto to a 'Mr. W. H.'.

Have we not after all a positive obligation as readers to decide whether this refers to the youth and later friend (if there is only one object of address between 1 and 126) of Shakespeare's sequence, and whether this young man is therefore William Herbert, Henry Wriothesley, William Haughton, Willie Hughes (the seductive boy-player invented by Oscar Wilde) William Hall, William Hathaway, the poet William Himself, or, as some have staunchly maintained, Queen Elizabeth in another guise? ... The answer is that, no, none of this matters much.[1]

To the contrary, it is an important part of Shakespeare's history and the identity of that abbreviated W. H. deserves better than the facetious proposal that it stands for 'Who He'.[2] It is an 'Uncle Tom Cobleigh and all' story with a jostle of men identified by a jostle of writers looking for and discovering their own 'begetter' of the sonnets.

In *Ecclesiastes*, the twenty-first book of the Old Testament, there is an admonition to those who undertake speculative research: 'Of making many books there is no end. And much study is a weariness of the flesh'.[3] In Shakespearian studies those are cautionary words for anyone wearily attempting to discover the person hidden behind the initials, 'W. H'.

One very obvious candidate was William Herbert, the young Earl of Pembroke, one of the two dedicatees in the 1623 *First Folio* of Shakespeare's plays:

TO THE MOST NOBLE AND INCOMPARABLE ... WILLIAM, Earle of Pembroke, &c. Lord Chamberlaine to the Kings most Excellent Maiesty

William Herbert, is one of the most strongly favoured persons to have been the abbreviated 'W. H.' but, just like the teasingly variety of 'eight' Dark Ladies, he is only one of many teasing alternatives to have been the 'Mr. W. H'. Yet the suggestion that William Herbert was the cryptic 'Mr. W. H.' seems convincing. He had the right initials in the correct order. He was close enough to Shakespeare to have the dramatist's *First Folio* of plays dedicated to him and to another nobleman. He was specially chosen as a dedicatee. The Earl of Southampton was not.

William Herbert was well-known to Shakespeare. His liking for available young spinsters and his almost notorious reluctance to marry was reflected in Shakespeare's 'commissioned' sonnets, numbers 1 to 17, urging the youth to take a wife and have children. Herbert ignored the advice for years. Man about town he may have been but he was also a very generous patron of the arts. According to John Aubrey:

> He was handsome, and of an admirable presence. He was the greatest Maecenas to learned Men of any Peer of his time; or since. He was very generous and open-handed: He gave a Noble collection of Choice Bookes to the Bodleian Library at Oxford, which remain ther as an honorable Monument of his Munificence.[4]

The identification of William Herbert as the 'Mr. W. H.' has much to support it. But there is an important caveat – Elizabethan etiquette. Even under a soubriquet it would be a considerable lapse in courtesy to address a peer of the realm as 'Mr.'. He would always have been addressed by his title whether by mouth or by letter. In reply, supporters of Herbert as the elusive 'Mr. W. H.' have stressed the fact that William Herbert did not become an earl until 1601. Before that time he had no noble title. To those adherents, therefore, there is a very strong case for identifying him as the 'Mr. W. H'. of the sonnets.[5] That very confident identification did not convince everyone. To Eric Sams:

> There are other candidates for the recipient of the Sonnets, just as there are for their writer. But William Herbert, 3rd Earl of Pembroke, for the former is on the same astral plane as Bacon for the latter. 'Mr. W.H.', the only factual connection, was always a red herring; he was the publisher's dedicatee, not the poet's.[6]

There is another red herring. There happened to be a second William Herbert, a cousin to the first. He became a peer in 1629 as Baron Powys of Powys but in 1609 when the sonnets were published he was simply William Herbert. That he could have been the elusive 'Mr. W. H.' was an idea offered by Ulric Nisbet in his *The Onlie Begetter* of 1936. But Nisbet was over-optimistic. That second William Herbert had been born in 1572 and was thirty-seven years old when the sonnets published. He could not have been the youthful William Herbert, the 'W. H.' of the sonnets.[7]

There was an alternative to Herbert as 'Mr. W. H.'. It was Shakespeare's patron, Henry Wriothesley, but, as Duncan-Jones pointed out, that earl's initials were the wrong way round.[8] Even the most careless printer's apprentice would not have been so slipshod as to deprive an earl of his proper title.

The first 'identification' of the Earl of Southampton as the 'Mr. W. H.' of the sonnets' was badly mishandled by Thomas Tyler who was too obsessed with his belief that Mary Fitton had been the Dark Lady to be bothered with the tedious details of explaining why Southampton must have been the enigmatic 'Mr. W. H.' For many years Tyler's blunders and omissions misled scholars searching for the tenuous 'Mr. W. H.'. Southampton was ignored until he was resurrected by a country doctor at the beginning of the nineteenth century. Today strong arguments have been put forward favouring Henry Wriothesley both as the 'fair youth' of the sonnets and the 'Mr. W. H.' of the poems' publication in 1609.

The conversion began in 1817 when Nathan Drake, a doctor in Suffolk and a member of the Royal Society of Literature, published two huge and very heavy volumes entitled *Shakespeare and His Times, including the Biography of the Poet*. It was an uneven work, full of anecdotes, too trusting of eighteenth-century Shakespearian guesswork, but it was the first to connect the Earl of Southampton firmly with the sonnets to whom, clearly, they must have originally have been dedicated: 'to Lord Southampton, the bosom friend, the munificent patron of Shakespeare, the noble, the elegant, the brave, the protector of literature, and the theme of many a song'.[9] Drake was a pioneer of 'Mr. W. H.' studies and as Schoenbaum explains:

> to Drake credit is due for devising a structure that could accommodate the synthesis for which a century of Shakespearian scholarship [had] supplied the materials, and one can only admire the systematic energy which enabled him to complete his monumental and self-appointed task.[10]

The Suffolk doctor was a pioneer but his research did not prove that the Henry Wriothesley was the 'Mr. W. H.'. It did not explain why the two letters, W and H were interchanged, as H and W, nor is it certain that Shakespeare had any further association with the young Earl of Southampton after 1594, a long and empty fifteen years before the sonnets were piratically printed. There is no evidence that the earl had any dealings with the poet/playwright after they met late in the sixteenth century and the complete absence of any reference to him in the dedicatory material of the *First Folio* suggests that their acquaintance had ended years before. Eric Sams considered much of the 'W. H.' so-called mystery no more than wishful thinking:

> A penchant for identifying this plain Mr. with an exalted Earl, and then converting both together into the Fair Friend ['To me, fair friend, you never can be old'] exemplifies the anti-historical approach preferred by many *literati*, going on to decry the wishful thinking that converted 'W. H.' into 'William Himself.[11]

But who 'Mr. W. H.' was has caused headaches, heartaches and despair. Not content with two earls researchers have proposed no fewer than nine other candidates, all of them with good credentials. Succeeding Henry Wriothesley, Earl of Southampton whose initials had been deliberately reversed to conceal his identity; and William Herbert, Earl of Pembroke, with his liking for young ladies and dislike of the altar, there were other possibilities for the elusive 'Mr. W. H.', all of them with the W and the H in the correct order. Among them was a law student, a publisher, a writer of plays, an engraver, Anne Hathaway's brother, Shakespeare's nephew, Shakespeare himself, and even a ship's cook. Any one of that motley may have been 'Mr. W. H.'

One feverish interpretation of 'W. H.' was it was intended to be 'W. S.', an abbreviation of Shakespeare's own name but there had been a typographical blunder by the printer. If so, it must have been by an even more clod-brained apprentice than the clown already mentioned. A second suggestion for 'W. H.', not quite as desperate as the first, was that it was an in-joke by the playwright, an egocentric play on abbreviations, 'W. H.' standing for 'William Himself'.

For anyone seriously hoping to understand what 'W. H.' represented those frantic explanations can be disregarded as both unhelpful and mistaken. But that the cryptic letters, 'W. H.', were the initials of someone intimately connected with the illicit publication of the sonnets is a probability. Several culprits have been put forward and are discussed in the alphabetical order of their surnames. The first is a publisher, William Hall. Sidney Lee was confident that it was that almost unknown man who had been the hard-to-find 'Mr. W. H'. William Hall had been an undistinguished London theological publisher in London, known to have been working there between 1577 and 1620. Elected a freeman of the Stationers' Company in 1584 he was a friend of Thomas Thorpe in the printing trade. Because of Hall's convenient initials, W and H, Lee believed that he must have been the slippery 'Mr. W. H.', stating:

[Mr. W. H.] is best identified with a stationer's assistant, William Hall, who was professionally engaged, like Thorpe, in procuring 'copy' ... When Thorpe dubbed 'Mr. W. H.' with characteristic magniloquence, 'the onlie begetter of these ensuing sonnets' he merely indicated that that personage was the first of the pirate-publisher fraternity to procure a manuscript of Shakespeare's sonnets and recommend its surreptitious issue. In accordance with custom, Thorpe gave Hall's initials only, because he was an intimate associate who was known by those initials to their common circle of friends.

To Lee the identification was confirmed by Hall's initials, W. H. Not only the same initials but the entire name was recorded in the third line of Thorpe's dedication if one full-stop was omitted. That line read, 'Mr W.H. all happinesse', which, withdrawing the second full-stop, became 'Mr. W. Hall', confirming that 'Mr. W. H.' was the once-unknown William Hall. Lee expanded his argument in his 1908 book, *A Life of William Shakespeare*, with Appendix V, 'The True History of Thomas Thorpe and "Mr. W. H."'. As the Palmers observed about the omission of the full-stop in the dedication, 'There is no evidence for Hall's connection with the work otherwise'.[12] The search for the evanescent 'Mr. W. H.' has a long history from as early as the mid-eighteenth century into the present day.

A William Hart, a known nephew of William Shakespeare, was proposed as that hard-to-find abbreviated 'W. H.' by Richard Farmer, Master of Emmanuel College, Cambridge, where in 1767 he had a 'joyous meeting' with Samuel Johnson. Richard Farmer was an iconoclast. In his only published work, *Essay on the Learning of Shakespeare* of 1767, extensively rewritten in the same year, he declared that Shakespeare had never been conversant with the classical languages of Latin and Greek. He had relied on contemporary translations. Farmer was also perceptive. He went on to state that Hart was a family relative of Shakespeare's. 'Many of these Sonnets are addressed to our author's nephew, Mr. William Hart'.

Farmer wrote nothing else. 'Invincible indolence prevented him from achieving other literary triumphs'.[13] But he had been correct about the family relationship between Hart and Shakespeare. William's young sister Joan, born in 1569, married William Hart, a Stratford hatter, in the late 1590s when she was already thirty years old. They went to live in the 'birthplace', the old house in Henley Street, Stratford-upon-Avon where they had five children, two daughters, Joan and Margaret, both of whom, almost predictably in those diseased days, died in infancy. Three sons William, Thomas and Michael survived to manhood. The first son, William, was born in 1600 and baptised on 28 August. His father, also a William, had been born in the 1580s. He died on 17 April 1616, a week before Shakespeare, probably succumbing to the same epidemic.

In his book Richard Farmer claimed that William Hart had been the semi-anonymous 'Mr. W. H.' of the sonnets. His contemporary, the eminent Shakespearian scholar, Edmund Malone, disagreed, pointing out that Hart had been far too young. Born in 1600, that year was much too late for a little boy to have been the plagiaristic 'Mr. W. H.' of the sonnets published in 1609 only nine years later.[14] Shakespeare left each of the three Hart sons £5.

Hart may have been too young but for the next person suggested as 'Mr. W. H.' his age would not have disqualified him. William Hatcliffe from Lincolnshire studied at Jesus College, Cambridge, and then became a law student at Gray's Inn, London. He was good company, so well-liked that at Christmas 1597 he was elected the Prince of Purpoole, an idiotic title for the leader of student pranks and mischief. Hatcliffe enjoyed the social life of London and 'It was now, as I think, that he met the rising poet-player, Shakespeare'.[15] The good life did not last. Hatcliffe squandered his inheritance recklessly, lost everything and was chronically in debt. Desperate for money he purloined copies of the sonnets from his friend, Shakespeare and sold them to Thorpe.

Leslie Hotson provided evidence for the theft and also how Shakespeare had displayed evidence of his friendship with William Hatcliffe by putting his name into the sonnets, two of many examples being:

In Sonnet 10, line 14:
That beauty still *live* in thine or thee. ... [*hatlive*]
And in Sonnet 13, lines 1 and 2:
O *that* you were yourself, but, love, you are
No longer yours than you yourself here *live*. ... [*hatlive*][16]

It was ingenious, it was contrived and it was not convincing. The Palmers criticised it both for its ingenuity and its chronology. The 'evidence is internal and cryptographic and depends on Hotson's own dating of the Sonnets, which assigns them to this period, far earlier than is generally been accepted'.[17] Hotson's was an unfortunately edited book from its very beginning with a mistake on the page listing the chapters. Chapter IX about the Dark Lady was misplaced. It became the first of two Chapter XIs of which only the second was in the correct order. From the almost sensible to the nearly unbelievable can be no more than a short sentence in the desperate search for 'Mr. W. H.'

On 19 December 1986, Dr Barbara Everett, of Somerville College, Oxford, wrote an article, 'Mrs. Shakespeare', suggesting that it was Shakespeare's wife who had sold his sonnets to a printer.[18] That wife, the former Anne Hathaway, was described:

> as a powerful, even attractively masculine woman, eight years older than the writer [Shakespeare] ... this perhaps ambitious, clever and wilful woman impatiently sent her brother [William Hathaway] off to London with the bundle of fair-copied, brilliant, confused poems which her obstinate husband wouldn't publish but which she believed were all about her.

Her generosity was acknowledged in Thorpe's thankful 'Dedication' to 'Mr. W. H.', the printer knowing that his mysterious 'Mr. W. H.' was Shakespeare's brother-in-law, the almost unknown Mr William Hathaway. Everett's theory had a mixed reception but the majority of critics agreed with Rowse: 'Rubbish! Absolute rot! Is there no end to human foolery?' And that derision was outdone by Katherine Duncan-Jones' quiet condemnation of Everett's fantasy: 'In its bold creativity and defiance of documentary evidence this article merits comparison with Rowse at his most imaginative'.[19]

'Of making many books ...' There are yet more theories about the various men who have been 'identified' as 'Mr. W. H.'

In 1953 John Berryman, 'one of America's most talented and influential modern poets', defended his own candidate, a William Houghton. There are problems within problems. There is confusion in the search for the surname of 'Mr. W. H.' Berryman's 'Houghton'. For several other writers 'Houghton' could be a misspelling of the proper name, 'Hoghton' or even 'Haughton'. Here 'Houghton' is preferred. To Berryman he was a young playwright 'whom I consider ... from 1597 in the London theatre, to be the best candidate ever proposed as the young man to whom most of Shakespeare's sonnets were addressed'. William Houghton from Lancashire did write plays and he has been suggested as a co-author with Shakespeare of *The Taming of the Shrew*. He was prolific, writing plays for the Admiral's Men and collaborating with other young Elizabethan playwrights, Chettle, Day and Dekker among them. Hardly one of them was forty years old.

A Woman will have her Will was the nudge-nudging title of Houghton's 'pleasant comedy' of 1597, a play that was so popular that it was acted on and off for forty years. Elizabethans chuckled at both the innuendo of its title about 'will' and its catchphrase, 'Women, because they cannot have their wills when they dye, they will have their wills while they live'. It was ambiguous, a risqué pun on the double meaning of 'will', slang for both the male and female sexual organs. The quotation about 'wills' was so popular for its crudity that Manningham copied it into his *Diary* of 1612.

Houghton was admired for his plays. Less creditably he borrowed money from Henslowe in 1600, failed to repay the loan and was imprisoned in the Clink for debt. And, sadly, except for Berryman's intuition there is not one piece of evidence to prove that William Houghton was the man disguised under an acronym as 'Mr. W. H.'[20] Nor is it likely that 'W. H.' was an abbreviation for 'William Himself', short for Shakespeare.

'Could not 'W. H.' stand for William Himself?', was a suggestion made by the German scholar, D. Barnstorff, in his *Schlüssel zu Shakspeare's Sonnetten*, 'The Key to Shakespeare's Sonnets', of 1860. Barnsdorff's 'abbreviation' was not well received. There were jeers from France. 'What a recondite conclusion! And if it is not very german[e] to the matter, at least eminently German!' But as Schoenbaum observed, 'The *Variorum* editor of the sonnets is correct in saying that this in fact is not the most idiotic guess ever made'.[21] Nor is the down-to-earth suggestion that 'W. H.' was a careless mistake for 'W. S.'. But that very ordinary human blunder is beyond proof.[22]

Not all searchers for the identity of the tantalising 'begetter' of the sonnets believe they are successful. Peter Levi observed that:

> One further W. H. ought to be recorded, though I do not believe he is the right one: William Hole, who was appointed in 1618 'Head Sculptor of the iron for money in the Tower and Elsewhere for life.

Hole was the first English engraver of music and knew many writers and scholars including Florio and Drayton. Moving among them he may also have met Shakespeare and if the word 'begetter' meant the procurer of Shakespeare's sonnets then Hole could have obtained them through one of his musical friends since some of the poems had been set to music. It is possible. It is not a probability.[23]

Almost the last of the possibilities for being the intangible 'Mr. W. H.' was a nondescript sailor and sea-cook, William Hughes. His names were deduced from a clue in the sonnets by Thomas Tyrwhitt, an eighteenth-century Shakespearian scholar. Writing to Edmund Malone he pointed out that line 7 in Sonnet 20 'inclines me to think that the initials W. H. stand for W. Hughes ...', the line being 'A man in hew, all Hews in his controwling'. Several sonnets, moreover, in particular Sonnet 135, played on the name, 'Will', the combination of the Christian and the surname being far too coincidental unless they did refer to a William Hughes.[24]

Optimistic believers searched for the unexpected William Hughes in the City of London records, among manuscripts at Dulwich, in the Records Office, and scoured the Lord Chamberlain's books. They found nothing. With a shrug of scholarly shoulders they decided that Hughes had probably been a lovely boy off the streets of London who became Shakespeare's 'apprentice'. Later search did discover a real William Hughes but one born in 1567 or 1568 who became the Bishop of Asaph when he was in his forties. He was too old 'and a lot too venerable'. And the real 'Mr. W. H.' would have made an unlikely bishop.[25]

In the following centuries contributors to *Notes and Queries* optimistically identified seven William Hughes, all roughly contemporary. The writer, Samuel Butler, found four more: a man who signed a lease in 1630; a man who repaired the church of St Mary Cray in Kent; a Shropshire man who denied a Christian burial to a person in Burford; and a man who threw a human corpse into a pigsty. None appears a likely literary associate of Shakespeare.[26]

Samuel Butler, a contemporary of Oscar Wilde, was the author of *Erewhon* in 1872, a book whose title in reverse slightly misspelled 'Nowhere', an imperfect example of anastrophe or 'turning backwards'. He later wrote a book about Shakespeare, *The 10 Sonnets Reconsidered ...* It 'identified' the 'Mr. W. H'. 'Butler's best guess at Shakespeare's friend was a humble naval rating named William Hughes, who ended up as a sea cook'.[27]

Butler did not provide details about Hughes. Oscar Wilde did. He became obsessed with the search and meticulously considered all the suggested candidates for 'Mr. W. H.' including William Herbert; a misprint for 'Mr. W. S.; Mr. W. Hall; Mr. William Hathaway; and decided that none was anything more than speculation. Wilde became engrossed with the nameless 'Mr. W. H' and wrote a 12,000 word story, 'The Portrait of Mr. W. H.', about him. It was published in July 1889 in *Blackwood's Edinburgh Magazine* having previously been rejected by the *Fortnightly Review*. Wilde rewrote it to twice its length but it was left unpublished until 1921.

The obvious clues to the name of the unknown 'Mr. W. H.' were that the 'W' stood for the Christian name, 'William' and that the 'H' was the first letter of the man's surname. Shakespeare could not have resisted playing with that name in his sonnets and Wilde thought he had discovered it as a joke in Sonnet 21's seventh line: 'A man in hue all hues in his controlling' which was an interesting deduction that might have been convincing had it not been that the entire sonnet was about a young man who was as lovely as a woman. Given Wilde's homosexual tendencies the sonnet would have been all the more appealing because of that ambiguity. It was characteristic of Wilde that he liked his story about his discovery that William Hughes was the undiscoverable 'Mr. W. H.' 'although "there is no evidence at all", I groaned'. Yet the very last sentence of his story was: 'I think that there really is a great deal to be said for the Willie Hughes theory of Shakespeare's Sonnets'. Others disagreed:

> The premise of the story, that W. H. is a boy actor named Willie Hughes, whose name is punned upon in Sonnet 20 – 'all hues in his controlling' – comes close to the speculations of less avowedly fictional writing.[28]

The initials 'W' and 'H' did not belong to any of the men already mentioned. They were no more than unjustified typographical conjectures. The man 'W. H.' wanted by frustrated scholars had to be someone who had access to the sonnets and who had a reason for passing them on to Thorpe. That man's name is known. He was William Hervey, the young Earl of Southampton's stepfather. The surname is interchangeably presented as 'Harvey'. 'Hervey' is preferred here as it is the accepted form in the *Dictionary of National Biography*.[29]

Mary, Southampton's mother, had married three times, first to the morose second Earl of Southampton; then to Sir William Heneage, Elizabeth's Vice-Chancellor; and, finally, in May 1598, to her third husband Sir William Hervey 'of Armada fame', who had gallantly boarded a Spanish galleon and killed its commander, Hugh Monçado, in single combat. He had also taken part in the raid on Cadiz where he was knighted on 27 June 1598.

Through his marriage to Southampton's mother Hervey had access to the manuscript of the sonnets that Shakespeare had left at Titchfield. They were fair copies with some errors in the handwritten sheets: 'my sinful earth' occurring twice in Sonnet 146, 1, 2. In others 'you' and 'your' were interchangeable, and so were 'thy' and 'their'. It is probable that they were the first, sometimes corrected, copies but when they were printed it is clear that their occasional italicised words had been changes intended by Shakespeare.

Sir William Hervey would have been addressed as Mr Hervey unlike an earl or a baron who would never have been called 'Mr'. Precedents certainly existed for addressing a knight as 'Mr'. The Countess of Southampton herself did so in her letters. She customarily referred both to Heneage and Hervey as 'Master' or 'Mr', following the usual custom 'for persons of recognised status' such as any man from an MA to a knight. So, on the title-page of the *Sonnets* William Hervey was acknowledged as 'Mr. W. H.', the person who had taken the poems to the printer. He had them.

On her death in 1607 the countess had left Hervey most of her possessions, including the manuscripts of the sonnets. After he remarried the following year he sold the sonnets in 1609. The poems were of no use to him except as articles to sell for money. That it was Sir William Hervey who sold them to Thorpe, is confirmed by the printer's words in the Dedication set in Thorpe's idiosyncratic full-stop punctuation that clearly referred to Hervey's new and advantageous marriage:

> Mr. W. H. All. Happinesse.
> And. That. Eternitie.
> Promised.
> By.
> Our.Ever-Living.Poet.
> Wisheth.
> The. Well-Wishing.
> Adventurer. In.
> Setting.
> Forth.

There is a final note. It was only after Hervey's first wife, the Countess of Southampton, had died that the publication of the poems became permissible. Because of the sonnets' candid revelation of the very close friendship between her son and Shakespeare the countess had considered the sonnets 'too intimate to share with the public during her lifetime'.[30] Her fears were justified. Those sonnets were the key to the identity of the Dark Lady.

13

The Rival Poet: Nine Sonnets &
a Name

The identity of the rival poet cannot, of course, be proved in the conclusive way that the dedicatory letters together with sonnet 26 prove that Southampton was the patron and friend. However, what anyone who has ever worked with poets would find powerfully convincing are those words 'a better spirit' and 'his great verse' applied by Shakespeare to the rival, while he calls his own gifts 'inferior'.

Robert Giroux, *The Book Known as Q ...*, 1982, p. 190.

Shakespeare's sonnets were published in 1609 without his permission and probably not in the order he intended – if there had been one. The printed collection of poems was a turmoil, a mixture of a conjectural beginning, an ill-arranged centre and an end that would not have been out of place in a jumble-sale. The 'sequence' was a hotch-potch, a ragbag of items scattered across a dozen different stalls.

The history of the previously unpublished sonnets is hazy. Probably left unprotected at Titchfield the unnumbered sheets may have been picked up, read, dropped and scrabbled together before Hervey took them to Thorpe. And the printer, Thorpe himself, may have 'tidied' them for publication. A. D. Wraight:

Among the publishing fraternity T. T. was a sly one. In 1600 he had boasted gleefully to his fellow publisher, Edward Blount, of his acquisition of Marlowe's translation of the first book of Lucan's *Pharsalia* which had once been in Blount's copyright. T. T. enjoyed a bit of one-upmanship.[1]

The book, *SHAKE-SPEARES SONNETS. Never before Imprinted*, started with the poems that had been commissioned to persuade a young man, the 'Fair Youth', to marry. At the end of the book the final poems were two cherubic Cupid verses extolling the virtues of venereal disease. The major part of the work were poems about the friendship, even love, between two men. There were others about a woman of the night, the Dark Lady who tantalized and taunted both those men. Near the middle of the more than 150 sonnets were ten – actually nine as one was an intruder, a poem about the Fair Friend – concerning a poet whom Shakespeare had both envied and admired, the Rival Poet.

To describe that collection of unrelated poems as a 'sequence' is to misuse the word. It was not a unity. Some sonnets were pedestrian afterthoughts written to link the originals into an apparent continuity. The poet, W. H. Auden, observed that there was no neat plan, just two very uneven halves in no obvious chronological order.[2] The compilation of sonnets had been mingled together by 1603 or shortly afterwards by an unknown person, perhaps Hervey, or some other well-intentioned enthusiast unaware of the order, if any, intended by Shakespeare.

Sonnets 78 to 86 about the Rival Poet were characteristic of this confusion. A completely irrelevant sonnet, 85, about the Fair Friend, had been inserted between sonnets 84 and 86 without any explanation or thought of its relevance. The year 1603 was not a good year for whoever it was that 'arranged' the sonnets. It was also the year when Queen Elizabeth I died. For her there was to be no more dancing with Mall Fitton, or Lucy Morgan, no arguing with Penelope, Lady Rich about her treacherous brother, no whispering scandal about the 'accidental' death of Amy Robsart, no more foreign wooers and 'frogs', nothing but a 'heavy dullness'. The stubborn Tudor queen would not go to her bed despite pleas and protestations, for 'if she once lay down she would never rise'. She died in Richmond Palace on 24 March 1603 which may also have been the year when the sonnets were assembled in the order that is known today. Katherine Duncan-Jones:

> Though we may never discover how early some individual sonnets or versions of sonnets were composed, there is good reason to believe that the whole sequence as published in 1609 was put into its final shape after 1603, and possibly quite close to its printing.[3]

But the year of printing was not an indication of when the sonnets had been written. Rowse believed that the majority had been composed in the earliest years around 1590. Sidney Lee thought that they may have been much later because one of the poems, Sonnet 107, contained a reference to Queen Elizabeth's death in 1603, one of its lines announcing that 'the mortal moon hath her eclipse endured'. It was plausible but it was not proof. As Schoenbaum, sighed: 'Quite likely so, but other scholars have variously assigned the sonnet to 1594, 1595, 1596, 1598, 1599 or 1600, 1602 and 1609. So much for certainties.'[4]

As one example of an interpretation different from Lee's death of the queen G. B. Harrison believed that the 'mortal moon' referred to the year 1595 when:

> many, and especially scholarly persons, who had observed or read how God was wont to deal in times and seasons, were alarmed because on September 6th, the Queen entered upon her ninth, or grand climacteric – that is her sixty-third year, when the mystic numbers were united ... the ninth [climacteric] was astrologically far more alarming.[5]

It also happened to be the ominous year when the moon did actually undergo a total eclipse. Shakespeare himself knew how fickle the moon could be. He had Juliet reprove Romeo for vowing by the moon his everlasting love. 'Swear not by the moon', she cried, 'th'inconstant moon'. It could not be trusted.[6]

'Clues' to the date of the sonnets have been found in the poems by enthusiasts who customarily read between the lines. Unfortunately, by custom, there is always a space between those lines. As an example, for one 'clue' there is no certainty that 'the mortal moon' of Sonnet 107 did refer to the queen's death or to her physical condition or even to the eclipsed moon. It has been suggested that it referred to the defeat of the crescent-shaped lunar formation of the Spanish Armada as it sailed up the English Channel in 1588. It is a disappointing but inescapable fact that the 'mortal moon' has been given a place in almost every year from 1588 to 1609, something that does not help today's frustrated reader of Shakespeare's sonnets presented with a confusion of order in the poems and a confusion of time as to when they were written.

Some sonnets were composed as early as 1582 at the time of the Whateley/Hathaway matrimonial chaos in Stratford-upon-Avon. Others could refer to happenings around 1588 and the Spanish Armada, or to 1603 and the death of the queen, and some may even hint at the Gunpowder Plot in 1605, all of which provides almost a quarter of a century of speculation about the sonnets. To add to the chronological problem is the contradiction of the time of events in the sonnets. Shakespeare's association with the young Earl of Southampton occurred in the early 1590s. Almost ten years later there was his possible friendship with the similarly young Earl of Pembroke. The majority of the poems were probably composed at any time within that decade.

As always with matters Shakespearian there is disagreement. Although the sonnets had been organised into their present order in the early seventeenth century there is a general scholarly agreement that the majority were written in the early 1590s over a brief period of some three or four years.[7] But whenever, even wherever the sonnets were written, there is nothing obvious in them to date the years when the Dark Lady brought anguish to Shakespeare. If he left a hidden code in the poems it remains undetected and undeciphered.

There is, however, an indication of when that time might have been in nine sonnets that refer to an unnamed rival poet.

Shakespeare was awed by him:

> O how I faint when I of you do write,
> Knowing a better spirit doth use your name,
> And in the praise thereof spends all his might
> To make me tongue-tied speaking of your fame ...[8]

Which one of so many Elizabethan poets that anonymous man was is fundamental to the story of Shakespeare and his Dark Lady. Many have searched. Many poets have been joyfully discovered. None has been unanimously accepted. Schoenbaum:

> The identity of the Rival Poet, the least prominent personage of the Sonnets, has mercifully occasioned the least speculation, most of the contenders for the honour being named before the century [the nineteenth] ended.[9]

There is also the challenging possibility that this enigmatic writer of poetry, so superior to Shakespeare, was not a person in real life but a projection, an amalgamation of ideas and memories created by Shakespeare's own imaginative mind. Duncan-Jones:

> Perhaps, indeed, the 'rival poet' is a composite figure, and the mini-sequence 76-86 should be seen as exploring the theme of the speaker-poet's sense of being threatened by other poets through a fictionally amalgamated writer, drawing on several individuals, rather than as embodying any single thread of allusion.[10]

It is more probable that there really was a person at some time in Shakespeare's career that he regarded not only as a rival but also as a much better poet. Several of his contemporaries have been suggested as that man of the shadows. 'He' could be anyone or no one. Such a non-existence is improbable given the physical evidence suggested by the first line of Sonnet 80: 'O how I faint when I of you do write'. It seems unlikely that Shakespeare was addressing a fantasy. There was a mysterious competitor to Shakespeare. His identity is the pathway to the Dark Lady. Charles Boyce:

> Speculation has similarly surrounded the 'rival poet' … Most poets of the period have been named, George CHAPMAN and Christopher MARLOWE most often, with honorable mention of Barnabe BARNES and Gervase MARKHAM. However, none of these questions can be profitably pursued: not only is evidence entirely lacking, it is not even clear that Shakespeare had any real people in mind.[11]

Barnabe Barnes was not a great poet. He was a prolific sonneteer who wrote flattering verses to the Earl of Southampton whose 'gracious eyes, those heavenly lamps which give the Muses light'. Sidney Lee believed him a possibility as the rival poet but Barnes was never to be good enough even though some contemporaries believed him 'certain to prove a great poet'. He wrote a childish melodrama, *The Devil's Charter* with such a large cast that the Chamberlain's Men was forced to use Shakespeare himself as one of the actors. The playwright had his revenge, rewriting the play as *Pericles*. Barnes has been described as 'one of the most despised of English versifiers'. He was. He was not the Rival Poet.[12]

Nor was Gervase Markham, a man best described as a doppelgänger or apparition, the double of a living person because of his varied 'lives'. He was first proposed as the Rival Poet 'with a contagious lack of enthusiasm' by Frederick Gard Fleay of the New Shakespearian Society in the late nineteenth century. The identification was repeated by Robert Gittings in 1960 who suggested that Markham had also been portrayed as 'Armado' in *Love's Labours Lost*. Markham was versatile, a soldier who wrote religious poetry as well as some plays for the Admiral's Men. He also imported the first Arab horse into England. Like Barnes he has been proposed as the Rival Poet of the Sonnets, largely because in the introduction to his poem about the sinking of the *Revenge* there was a complimentary sonnet to the Earl of Southampton.

Every book needed a patron to whom it could be dedicated and an experienced man of letters like Gervase Markham could often pack several into a single book. When Markham wrote a poetic narrative on a sea-fight, he opened with a dedication to Lord Mountjoy and announced that he was 'eternally' his Lordship's. He then, on the next page, offered his work to the 'sacred hand' of the Earl of Sussex. That was followed with a dedication to Sir Edward Wingfield and another 'to the right honorable Henry Wriothesley, Earl of Southampton and Baron of Tichfield', whom he implored to favour his work.

> Vouchsafe to sweet it with thy blessed tongue …
> So shall my tragic lays be blest by thee
> And from thy lips suck their eternity.

To complete the confusion the American scholar, C. W. Wallace, who with his wife discovered important documents about the *Globe* and *Blackfriars* theatres, suggested that there may have been two separate Markhams, the poet and playwright being a different person from the Nottinghamshire horse enthusiast.[13]

If not Markham then it may have been the lyrical poet, Samuel Daniel, who had been the Rival Poet. James Boaden, the eighteenth-century English playwright scholar who had initially been deceived by Ireland's forgeries before condemning them as fakes, was the first person to claim that the youthful Earl of Pembroke had been the Fair Friend, and that Samuel Daniel, who had been brought up in Pembroke's home at Wilton, was the Rival Poet. Neither of the identifications, whether Pembroke or Daniel, has been popularly accepted. Samuel Daniel is an unlikely Rival Poet and becomes an irrelevance. That is not true of his sister. Married to the Italian translator, John Florio, she remains one of the most suspicious of all the Dark Ladies in this book. Yet even her Christian name is doubtful.[14]

Of the many suspects as the Rival Poet, Francis Davison was a sonneteer and lawyer who in 1595 was at the rowdy Gray's Inn masque. He was a friend of the Earl of Essex but did not become entangled in those perilously mutinous years. With his brother, Walter, he published *A Poetical Rhapsody* in 1602, an anthology of poems by Ralegh, Spenser and others. The book was dedicated to William Herbert, Earl of Pembroke.

Henry Brown proposed the well-born Davison as the rival poet. His father, William, had been the Secretary of State who had been imprisoned by Queen Elizabeth in 1587 as a scapegoat for having delivered the death-warrant of Mary Stuart, Queen of Scotland. As the son of an eminent statesman Francis Davison was socially far superior to Shakespeare, 'a better spirit', and according to Brown a plausible candidate for the role of Rival Poet. Rollins, the 1944 editor of Shakespeare's sonnets, considered the identification ludicrous:

> Henry Brown, the only scholar to have proposed Francis Davison as a candidate for the 'rival poet' has been dismissed with utter contempt and disbelief. Yet in certain respects Davison seems a distinct possibility.[15]

A possibility, perhaps. A probability much less appealing.

Like Samuel Daniel, John Davies, a Hereford poet, was also thought to have been the Rival Poet because of his tenuous connection with the Earl of Pembroke. He included a poem to the earl in his *Wittes Pilgrimage*, and addressed him as 'Faire featurd Soule! Well-shapen Spright'. It is very far indeed from conclusive evidence. As well as Daniel and John Davies both Ben Jonson and George Chapman are: 'plausible candidates for the role of 'Rival Poet'. All were protégés of Pembroke, and any or all might have been viewed by Shakespeare as offering a threat or competition to him the pursuit of Pembroke's favour.[16]

It should be added that discussing the identity of the Rival Poet an anonymous 'J.G.R.' in *Notes & Queries* of 12 February 1869, observed that Ben Jonson was 'perhaps an inevitable although never a popular candidate'. With such a lack of enthusiasm Jonson can be eliminated. So can Thomas Nashe and Edmund Spenser, a poet famous for the complexity and richness of his unfinished *Faerie Queene*. Spenser died in

January 1599, 'for lack of bread' according to Ben Jonson. The Earl of Essex paid for his funeral in today's Poet's Corner of Westminster Abbey, attended, wrote Camden, 'by poets, and mournful elegies and poems, with the pens that wrote them, thrown into the tomb'. Despite the queen's command there was no monument to 'the prince of poets' until 1619 when the resolute Lady Anne Clifford, who had been taught by Daniel, had a memorial erected in his honour. Sadly, both the dates of his birth and death were wrong. The monument was restored in marble in 1778.[17]

Yet one more of the supposed rival poets was the French-born Thomas Watson, Oxford-educated and learned, a 'university wit'. In his *Palladis Tamia* Francis Meres described him as 'the equal of Theocritus, Petrarch and Virgil'. In 1590 Watson published a set of Italian sonnets that he had translated. In Shoreditch a year earlier on 28 September 1589 he had become involved in a sword-and-dagger fight between Christopher Marlowe and a quarrelsome innkeeper's son, William Bradley. Watson intervened to separate them. An expert swordsman he killed Bradley 'with a thrust that went six inches deep into his chest'. Having been lightly wounded himself it was deemed proof of his innocence and he was pardoned after some months of imprisonment. His 'identification' as the Rival Poet, however, has been proposed with only the most tepid of enthusiasm.[18]

Of all the possible rival poets literally the most outlandish was Torquato Tasso, an Italian poet of Sorrento some 500 European land-covered miles south-east of London. He was unearthed by the encyclopaediacally-minded Samuel Schoenbaum who found an account of him in the 1897 issue of the *Westminster Review*. Tasso was a native of Sorrento who had a nomadic life, drifting from town to town until imprisoned for seven years as insane in Ferrara. It was there that he wrote his famous poem, *Gerusalemme Liberata*, 'Jerusalem Liberated'. He managed to escape and eventually was summoned to Rome by Pope Clement VII to be crowned poet laureate. Sadly, ill on arrival, he died in Sant' Onofrio monastery in 1595. Tasso is the most improbable of all the unlikely rival poets. But, as Schoenbaum sardonically remarked: 'After all, does not the mention in Sonnet 78 of an 'alien pen' point unmistakably to a foreigner?'[19]

That was not true of the very English poet and scholar, George Chapman, a somewhat pedestrian playwright who also started to make a translation of Homer. He was first put forward as the Rival Poet by the Scottish scholar William Minto in his *Characteristics of the English Poets from Chaucer to Shirley* of 1894. Several later writers have accepted that identification. Paterson was one:

> Why? Because Shakespeare will have been jealous of his success, and – with his little Latin and less Greek – of his classical learning: he translated the *Iliad*, bragging that he had been inspired by the ghost of Homer himself – 'by spirits taught to write'.[20]

As a young idealist and protestant Chapman may have fought in the Low Countries against the Catholic Spanish invaders. Among English soldiers recuperating in Middelburg in 1586 was a 'Joris Schampen', perhaps a garbled Dutch version of his name.[21] Being one of the young English poets and playwrights he was, like Marlowe and others, a member of Ralegh's School of Night debating the meaning of life, religion and the value of poetry. And as a writer he was good enough to be respected but not great enough to be admired.

By nature melancholy and disputatious Chapman was a close acquaintance of Ben Jonson whose own argumentative personality probably appealed to him. Conversely, Shakespeare who probably disliked him for his pretentions may have mocked him for his pomposity as the emptily verbose pedant, Holofernes, in *The Merry Wives of Windsor* who described the conceited Don Adriano de Armado as: 'He is too picked, too spruce, too affected, too odd, as it were, too peregrinate as I may call it'. It may have been a caricature of Chapman himself.[22]

Chapman's first published work was the 1594 *The Shadow of Night*, a long and verbose philosophical poem, about occult nocturnal inspiration. It was derided in *Love's Labours Lost*. His final work, his ambitious Homer took almost twenty years of translation and writing from 1598 to 1615 onwards. It was never completed. He was not an easy man, resentful of more successful rivals. In his Iliads of 1611 he may have referred to Shakespeare as 'a certain envious windsucker that hovers up and down, laboriously engrossing all the air with his luxurious ambition, and buzzing into every ear my detraction'.[23] If so, and if it had been an insult it was not one that Shakespeare was ready to ignore. In his *Love's Labours Lost*, he replied:

> Beauty is bought by judgement of the eye,
> Not uttered by base sale of chapmen's tongues.[24]

This was a rebuke to Chapman's insulting reference in his *The Shadow of the Night*, about how 'great men's fancies take upon them as killing censures as if they were judgement's butchers', a demeaning allusion to Shakespeare as a butcher's son.

Three hundred years after his death Chapman is probably best remembered for his laboured completion of Marlowe's epic 'Hero and Leander'. Marlowe's unfinished one and a half thousand words were appended by Chapman's almost twice as long and almost resentful completion, being 'drawn by strange instigation to employ some of my serious time in so trifling a subject'. It was plod rather than poetry.

> No one comparing Marlowe's beginning to 'Hero & Leander' with Chapman's completion of it, could have spoken of the 'proud full sail' of Chapman's verse without putting himself out of court as a judge of poetry.

Milton's nephew thought it 'fell short of the spirit and invention with which it was begun'. Havelock Ellis considered it, 'Scarcely a happy thought'. And Katherine Mansfield condemned Chapman for putting Marlowe's 'divine poem into a blouse and skirt'.[25] George Chapman was not good enough to have been the Rival Poet. He died in 1634 was buried in the churchyard of St-Giles-in-the-Fields in an unmarked grave. His friend, William Habington, thought it disgraceful.

The Rival Poet was Christopher Marlowe. Elizabethan poet, playwright and quarrelsome genius. To Tennyson he was the 'morning star' to Shakespeare's 'dazzling sun'. It was a morning that never reached noon. A dagger ended the comparisons between the two dramatists. To a physicist, Thomas Corwen Mendenhall, Marlowe/Shakespeare was one and the same man! In 1900 he analysed the writings of some twenty authors including Byron and Shelley attempting to quantify their distinctive styles through their personal choices of vocabulary, grammatical construction and imagery. He concluded that it was almost impossible for any writer perfectly to imitate the style of another. Except for Marlowe and Shakespeare! They were identical.

From that he argued that until Marlowe had been murdered Shakespeare had done nothing. But after the death in Deptford Shakespeare emerged as the poet who wrote 'Venus and Adonis', 'a verse that works perfectly as a continuation of the theme in Marlowe's last work, the idyllic love poem, 'Hero and Leander'. The two styles are identical'. To Mendenhall it followed that Marlowe had never been killed but went into hiding, continuing to write under the pseudonym of 'Shake-Speare' to avoid government persecution and torture as an atheist and secret agent.

Mendenhall's theory has not received general acceptance although half a century later Calvin Hoffman also argued for the same resurrection 'having roamed through graveyards, I crawled into dusty tombs, I shivered in the dampness veritable archives, and in the musty atmosphere of libraries whose book-lined shelves had remained undisturbed for centuries'. Hoffman was refused permission to dig into Shakespeare's 'supposed' grave in Stratford-upon-Avon [26]

There has been no consensus about the identity of the Rival Poet but there is general agreement that in 1593 any comparison between the two men Marlowe would have been considered by far a better writer than Shakespeare. The man that Shakespeare had said was 'polished' with a 'well-refined' pen' and was his superior was Christopher Marlowe, his rival. He was first suggested as the Rival Poet by Robert Cartwright, the editor of *The Sonnets of William Shakspeare Rearranged*, in 1859. The book had no Index, no author's name on the title-page nor anywhere else. But it did name Marlowe as the Rival Poet.[27] Using the same publisher Cartwright followed it three years later with *The Footsteps of Shakespeare, or a Ramble with the Early Dramatists, Containing Much New and Interesting Information Respecting Shakspere, Lyly, Marlowe, Greene and Others*. The book did not discuss the Rival Poet but Robert Giroux remarks that:

> The one poet Shakespeare might have regarded as 'great' and 'a better spirit' than himself in 1592–3, and to whom he might have acknowledged himself to be 'inferior' was Christopher Marlowe. 'Hero and Leander' which Marlowe was busy composing at Scadbury in Kent in the early months of 1593, is also the one poem Shakespeare might have considered superior to 'Venus and Adonis'.[28]

Marlowe had many advantages over Shakespeare. He had a university education, he knew Latin well enough to translate some Ovid and Martial, he was in London several years earlier than the man from Stratford and had his dramatic play of the conqueror, *Tamburlaine the Great* first performed at Henslowe's *Rose* theatre as early as 1588. Since that year sweating audiences had packed shoulder to shoulder to hear his 'mighty line' declaiming the murderous Jew of Malta or the tormented Edward II. Superstitious men crossed themselves as Faustus made his doomed pact with the Devil.

The theatre-owner Philip Henslowe appreciated the popularity and the profit of Marlowe's plays and provided imaginative props to add to their attraction: a 'cage' for Tamberlaine's captive kings; a 'cauldron' filled with boiling oil for the tormented Jew of Malta; a flaming 'hell-mouth' to receive the damned soul of Dr Faustus.[29] The groundlings squashed into the *Rose* gawped and clapped, shuddered at the prospect of damnation: 'Why, this is Hell, nor am I out of it,' groaned the fiend, Mephistopheles, disguised in friar's robes.

The *Rose* played to perspiring penny-paying, profitable crowds. Marlowe was a magnet. And he was a poet. At Cambridge he had 'translated', 'transmuted' would be better, one of Virgil's *Eclogues* in which an imaginary shepherd, Corydon, tried to seduce a reluctant boy, Alexis. Marlowe turned the Latin into English loveliness. He wrote the charmingly innocent pastoral that his young shepherd sang to his love:

> Come live with me and be my love,
> And we will all the pleasures prove
> The valleys, groves, hills and fields
> Woods or steepy mountains yield ...

To which the world-weary Sir Walter Ralegh sighed:

> If all the world and love were young
> And truth on every shepherd's tongue
> These pretty pleasures might me love
> To live with thee and be thy love ...

Marlowe's pastoral was a delightful thing and, unsurprisingly, it was pirated in the *Passionate Pilgrim* of 1599, although imperfectly and with only the first three of the original six verses. Several years later, when he himself had become an established playwright, Shakespeare remembered those verses being recited in the streets of London. Half-enviously he parodied it in his *Merry Wives of Windsor*, with the absent-minded Parson Evans declaiming:

> Melodious birds sing madrigals. –
> When as I sat in Pabylon
> And a thousand vagram posies.
> To shallow etc ...[30]

That was later. In the beginning in the early 1590s Shakespeare, a young, inexperienced playwright envied Marlowe, was half in awe of him and complimented him in verse in Sonnet 78:

> So oft have I invoked thee for my Muse
> And found such fair assistance in my verse
> As every alien pen hath got my use
> And under thee their poesy disperse ...

Marlowe's work had taught him how to write:

> But thou art all my art and dost advance
> As high as learning my rude ignorance.

It was honest praise but Shakespeare was still learning and improving. By 1593 he and Marlowe were vying against each other for the patronage of the youthful Earl of Southampton. Both were composing long poems to be offered to him, Shakespeare with 'Venus and Adonis', Marlowe with 'Hero and Leander'. They were becoming equals. But that rivalry ended in May 1593 when Marlowe was killed in Deptford over a drunken argument about the payment of a bill. Shakespeare grieved publicly in one of his plays:

> When a man's verses cannot be understood, nor a man's good wit
> seconded with the forward child, understanding, it strikes a man
> more dead than a great reckoning in a little room.[31]

'Come live with me and be my love' had been the plea of the young shepherd to his chaste would-be bedfellow. Now Marlowe was the murdered shepherd and Shakespeare remembered a line in the unfinished 'Hero and Leander' about the ecstasy of falling in love. And mourned:

> Dead Shepherd, now I find thy saw of might,
> Who ever lov'd, that lov'd not at first sight?[32]

In one of the saddest of his Sonnets, 86, Shakespeare grieved at the loss of a rival, a colleague and a genius:

Was it the proud full sail of his great verse,
Bound for the prize of all too precious you,
That did my ripe thoughts in my brain inhearse,
Making their tomb the womb wherein they grew?
Was it his spirit, by spirits taught to write
Above a mortal pitch, that struck me dead?
No, neither he, nor his compeers by night
Giving him aid, my verse astonishèd.
He, nor that affable familiar ghost
Which nightly gulls him with intelligence,
As victors, of my silence, cannot boast;
I was not sick of any fear from thence,
But when your countenance filled up his line,
Then lacked I matter, that enfeebled mine.

Of all the men suggested by writers searching for the Rival Poet, some in near desperation, the only one who can be confidently accepted as that poet is Christopher Marlowe. And that identification provides the time when most of Shakespeare's sonnets were written.

Some, a few, of those poems were irrelevant to the question of which woman had been the Dark Lady. There was the pair of suggestive Cupid verses, the isolated sonnet of despair to Anne Whateley when William Shakespeare was trapped into marrying Anne Hathaway. Perhaps as many half a dozen other sonnets were related with less personal matters. Those about the Dark Lady form a group at the end of the long sequence, about a sixth of the total. Those sonnets directly connected with the woman contain nothing to suggest their date. Those concerned with the Earl of Southampton relate to a period in the early 1590s, those with the Earl of Pembroke to the end of that decade. Neither indicates when the Dark Lady sonnets were composed.

But the discovery that the rival poet was Christopher Marlowe who was killed in 1593 reduces the number of women 'discovered' as the Dark Lady from eight to the four known to be associated with William Shakespeare in the early years of the 1590s. With the death of Marlowe the Rival Poet disappeared. The Dark Lady sonnets were probably written within a few years of that death.

14

The Dark Lady of the Sonnets

She was 'the faithless, dark-haired woman with 'raven-black' eyes to whom Shakespeare addressed the later sonnets (127 to 154) and who, despite scholarly conjecture, has remained unidentified. She may have been a composite invention of the poet or a real person. It has even been proposed that the Dark Lady may have been a young man and the object of Shakespeare's homosexual love ... We know from the sonnets that the Dark Lady played a musical instrument ... The only other personal details that can be gleaned from the poems are that she was married and that she had an adulterous relationship with the poet, among other men, that was marked by bitterness and feelings of guilt.

Louise McConnell, Exit, pursued by a bear, 2003, p. 83.

The year when Shakespeare first met that mysterious woman can be deduced from evidence hidden in his sonnets, particularly those from number 127 to number 152. None contains her name.

There were eight very desirable women in Shakespeare's theatrical life from as early as 1589 to as late as 1604. The first was the lovely Jacqueline Field, French wife of the London printer with whom the young Shakespeare from Stratford had lodged. Gossip muttered that he had also lodged in her bed while her husband was away on business.

A year or two later at Titchfield Court there was the wife of

John Florio, the man who was acting as a tutor to the Countess of Southampton's son. In reality, he was a government spy sniffing out Jesuit priests. William Shakespeare was a friend of the young earl. He was also an even closer friend of Florio's wife. Although respectably married she did sometimes smile or murmur a word or two to him. She was a mystery. He pursued her. Flattered, maybe bored, she did not repulse him. Titchfield had comfortable beds.

A year or two later in the *Theatre* Shakespeare noticed the beautiful Emilia Lanier as she stood by her lord and keeper. Shakespeare stared at her, noticing how graceful she was, listening to her quiet voice with its faintly foreign accent. She had inherited her father's dark hair. To Shakespeare she was irresistible. She did not resist.

One of Queen Elizabeth's maids of honour, the Welsh Lucy Morgan, had lost her place in court for an unpardonable *pas de deux* with a persuasive pursuer. She became a high-class courtesan in London and Shakespeare met her. She welcomed him. To his disadvantage. The final line of Sonnet 144 told of his disgust and dismay: 'Till my bad angel fire my good one out', because she had contaminated him, perhaps also his friend, Southampton, with venereal disease. They had been sexually infected with the 'clap', gonorrhoea with its lingering symptoms of aching bones, decaying flesh and loss of hair.

Another woman in Shakespeare's love-life had been Penelope Devereux. Hints in the sonnets suggest that she had been the real Dark Lady, 'a well known person ... of superior social standing to Shakespeare'. It accurately described Penelope, Lady Rich. She neither patronised the poet nor turned him away. Unlike the virginal Penelope of Homer's *Iliad* waiting for her husband to return from Troy, Penelope Devereux, her surname derived from the French *de vereux*, 'rotten' or 'corrupt', did not reject her passionate suitors. Nor did she reject Shakespeare.

Some years later, at the end of the century, Mary Fitton, a maid of honour at the royal court, also went to the *Theatre*. She met the famous playwright. Two sonnets murmur of her affair with Shakespeare, with delicate half-puns on her name, 127's 'or if it' and the entire Sonnet 136 in which both Mary Fitton and William Shakespeare are named coupled suggestively in the lines: 'Swear … that I was thy *Will* …; *fulfil* …; *Will* ful*fil* the treasure of thy love …; *fill it* full with wills, and my will one …; And then thou lovest me for my name is *Will*'. It was clumsy but it was flattering. It succeeded. She consented. But Mary Fitton's life was very soon to be disgraced by an indiscreet and disastrous affair.

Two or three years later Shakespeare was lodging with, and sleeping with, Marie Mountjoy, a wig-maker's wife. She was a paradox. Her husband was successful but she was neglected. She was lovely but not virtuous. She was emotional but not faithful. Her surname of 'mount' and 'joy' was an accident of marriage but, by a joyful coincidence, it was also an indication of her enthusiasm for the pleasures that human bodies could provide. Any affair, however, between the poet and such contrasts in that woman could have no stability. His sonnets said so. There would always be a conflict between the fair and the dark, the contrast between her naturally almost black hair and the near-golden wig, the 'tire' that covered it when she appeared in public. He wrote a punning sonnet, number 127, teasing his dark-haired, occasional mistress about her struggle between her naturally almost black hair hidden under a fair wig:

> In the old age black was not counted fair …
> Fairing the foul with art's false borrowed face

But of all the suspected Dark Ladies and their forbidden pleasures the last one may have been Jane Davenant, wife of an Oxford wine merchant in whose tavern Shakespeare regularly stayed on his twice-yearly journeys to and from London to Stratford. There were street-corner whispers that the lovely, vivacious but unsatisfied 'Jennet' had found comfort with Shakespeare and that that witty, beautiful and accessible woman had given birth to a possibly illegitimate son. For Jane Davenant the slanders were malignant and unfair. She was not a trollop selling her body. She was a woman who 'had a very light report', wrote an indignant John Aubrey, 'whereby she was called a Whore'. Two hundred years later George Bernard Shaw believed that Jane Davenant was the woman most likely to have been Shakespeare's Dark Lady. If so, she was the eighth.[1]

For William Shakespeare, as the 1590s passed into the 1600s, those long years of so many suspected dalliances can be reduced sharply. The death of Shakespeare's Rival Poet, Christopher Marlowe, in 1593 proved which half of the sixteenth century was relevant to the date of the majority of sonnets. It was the beginning rather than the end because a short group of those sonnets referred to that murder. And almost all the other poems belonged to that one short period of four or five years around 1593.[2]

It follows that the Fair Youth of the sonnets had been Henry Wriothesley, Earl of Southampton, rather than the years-later, much younger, William Herbert, Earl of Pembroke. And that reduces the search for the Dark Lady to four women: Jacqueline Field; Mrs Florio; Emilia Lanier, and Lucy Morgan. They were the contending, and contentious possibilities for the harpy who would bestow delight, disappointment and depression to the no longer youthful playwright. And they all had lived in the city of London.

London didn't care about them. Bells tolled the hours. Horses and carts splashed through puddles. Mud fouled the cobbles. Shopkeepers shouted their wares. Prostitutes flouted theirs. Dogs barked, snarled from their straining leashes. London was not Utopia. It was a dirty city, noisy, busy with crowds hurrying, unmindful of the lives around them. Puritanical authorities raged, shook impotent fists at the bawdiness of unseemly plays and the drunken men and lecherous women who went to the playhouses. Shakespeare's tormented mind was a rabble of hope, worry, despair, rage, a turmoil of poetry about the woman who was agony to him. But not every critic has considered that the agonised sonnets that he wrote about her were sincere. They were not great poetry:

The 'Dark Woman' Sonnets drag their unwholesome length like some wounded and weary reptile, leaving an impression of misery and defeat. Whatever nastiness there is in the Sonnets is concentrated in them. They are often the ravings of a thwarted soul tortured by jealousy. They have been called the 'Back Slums' of the Sonnets, and a 'disordered Appendix'. A few of them give the very definite impression that they are from the pens of other authors ... A thread of peevish, thwarted querulousness which is the antithesis of Shakespeare's characteristic attitude, runs through the 'Dark Woman' series.[3]

The majority of critics disagree with that negative opinion of William Thomson. The Dark Lady sonnets are not comfortable reading but many of them are sharp revelations of a tortured mind, 'the ravings of a thwarted soul'.

Quite intentionally the group of Dark Lady sonnets provide no direct clues about that woman of the night except that she was 'dark', and that her moods were changeable. Shakespeare endured her for several clamorous years. Evidence from the sonnets shows that she was: married, musical, had children, was faithless, enjoyed sex, and was egotistically self-centred. It does not give her name.

Shakespeare's affair with that tenuous woman had begun around 1592. His poetry was the proof. In Sonnet 104 to his young friend, Southampton, 'To me, fair friend, you never can be old', he wrote of three winters, three springs, and three Aprils, the last of them in 1594. At the start of that brief period the Dark Lady had been his alone until Southampton selfishly, obsessively indifferent to the loss of his friend, an ordinary man, decided to dally with her. For both the poet and the youthful earl it was to become a dalliance as pleasurable as playing with a poisonous asp.

For her part, eventually she had chosen to associate with nobility and wealth rather than with an ageing commoner who worked in a playhouse. For Shakespeare, having raged for a few impotent years, it was over by 1595. It is all in a short section of the sonnets, the Dark Lady sequence from Sonnet

127 to the final number 152. She was not only in the sonnets. Shakespeare's early plays are full of dark-haired women and their power over men as Charles Nicholl explains:

> These genial comedies of the 1590s discuss the delights of sultry, black-browed women, and their exciting difference from conventional ideals of fairness – ideas explored more sourly and obsessively in the 'Dark Lady' sequence. Is this a genuine predilection of Shakespeare's? The 'I' of the sonnets is not exactly William Shakespeare, and the poems are not just a protracted emotional diary, but to divest them of all personal meaning makes them a bloodless set of literary variations, which they palpably are not. Then there is Cleopatra herself , the embodiment of sultriness, described as 'tawny' and 'gipsy' and 'riggish' [highly-sexed] in the late tragedy *Antony and Cleopatra* (*c.* 1607–8) – now an ageing 'Dark Lady' but still full of erotic 'witchcraft'. And it seems that, in the author's imagination, the impeccably English Alice Ford in the *Merry Wives* is also dark-haired, for Falstaff woos her somewhat indelicately as 'my white doe with the black scut'. The scut is the hindquarters of a female deer, and here stands for the triangle of pubic hair'.[4]

'Scut' can also mean something different but still related to those hindquarters. Dictionaries provide another definition, that the word was the short, erect tail of a hare, rabbit or deer resembling an aroused penis. To avoid any suggestion of such indecency the word 'scut' was excluded from Robert Cawdrey's first English dictionary of 1604 which passed decorously from 'scurrilitie' to 'seclude'. [5] Nor is it anywhere in the twenty-five sonnets to the Dark Lady. From the first line of the first sonnet, 127, 'In the old age black was not counted fair' to the very last line of the final sonnet 152, 'To swear against the truth so foul a lie' the offensive word is absent. Nor did Shakespeare ever use it again in any of his later plays.

In the Dark Lady sonnets the themes slowly but irreversibly decline in mood from a first joyful time of meeting and love into darkening stages of worry, jealousy, hate, brief hope and, finally, despair. Some subjects persistently recur. 'Eyes' predominate, mentioned more than twenty times in the poems, stressing that of the beautiful woman's appearance it was the loveliness of her dark eyes and the way that they looked at him that had most drawn Shakespeare to that lady of the night. There are other significant repetitions. The words 'Will' or 'will' have twelve entries; 'heart' has eleven; 'black' and 'fair', are mentioned nine times; 'friend' and 'beauty' seven. There are several occurrences of 'hell', 'lips', 'realism', and 'soul'. But 'self-deception' is no more than a rare and reluctant afterthought. The Dark Lady sonnets are not records of a joyful love-affair.

Their beginnings were happy. Shakespeare praised her and reassured her that the colour of her hair was beautiful despite the Elizabethan faddish preference for the fair and the blonde. Remember, he wrote:

> In the old age black was not counted fair,
> Or if it were, it bore not beauty's name[6]

To him black would always be lovely. He praised her for being musical, delighted at the delicate skill with which she played the virginals, her gentle fingers:

> Making dead wood more blest than living lips.
> Since saucy jacks so happy are in this,
> Give them thy fingers, me thy lips to kiss.[7]

Every thing about her was a wonder, a woman beyond comparison, her eyes, her lips, her breasts, her hair, the delicacy of the colour of her cheeks, the music of her voice, even the way that she walked. She was a woman of wonder. By the light of late night candles he wrote the laughing words that sang of her imagined shortcomings:

> My mistress' eyes are nothing like the sun;
> Coral is far more red than her lips' red;

If snow be white, why then her breasts are dun;
If hairs be wires, black wires grow on her head.
I have seen roses damasked, red and white,
But no such roses see I in her cheeks,
And in some perfumes is there more delight
Than in the breath that from my mistress reeks.
I love to hear her speak, yet well I know
That music hath a far more pleasing sound.
I grant I never saw a goddess go;
My mistress when she walks goes on the ground.
And yet, by heaven, I think my love as rare
As any she belied with false compare.[8]

'Thus conscience doth make cowards of us all', he was to write years later, remembering how he had loved and made love to her even though he was married with children. So was she. It could not be called love. It was lust. And lust was shameful.[9]

Th'expense of spirit in a waste of shame
Is lust in action; and, till action, lust
Is perjured, murd'rous, bloody, full of shame
Savage, extreme, rude, cruel, not to trust; ...
Before, a joy proposed, behind, a dream.
All this the world well knows, yet none knows well
To shun the heaven that leads men to this hell.

It was savage self-criticism. George Bernard Shaw considered it 'the most merciless passage in English literature'.[10]

Below heaven there is hell. Love binds a bandage around adoring eyes. To make love to a goddess is a deception of the mind. He was in love. She was perfection. And yet Shakespeare's conscience told him that it was sin. Then, not long after he had met her, his mind warned him that he was being deceived. The woman of his sonnets was a slattern who was sleeping with another man. She had told him that she loved him but she was a tyrant, demanding, treacherous and black of heart. It was hell:

… thinking on thy face,
One on another's neck, do witness bear
Thy black is fairest in my judgement's place.
In nothing art thou black save in thy deeds,
And thence this slander, as I think, proceeds.[11]

He raged. Wrote in anger, tore up the lines, hoped briefly, worried, cursed, 'My love is as a fever, longing still …', tried to work, idled around the playhouse, hid in shadowed streets hoping to see her, sent her a poem:

In loving thee thou know'st I am forsworn,
But thou art twice forsworn, to me love swearing;
In act thy bed-vow broke, and new faith torn
In vowing new hate after new love bearing[12]

He was defeated. He had lost her. She would never return. She would stay with her new lover who was younger, more wealthy, of better blood. And even worse, he was an old friend of Shakespeare's. That is how she had met him.

Myself I'll forfeit, so that other mine
Thou will restore to be my comfort still.
But thou wilt not, nor he will be free,
For thou art covetous, and he is kind;
He learned but surety-like to write for me
Under that bond that him as fast doth bind.
The statute of thy beauty thou wilt take,
Thou usurer that put'st forth all to use,
And sue a friend came debtor for my sake;
So him I lose through my unkind abuse.
Him have I lost, thou hast both him and me;
He pays the whole, and yet I am not free.[13]

Ivor Brown:

The Sonnets, in short, give a precise picture of a pale-skinned, red-lipped, black-haired woman, with eyes of gleaming black, witty, fond of music, alluring, maddening, magical, utterly wanton. She has broken her 'bed-vow' with her husband and betrays lovers no less lightly. The later Sonnets were mostly written in resentment and in contrite loathing of the weakness that enslaves men and keeps them vassals to such 'daughters of the game.[14]

Four candidates remain as possibilities to have been the Dark Lady: Jacqueline Field; Mrs Florio; Lucy Morgan, and Emilia Lanier. Facts known about them eliminate three. The woman was married with children proving that she had to be Mrs Florio, wife and mother, who knew Titchfield where her husband was employed, where the young Earl of Southampton was living, and where William Shakespeare had been invited by the earl's mother.[15]

The earl was mentioned frequently in the sonnets where his family name, Wriothesley, 'rose-lee', was often used as an affectionate pun in three-quarters of Shakespeare's sonnets. It was a private joke between the two friends about the pronunciation. In the sonnets there are many allusions to Southampton as 'Rose': 'roses have thorns' 'the rose looks fair', 'perfumèd tincture of the roses', 'sweet roses'; 'roses of shadow, since his rose is true', 'the roses fearfully on thorns did stand' and 'save thou, my Rose; in it thou art my all'.[16]

In contrast, almost unremarked upon, there is only 'rose' in the entire Dark Lady sonnets from the first, 127, to the last, 152. The exception occurs in Sonnet 130 in which the flower appears twice. Significantly that sonnet is in the Dark Lady sequence and, just as significantly, it refers not to the earl but to the woman and her appearance:

I have seen roses damasked, red and white,
But no such roses see I in her cheeks.

It was as though Shakespeare had forsaken his first 'Rose', the Earl of Southampton, for a second love, the Dark Lady. From what he had written about her at that time it can be seen that she was a woman called Aline, a name meaning 'noble' that was becoming popular in the sixteenth century. The combination of Southampton, 'Rose', and the Dark Lady 'Aline', created 'Rosaline', an enticing woman who would be immortalised in Shakespeare's plays.

Two of Shakespeare's early plays, *Love's Labours Lost*, and *Romeo and Juliet*, include a Rosaline as though there had been an emotional association in the poet's mind between a 'rose', and an 'Aline'. Both plays provide an answer. *Love's Labours Lost*, written around 1594, had not been written for the general public. It was for a higher class of audience who would understand and enjoy the topical allusions and references to persons that they knew even when those people were disguised as characters in the play. Associates of the Earl of Southampton would know of Shakespeare, John Florio and their associates. If the Dark Lady happened to be connected to one of those acquaintances then the descriptions of her in the play as the heroine, Rosaline, would have had all the more significance. It is probable that Shakespeare, enjoying her favours, also enjoyed writing the play. It contained in-jokes.

The fictitious Rosaline of Shakespeare's 1594 *Love's Labours Lost* was a well-born French lady attending her princess on a visit to the royal court of Navarre. One of her admirers, Berowne had been immediately attracted to her. But when he asked, 'Is she wedded, or no?' he received the astonishing reply, 'To her will, sir, or so', meaning, no, she was not married but she had enjoyed unmarried sex with 'her Will'. It was a jest that the *Love's Labours Lost* knowledgeable audience would have enjoyed.[17]

In his plays Shakespeare seldom described his characters in detail but he treated Rosaline differently. She was given a personality. She was witty, proclaiming the virtues of courtly love. She was also charming and mischievous. 'Rosaline is described as having a dark complexion and it has been speculated that the character is associated with Shakespeare's Dark Lady of the Sonnets'.[18] One of those poems was number 127:

Therefore my mistress' eyes are raven-black,
Her eyes so suited, and they mourners seem

And in Sonnet 132 her eyes

> ...have put on black ...
> Then will I swear beauty herself is black
> And all they foul that thy complexion lack.

Like the Dark Lady the Rosaline of *Love's Labours Lost* had beautiful eyes. They fascinated Berowne. 'O but for her eye, by this light, but for her eye, I would not love her, but for her two eyes'.[19] Towards the end of the play he was taunted by the king that his beloved was as 'black as ebony'. Berowne replied that if it were true then:

> Is ebony like her? Oh wood divine
> A wife of such wood were felicity!

Tauntingly the king insisted that, 'black is the badge of hell ...' but the love-sick Berowne insisted that 'No face is fair that is not full so black'.[20] Shakespeare was enjoying writing about the appearance of the woman he loved.

But there were two Rosalines. The Rosaline of *Love's Labours Lost* was a lovely, dark-eyed, desirably available woman. The Rosaline of Shakespeare's a year or so later *Romeo and Juliet* had the same appearance but something bitter had happened in Shakespeare's life. In the play he got rid of her as he would try to get rid of his flesh-and-blood Dark Lady in life.

The Rosaline of *Romeo and Juliet* was a ghost. She never appeared on the stage but she was described in detail, her face, her foot, the paleness of her skin and, most of all, her eyes. Exactly the same emphasis was placed on eyes in the Dark Lady sonnets. Shakespeare teased her about them in Sonnet 130: 'My mistress' eyes are nothing like the sun'. Both in *Love's Labours Lost* and in *Romeo and Juliet* the hidden woman is the real-life Dark Lady with her dark hair and her attractive eyes. Her sonnets emphasise the loveliness of her eyes, mentioned a score of times in eleven sonnets: five times in each of sonnets 137 and 148, and more than once in 139.

In *Romeo and Juliet* Mercutio teased Romeo about his obsession with eyes: 'Alas, poor Romeo, he is already dead, stabbed with a white wench's black eye, run through the ear with a love song'. It was Shakespeare talking to himself.[21] Overlooked in accounts of that well-known tragic love story there is almost no description of the play's heroine, Juliet. But even though Rosaline never appears there is an indelicate word-picture of her by Mercutio:

> I conjure thee by Rosaline's bright eyes:
> By her high forehead, and her scarlet lip,
> By her fine foot, straight leg, and quiv'ring thigh,
> And the demesnes that there adjacent lie.[22]

The word 'demesnes', might have puzzled the groundlings but Mercutio's crude gesture and thrusting hips explained the indecency, near her legs and thighs were 'her lap and vagina'. They guffawed.

Who was the Dark Lady? Rowse thought that 'she seems to have been a woman of the courtesan type' and 'We seem to find that Shakespeare was sexually drawn to dark, foreign-looking women'. She was 'Rosaline'. Mercutio condoles with poor Romeo:

> Ah that same pale, hard-hearted wench, that Rosaline,
> Torments him so that he will sure run mad.

Ivor Brown again:

> There is no good reason for this little flow of detail, no dramatic cause for recording the facial items, the pallor, the high forehead, the jet-black eyes, the alluring foot ... The only explanation is that Shakespeare was himself haunted by such a mask.[23]

In Shakespeare's imaginative mind 'Rosaline' was an intentional combination of 'Rose', the Earl of Southampton, and Aline, the wife of the Italian translator, John Florio. She was the Dark Lady. Gareth and Barbara Lloyd Evans:

Shakespeare's sonnets, numbers 126-52, seem to refer to a 'dark lady'. But did she exist in fact, or in his imagination? Lack of knowledge has not deterred the most astonishing scholarly and not-so-scholarly activity to fix her identity. Some have claimed her to be Queen Elizabeth ... One believes her to be, literally, a dark lady – a negress ... but this is as much conjectural, and fanciful, as most theories about the strange lady.[24]

The Dark Lady was Florio's wife, born Aline Daniel, who probably first met William Shakespeare at Titchfield. They met again in London at Florio's home in Shoe Lane near the River Fleet. But to her Titchfield also meant the Earl of Southampton, temptation and her callously self-satisfied betrayal of her husband, her children, Henry Wriothesley and William Shakespeare. She lived for her own gratification. She hurt and harmed poets and earls. Yet today after so many centuries and after so many people have searched the records for her identity to those seekers she has remained until now the mysterious woman of darkness.

Aline Florio died late in the sixteenth century. Shakespeare died in 1616. The following year Giovanni Florio married again. By an ironical coincidence of names his second wife's Christian name was Rose. It was a name that carried sexual associations. In Eric Partridge's *Shakespeare's Bawdy* the word 'rose' is defined as 'pudend', 'maidenhead', adding that in *As You Like It* the court jester, Touchstone, says:

He that sweetest rose will find
Must find love's prick and Rosalind.[25]

It was a dirty joke. But that recurring Christian name of Rosalind/Rosaline contained the long-forgotten name of Shakespeare's Dark Lady, Mrs Aline Florio and her long-forgotten self-indulgent dalliance with William Shakespeare and Henry Wriothesley, Earl of Southampton.

Postscript: The Fourth Forger

The name of Florio's second wife, Rose, may have been a coincidence but another question about names has fact as an answer. In this story there had been two men with the initials 'W. H.' The Elizabethan 'Mr. W. H.' was the William Hervey who had been involved in the unauthorised publication of Shakespeare's sonnets. Quite differently, the Georgian 'Mr. W. H.' was a rascal, the young William-Henry Ireland, a late eighteenth-century forger of pseudo-Shakespearian documents.[1]

It has already been noticed that the Ireland family were questionable citizens. The gullible father, Samuel, had been duped into buying the 'original chair' on which William Shakespeare had wooed Anne Hathaway. The son, William-Henry Ireland, stole sheets of blank manuscript paper to fake Shakespearian documents. He was clever. Regrettably, he was also incompetent.

Born in 1775 William-Henry was a romantic, an introverted dreamer, a man of medium height, slender with curly brown hair.[2] Resenting his nondescript social background he was ambitious for fame and recognition. He was successful, becoming the most notorious of all Shakespearian forgers. Dissatisfied with his boring life as an accountant's assistant he took advantage of his post by stealing many unused sheets of parchment. Then creating some 'genuine' antique ink he mischievously decided to make some fake historical manuscripts to test the credulity of his father and acquaintances.[3] When those unsuspecting guinea-pigs uncritically and enthusiastically accepted the forgeries as genuine relics he became more ambitious and turned to much more notable forgeries. He 'recreated' some of the works of William Shakespeare.

In 1795 he announced that he had discovered some unknown correspondence between Shakespeare and Queen Elizabeth. The poet had presented her with a collection of sonnets. They had been written by the poet but those sometimes unpleasant poems were not about her majesty. She was not the hidden and unpleasant Dark Lady. Her royal majesty had simply been the recipient of a gift of a sonnet sequence that told a story of love betrayed and lost. Predictably the queen had been delighted to receive such a rare and valuable gift. There followed a letter of thanks from Elizabeth to Shakespeare for his sonnets:

> Wee didde receive youre prettye Verses good Masterre William through the hands off oure Lord Chamberlayne ande wee doe Complemente thee onne theyre great excellence. Wee shalle departe from Londonne to Hamptowne forre the holydayes where wee Shalle expecte thee with thye beste Actorres thatte thou mayste playe before ourselfe toe amuse uss bee notte slowe butte comme toe usse bye Tuesdaye nexte asse the lorde Leicesesterre willee bee with usse.
> Elizabeth R.

Shakespeare gratefully acknowledged such beneficence.

> Thys Letterre I dydde receive fromme my moste gracyouse Ladys Elizabethe ande I doe request itte maye bee kepte with all care possyble.
> Wm Shakspeare
> For Master William Shakspeare atte the Globe bye Thames.

Ireland had meticulously copied an original royal signature from a document signed by the great Queen Elizabeth. He had already made tracings of Shakespeare's signature from a mortgage deed of 1612 and from the poet's own Last Will and Testament. To complete the authenticity the forger had already made some 'Tudor' ink for writing on the 'spare' sheets of stolen paper.

The forgery was both feeble and ludicrous. It contained abundant errors as well as being written in preposterous 'Elizabethan' spelling. The queen would not have written the letter herself. The 'lorde Leicesesterre' of her letter was Robert Dudley, Earl of Leicester, who had for many years been the queen's favourite – and possibly her lover. But at the time of the sonnet sequence he was dead. He had died on Wednesday 4 September 1588, so the 'letter' must have been written earlier, no later than 1587–8, the very earliest years when Shakespeare had arrived in London as an unknown twenty-four year old.[4]

There were other mistakes in the letter. Shakespeare had not begun writing sonnets until 1591 at the earliest. And the *Globe* theatre had not been built until ten or more years after the letter. That playhouse on Bankside had been a replacement for the old Shoreditch *Theatre* that Shakespeare's Company had dismantled on 28 December 1598 and re-erected in 1599 on the other side of the Thames where it was no longer under the jurisdiction of the City of London.

But in the enthusiastic acceptance of Ireland's announcement in 1795 none of this factual history diminished the popular enthusiasm for the young man's 'discoveries'. Even more general belief was created by the discovery of a letter from Shakespeare to his beloved wife, Anne Hathaway proving that theirs had been a perfect marriage. The letter ended:

O Anna doe I love do I cheryshe thee innne mye hearte forre thou arte ass a talle Cedarre stretchynge forthe its branches ande succourynge the smallere Plants fromme nyppynge Winneterre orr the boysterouse Wyndes Farewelle toe Morrowe by tymes I wille see thee tille thenne.
Adewe sweete Love

Thyne everre
Wm Shakspeare[5]

To anyone conversant with the history of Shakespeare's life and professional career Ireland's 'discoveries' were nonsensical. His contemporary and eminent literary critic, Edmond Malone, violently attacked the forgeries, describing the letter as 'this namby-pamby stuff'. Many wishful thinkers contradicted him including the Scottish historian, George Chalmers, who wrote a long counterblast, 'Apology for the Believers in the Shakespeare Papers'.

It did not convince Malone. On 31 March 1796, he published a 400 page rebuttal of Ireland, the *Inquiry into the Authenticity of Certain Miscellaneous Papers*.[6] It was destructive in its sharp observations. In English history no known person had spelled as idiosyncratically as 'Shakespeare' was supposed to have done: not Chaucer; none of the numerous Paston letter-writers; not the Earl of Surrey in any of his poems; nor his contemporary and even better poet, Sir Thomas Wyatt; and, damningly, not one man or woman whose writings survived in the countless documents of Queen Elizabeth's reign. And there were dozens.

The 'spelling' in the discoveries was ludicrous. In Ireland 'almost every word is overladen with both consonants and vowels'. Ireland had overdone the 'antiquity'. In Elizabethan times spelling was variable but it was not ridiculous. A courtier like Sir William Knollys could write: 'I will no fayle to fulfille you desire in playing the Good Sheperd & will to my power dffend the innocent lamb from the Wolvyshe crueltye & fox-like subtlety of the tame bests off this place ...'. But it was not a parody of the English language like Ireland's: 'thou arte ass a talle Cedarre stretchynge forthe its branches ande succourynge the smallere Plants fromme nyppynge Winneterre'.

Malone mocked and massacred the mumbo-jumbo of mistakes in Ireland's work. Effectively the fraud was over. There were protests, arguments, letters in newssheets but William-Henry Ireland had been exposed as a fraud. People mocked. On the first of December 1797, the brilliant cartoonist James Gillray engraved a caricature entitled, 'Notorious characters' with 'No. 1', Samuel Ireland being the 'Fourth Forger'. The other cheats were William Lauder, James Macpherson, and Thomas Chatterton.[7]

William Mason, a friend of the poet, Thomas Gray, and a poet himself, derided the would-be deceivers:

> Four Forgers, born in one prolific age,
> Much critical acumen did engage.
> The First was soon by doughty Douglas scar'd.
> Tho' Johnson would have screen'd him, had he dar'd.
> The Next had all the cunning of a Scot;
> The Third, invention, genius, – nay, what not!
> FRAUD, now exhausted, only could dispense
> To her Fourth Son, their three-fold impudence.

Supporters and opponents of Ireland continued arguing for and against for years until in 1805, both exhausted with the controversy and newly married, Ireland wrote his *Confessions* admitting that he had forged the 'Shakespearean' manuscripts. He sent a letter to Chalmers apologising. He also informed his readers that he had made no money from the fraud, had harmed no one and had had no intention of causing any offence.

The Ireland 'affair' gradually became just one more of the many idiosyncrasies that accompany the long history of Shakespearian criticism. But William-Henry Ireland did not completely disappear as a writer. In 1808 in his *The Fisher Boy* he became the first person to provide a recipe for making the very English dish of fish and chips:

> And for his parents' eating dab supplies
> Which clean'd – in dripping pan he dextrous fries;
> Then adds potatoes slic'd, thin, crisp, and brown,
> Whereto he sets his silent mother down;
> Praises the dish, to coax her to the meal,
> The highest earthly transport he can feel

It was a good recipe and, at least, the spelling was impeccable. And William-Henry Ireland was not forgotten:

> The most spectacular forgeries of Shakespeare's works were perpetrated over 200 years ago, in 1795 and early in 1796, by a dim-looking youth of about nineteen, who had only a superficial knowledge of English literature and historical events, who initially spelt by ear, and who never punctuated – William-Henry Ireland. However, he kept England and beyond, in a state of feverish excitement for months on end, and managed to fool most of the experts. The unpromising lad had had great promise, had made his mark, and had survived. His statement to the world remains – 'I was here! I was somebody!

For readers wishing to learn more about the ingenious William-Henry Ireland, forger or fryer, full-length books by Grebanier; Mair; and Pierce are listed in the Bibliography.

There are also long accounts of Ireland's brief appearance in the history of English literature in parts of Nick Groom's *The Forger's Shadow. How Forgery Changed the Course of Literature*, Picador, London, 2002, pp. 217-55; and in Schoenbaum, 1991, pp. 135-68; in John Whitehead, *This Solemn Mockery. The Art of Literary Forgery*, Arlington, London, 1973, Chapter Two, 'Vortigern and Rowena – the new Shakespeare', pp. 20-35.

See also, 'William-Henry Ireland', in Joseph Rosenblum, *Practice to Deceive. The Amazing Stories of Literary Forgery's Most Notorious Practitioners*, Oak Knoll Press, New Castle, Delaware, 2000, Chapter IV, pp. 107-156,

For a compendium of the people involved in the Ireland forgeries see: Schoenbaum, 1991, Part III, 'Edmond Malone': George Chalmers, pp. 167-8; William-Henry Ireland, pp. 135-56; Edmund Malone, pp. 111-129, 157-67.

Notes

Preface
1. Sir Walter Ralegh: Dick, *John Aubrey's Brief Lives*, 1949, pp. 255-6; M. Irwin, *That Great Lucifer. A Portrait of Sir Walter Ralegh*, Chatto & Windus, 1960, pp. 75-6.

Introduction
1. Duncan-Jones, *The Sonnets*, 1989, vii.
2. Bernard Shaw's 'Dark Lady': Brown, 1968, p. 193.
3. 'superior social standing: Saunders, p. 328, note 661.
4. The Dark Lady and sexual infatuation: Burto, xxxv.
5. Francis Meres: Shakespeare's *'sugred sonnets'*: Honan, p. 264.
6. Jaggard's theft of two sonnets in 1599: Dowden, 1883.
7. Thorpe and 'Mr. W. H.': Weis, pp. 332-3; Thorpe's *SHAKE-SPEARES Sonnets*, 1609: Giroux, 1982, pp. 227-95.
8. The 'anonymous' women of other poets: Duncan-Jones, 2007, pp. 46-7.
9. Samuel Daniel: Lever, 1966, pp. 168-9.
10. Michael Drayton: Lever, 1966, pp. 154-60.
11. 'Many attempts': Marchette Chute, *Shakespeare of London*, pp. 343-4.
12. Auden, *The Sonnets*, 'Introduction', xxi. see also; Duncan-Jones, 2010, xiii-xv.
13. 'Embarrassing Phantom': Brown, 1968, p. 196.
14. Imposters: (i) Jane Daniel: R. Nield, *Breaking the Shakespeare Codes*, C. C. Publishing, Chester, 2007, pp. 116-17, the anagram, p. 153; (ii) Elizabeth Tudor: P. Pierce, *The Great Shakespeare Fraud. The Strange, True Story of William-Henry Ireland*, Sutton, Thrupp, 2004, pp. 81-4.
15. Winifred Burbage, the 'outsider': Kerrigan, p. 10.
16. The name of the Dark Lady: Kerrigan, p. 10.
17. 'wife of some rich City merchant': Quennell, p. 131.
18. Uncertainty of the sonnets' original layout: Kerrigan, pp. 1-10; Burto, xxi-xxiii.
19. Reproduction of the sonnets' original printing: Giroux, pp. 231-306.

1. Anne Whateley: Wraith or Rival to Anne Hathaway?

1. Vendler: in, Schoenfeldt, 2003, p. 33.

2. Whateley no more than a clerical error: Holden, pp. 66-9.

3. 'The rock': Wood, 1983, p. 87.

4. Anne Whateley, the phantom: Honan, p. 83; and many others.

5. The marriage bond/s: Weis, 2007, p. 54; Brown, 1968, p. 47; Wilson, I, 1993, pp. 56-7; Stopes, *Shakespeare's Family*, 1901, p. 63.

6. The Shakespeare/Hathaway bond: Brown, 1968, pp. 47-8; J. W. Gray, *Shakespeare's Marriage, his Departure from Stratford, and Other Incidents in his Life*, Chapman & Hall, 1905.

7. The dowry: Greer, pp. 16-17; Brown, 1968, p. 53.

8. Anne and Agnes: Holden, p. 66.

9. Bond for a special licence: Brown, 1968, p. 49; Lee, p. 20.

10. No Shakespeares in the bond: Lee, p. 21

11. The marriage bond: Brown, 1968, pp. 47-8. In Tudor times the average age for marriage in the Arden area was: women, about twenty-six; men almost thirty. Shakespeare was exceptionally young: Razzell, pp. 124-5.

12. Pre-marriage pregnancy: Wood, pp. 82-3.

13. Unscrupulous souvenir hunters: Brown, 1968, p. 59.

14. The Irelands: the father, Samuel: J. Mair, *The Fourth Forger. William Ireland and the Shakespeare Papers*, Cobden-Sanderson, London, 1938, p. 17. William-Henry the son: Mair, supra : P. Pierce, *The Great Shakespeare Fraud. The Strange True Story of William-Henry Ireland*, Sutton, Thrupp, 2004; Brown, 1968, p. 59.

15. Luddington: Levi, p. 38.

16. Temple Grafton and John Frith: Honan, p. 85; Wood, p. 86.

17. Birth of Susanna: Brown, 1968, p. 48.

18. The shepherd's warning: *A Winter's Tale*, III, 3, 62-4, spoken in prose. 'Affection': *Twelfth Night*, II, 4, 38-9.

19. Local legend: J. Harrison, *Shakespeare-Land*, ed. A. Crosby, Warwickshire Books, Warwick, 1995, p. 135.

20. Anne Hathaway's life and death: Wood, 2004, p. 81; Greer, p. 343.

21. The Worcester clerk's misspelling of a name: Stopes, 1901, p. 63.

22. Anne Whateley not a dim, sad shadow: Brown, 1968, p. 58.

23. Anne Hathaway's imaginary flight to Temple Grafton: Duncan-Jones, 201, p. 19; Greenblatt pp. 124-5; Honan, p. 83; Schoenbaum, *Documentary Life*, pp. 86-7; Weis, p. 207.

24. The 'blunder': R. E. C. Brinkworth, *Shakespeare and the Bawdy Court of Stratford*, Phillimore, London, 1972, p. 88.

25. The name 'Whateley': Weis, pp. 58-9.

26. 'Young men will do't': *Hamlet*, IV, 4, 58-64.

27. The enforced wedding: Wood, pp. 82-6.

28. Sonnet 145: 'trippingly light sounds': Duncan-Jones, pp. 144-5; 'amusing little curiosity': Paterson, pp. 443-6.

29. Wordsworth and Browning: Cheney, p. 131: Sonnet 145 and Anne Hathaway: Greer, pp. 58-9.

30. Sonnet 145 and Shakespeare's marriage: Paterson, p. 445; G. & B. Evans, p. 23.

31. For a novel about Anne Whateley see: K Harper, *Shakespeare's Mistress*, Ebury, 2009.

2. Ten 'Lost Years', 1582–1591

1. Shakespeare's youth according to what Beeston told John Aubrey: Clark, II, pp. 225-7.

2. Discovery of John Shakespeare's Will: Schoenbaum, 1991, pp. 80-1. For a general life of John Shakespeare, see: Razzell, pp. 8-73.

3. Katherine Hamlet: Harrington, 1933b, pp. 272-3; Sams, 1997, p. 42, p. 203, n. 101; Schoenbaum, 1991, p. 501; Weis, p. 32; *Daily Telegraph*, 6 and 8 June 2011.

4. 'There is a willow ...': *Hamlet*, IV, 6, 149, 151-2, 154.

5. Death of Hamnet: Wilson, I, p. 208; Weis, p. 119.

6. Susanna, a recusant: Doran, p. 165.

7. 'William Shakeschafte': Sams, 1997, pp. 36-54; Honigman, pp. 1-49.

8. Shakespeare and Sir Thomas Lucy: Rowe, I, v-vi; Schoenbaum, 1991, pp. 68-72; Lucy's deer park: Razzell, pp. 91-120.

9. Justice Shallow: *Merry Wives of Windsor*, I, 1, 22-5. 'Coat': Kiernan, p. 297. Codpiece: *The Two Gentlemen of Verona*, II, 7, 55-6.

10. Shakespeare's deer-stealing: Razzell, p. 120.

11. C. J. Sisson, *The Boar's Head Theatre. An Inn-Yard Theatre of the Elizabethan Age*, Routledge & Kegan Paul, London, 1972. see also: Sissons, in *A Companion to Shakespeare Studies*, Cambridge University Press, Cambridge, 1946, pp. 45-88.

12. Sim, p. 171, pp. 188-9; Harrison, *An Elizabethan Journal, I, 1591-1594*, p. 44. Pepys: Roud, p. 314.

13. Theatre admission prices: William Lambarde's *Perambulation of Kent, 1576*: Gurr, pp. 15-16.

14. Theatre attendances: Gurr, pp. 13-22.

15. Troupes in Stratford: Duncan-Jones, 2001, pp. 25-31.

16. Tarlton: Gurr, pp. 121-8.

17. Marlowe, *Tamburlaine, Part the First, Prologue*, 1-3.

18. The fight at Thame; and Knell's widow: Weis, pp. 83-4.

19. Hemminge: Connell, pp. 8-9.

20. Joining the Queen's Company: Southworth, pp. 24-31, Wilson, I, p. 67.

21. Philiomena and *The Two Gentlemen of Verona*: Sams: p. 58.

3. Jacqueline Field: The First of the Dark Ladies

1. Fat-jowelled Shakespeare: Dover Wilson, I., in Schoenbaum, 1987, p. 309.

2. Shakespeare's limp: Sonnet 37, line 3: Sonnet 89, line 3; and *Comedy of Errors*, II, 2, 9a; II, 67-8: (c) II, 2, 81.

3. His appearance: Duncan-Jones, 2001, p. 197; Honan, pp. 252, 324; Weis, pp. 8, 117, 163; Wilson, I., p. 407.

4. Performances of *Henry VI, I–II*: Norman, pp. 10-19; Nuttall, pp. 25-45.

5. Robert Greene, *Greenes Groats-worth of witte, bought with a million of Repentance ...*, William Wright, London, 1592 (no pagination). [Reprint: Benediction Classics, Oxford, 2007, p. 41].

6. Tiger's heart ...': *Henry VI*, III, Act 1, scene 4, 137.

7. Nuttall, p. 329.

8. Tolstoy and Landor: Jones & Guy, p. 26; today, p. 78.

9. 'smell as sweet': Sonnet 130, 5, 6; 'What's in a name?: *Romeo and Juliet*, II, 1, 90-1.

10. 'The rose distilled': J. Kerr, *Shakespeare's Flowers*, Kestrel.1969, p. 37.

11. Rosaline: Benvolio, in: *Romeo and Juliet*, I, 2, 77-8; Mercutio, in: *Romeo and Juliet*, II, 1, 19-22; 'medlar': II, 1, 34-40.

12. Mercutio, in: *Romeo and Juliet*, II, 3, 12-13.

13. Rosaline: *Love's Labours Lost*, III, 1, 153-6.

14. Sonnets 142, 152, and 147, 13-14. *Macbeth*, II, 1, 42.

15. H. E. Rollins and Sonnet 151: *A New Variorum Edition of Shakespeare's Sonnets*, two volumes, Philadelphia, 1944.
16. White, p. 476, and Tucker are both in Giroux, p. 177, footnote. R. Gibson, 1997, p. 174.
17. The physical sexuality of Sonnet 151 has received scholarly criticism: Blakemore Evans, pp. 253-4; Booth, pp. 525-9; Burrow, p. 682; Kerrigan, p. 383. In Schoenfeldt, 2010, the contributors are rather reticent: 'coy', p. 22; 'bawdy,' p. 30; 'an oddly tender note', p. 85; but there is an admission that the sonnet is 'frankly obscene', p. 142.
18. Wilhelm Jordan: S. Wells, *Is It True What They Say About Shakespeare?*, p. 138.
19. *Love's Labours Lost*, IV, 3, 258-61.
20. Stopes, *Shakespeare's Environment*, 1918, p. 155.
21. Jacqueline Vautrollier: Greer, pp. 187-9; Honan, p. 323; Nicoll, pp. 175-7; Wraight, 1994, pp. 350-1.
22. Richard Field: Palmers, p. 83.
23. Stonley: I. Wilson, I., pp. 133-4. Cost of a Bible: Tames, p. 100.
24. 'twixt his sheets': Burgess, p. 103; Holden, p. 114.
25. London deaths: Porter, 2005, pp. 75-7. George Withers: F. P. Wilson, I., p. 44.
26. Beauty is but ...': third verse of six of a song in Thomas Nashe's play, *Summer's Last Will and Testament*.
27. Mercutio: *Romeo and Juliet*, III, 1, 78.
28. 'rich in Will ...': Sonnet, 135, 11-14.
29. M. Wood, 2003: the dedication, p. 148; Venus's body, p. 150.

4. The Fair Youth of the Sonnets

1. Shakespeare and Marlowe: Giroux, pp. 187-91.
2. Dedication to 'Venus and Adonis': Burrow, p. 11.
3. Luisa de Carvajal: G. Redworth, *The She-Apostle: the Extraordinary Life and Death of Luisa de Carvajal*, 2008; Shoreditch: Stow, London, pp. 123-4.
4. M. Rukeyser, *The Traces of Thomas Hariot*, Gollancz, London, 1972, pp. 147-8; B. Woolley, *The Queen's Conjurer. The Life and Magic of Dr. Dee*, Flamingo, London, 2002; Shakespeare, *Love's Labours Lost*, IV, 3, 251-3.
5. Marlowe's blasphemy: D. Riggs, *The World of Christopher Marlowe*, Faber & Faber, London, 2004, pp. 326-9.
6. 'Hero and Leander': Sestiad I, 55, 61; Sestiad II, pp. 66-9, pp. 83-90.
7. J. L. Hotson, *The Death of Christopher Marlowe*, Nonesuch Press, London, 1925; C. Nicholl, *The Reckoning*, Jonathan Cape, London, 1992; M. J. Trow, *Who Killed Kit Marlowe?* Sutton, Thrupp, 2001.
8. Ralegh's 'School of Night': Weis, pp. 132-3.
9. Mourning for the death of Marlowe: *As You Like It*, III, 3, 8-9.
10. Marlowe: 'infinite riches in a little room', *The Jew of Malta*, I, 1, 37.
11. Leland and Titchfield: *The Itinerary of John Leland, the Antiquary*, Southern Illinois U.P., Carbondale, 1964, I, p. 281.
12. The architecture of Titchfield: Wilson, I., pp. 142-3.
13. Titchfield's history: A. Mee, *Hampshire*, Hodder & Stoughton, London, 1939, pp. 363-4.
14. Mary, Countess of Southampton: A. & V. Palmer, pp. 235-6; Rowse, 1965: many refs.
15. Her marriage to the second earl: Rowse, 1965, p. 29.
16. Southampton's father, Dymoke, and the widow: Rowse, 1965, pp. 37-9, 42.

17. The young Southampton's character: Rowse, 1965, p. 57. His life: 'Henry Wriothesley, 3rd Earl of Southampton': *Dictionary of National Biography*, II, 2334.

18. Nashe, Southampton, and 'catamite': Giroux, pp. 33, 204-5.

19. Clapham's 'Narcissus': Giroux, pp. 77, 99. Rowse, 1971, p. 74, interprets the poem differently as a plea for patronage.

20. Florio as a spy: Bate, p. 345.

21. 'A woman's face …': Sonnet 20, line 1.

22. 'Thy mother's glass': Sonnet 3, lines 10 and 9.

23. Southampton, the dandy: Honan, p. 176.

24. Florio: G. B. Harrison, 1928: 1591, pp. 24, 330.

25. Southampton with Piers Edmond: Honan, p. 177.

26. Nashe, Southampton, and 'catamite': Bate, p. 345.

27. Dedication to 'The Rape of Lucrece': Burrow, p. 41.

28. Sonnet 20: Paterson, pp. 60-4.

29. Steevens, Richardson: West, p. 76; Malone: Bale, 1998, p. 40.

30. A homosexual poem: Weis, 2007, pp. 121-2.

31. 'Pudenda': Partridge, 1961, p. 675.

32. 'Prick': *Henry V*, II, 1, 30; *Romeo and Juliet*, I, 4, 28.

33. Mercutio in *Romeo and Juliet*, II, 3, 85-6.

34. 'Lavinia's treasury': *Titus Andronicus*, II, 1, 136-8.

5. Titchfield: Treachery & Another Dark Lady

1. Ralegh in *Love's Labours Lost*, V, 1, 2.

2. The two undergraduates: *Willobie His Avisa*: Harrison, 1926, pp. 19-20.

3. Susanna: *The Apochrypha, Book of Daniel*, Cambridge University Press, 1989, verses 1-63, pp. 63, 64. The story was repeated in *Susanna, or, The Pistil of Swete Susan*, 1350–80, a North Midlands poem in alliterative verse.

4. The words *semper eadem*, 'always the same', in cantos in *Willobie*: DB, 32; DH, 41, 43; HW, 62, 74. see also: R. Rex, *Elizabeth. Fortune's Bastard?*, Tempus, Brimscombe Port, 2007.

5. Edith Sitwell, *The Queens and the Hive*, Macmillan, London, 1962, pp. 96, 97-8; Josephine Ross, *The Men Who Would Be King*, Phoenix, London, 2005.

6. Targets in Willobie: Nobleman, Cantos II-XIII; Caveileiro, XIV-XXII; D. B., XXIII-XXXIII; D. H., XXXIV-XLIII: Harrison, 1926, pp. 31-55; 56-73; 73-94; 95-115.

7. A detailed account of Elizabeth's suitors from Philip II to Alençon and others can be found in MacNalty, pp. 78-101.

8. Southampton and Willoughby: Rowse, p. 120.

9. Elizabeth, Willoughby and Southampton: Holden, pp. 131-2.

10. Florio on the theatre: Chute, p. 40.

11. The *Red Bull* theatre: Robins, p. 46; Porter, p. 241.

12. Brahe's nose: G. Uden & A. Pedley, *They Looked Like This* (Europe), Blackwell, London, 1967, pp. 34-5.

13. Florio as Burghley's spy: Bate, 1997, p. 345.

14. Florio's dedication to his work: Yates, p. 167.

15. 'Jennet Sheppard' and Florio: Schoenbaum, 1991, p. 60.

16. Florio and the *Bull* theatre: Greenblatt, p. 186; Wood, p. 128.

17. The 'Phaeton' sonnet: Giroux, pp. 120-2. see also: Levi, pp. 96-7; O'Connor, p. 124.

18. 'Phaeton' in Shakespeare's plays: *Henry VI*, 3, I, 4, 33; II, 6, 12. *Richard II*, III, 3, 179.

Romeo and Juliet, III, 3, 2. *The Two Gentlemen of Verona*, III, 1, 154.

19. Daniel at Oxford: Yates, p. 54; Palmers, pp. 59-60. 'pecking': Anthony à Wood, *Athenae Oxoniensis II*, pp. 268-74.

20. Daniel's wife: Anthony à Wood [Note 14], p. 269.

21. Florio's wife as the Dark Lady: Bate, pp. 54, 56, 57, 58.

22. 'Whitely wanton': Holden, p. 121.

23. 'Lo, as a careful housewife …': Sonnet 143.

24. Bate, pp. 54-5.

6. Emilia Bassano/Lanier: 'A Devil Incarnate'

1. The small world of London theatres: Wood, 2003, p. 195.

2. Rowse's 'discovery' of the Dark Lady: Rowse, 1973, ix.

3. Shakespeare's *femme fatale* : Duncan-Jones, 1997, pp. 50-1.

4. Psychological profile of Emilia Bassano: Wilson, I., 1993, p. 155.

5. Her appearance: Wilson, I., 1993, p. 155.

6. Emilia Bassano's childhood and upbringing, and as the Dark Lady: Schoenbaum, 1991, pp. 558-9; Weis, p. 148; Wood, p. 198: Nashe, 'Christ's Tears over Jerusalem', 1593.

7. Emilia Bassano and Lord Hunsdon: Weis, p. 149.

8. The bad reputation of playhouses: Harrison, 1931, p. 45.

9. R. Dutton, 'The Sonnets and Shakespearian Biography', in Schoenfeldt, pp. 121-36, 134.

10. The spurious letter: Giroux, p. 180.

11. Emilia Lanier consulted Forman: Cook, p. 102.

12. 'Married off': Cook, p. 102; Giroux, p. 180; Rowse, 1978, p. 15. Longditch: Rowse, 1978, pp. 13-14.

13. Lanier with Essex: Wilson, I., p. 239.

14. 'Trophies of my lovers gone': Sonnet 31, line 10.

15. Emilia Lanier's appearance: Wood, pp. 199-201.

16. Elizabethan sexual slang: J. Green, *Slang down the Ages*, Kyle Cathie, London, 2003, pp. 31-46; Partridge, *Shakespeare's Bawdy*, p. 284.

17. The Warboys 'witches': Harrison, 1928, pp. 224-8; James Sharpe, *Instruments of Darkness. Witchcraft in England, 1550–1750*, Hamish Hamilton, London, 1996, pp. 96-7; A. L. Barstow, *Witchcraft. A New History of the European Witch Hunts*, Pandora, London, 1994, pp. 193-4.

18. Plague deaths: Harrison, 1928, p. 269; Wilson, F. P., pp. 212-14.

19. Southampton and Emilia Lanier: Wilson, I, p. 155.

20. 'Love is my sin': Sonnet 142.

21. 'Except the last act': Ben Jonson, *Conversations with William Drummond of Hawthornden*, Edinburgh University Press, Edinburgh, 1966, p. 13.

22. Elizabeth Vernon: Rowse, *Shakespeare's Southampton, Patron of Virginia*, Macmillan, London, 1965, p. 124.

23. Forman the 'king of shysters': Weis, p. 221. Ben Jonson and Forman: Rowse, 1974, p. 16. For Forman and the occult, see: Traister, 2001. pp. 97-119.

24. Forman's background: Antony à Wood, *Athenae Oxoniensis, II*, 1692, pp. 98-101. see also: Cook, 2001, pp. 100-2, 107-8, 140-1; Rowse, 1974, pp. 15-16, 99-117.

25. Forman the theatre-goer: Baker, p. 30; Rowse, 1974, pp. 303-7. For *Richard II* see, Cook, pp. 188-9.

26. Forman's address: Cook, p. 50; Stowe, pp. 267-8.

27. Travelling across Elizabethan London: by foot, Picard, pp. 34-5; by boat, Picard, pp. 7, 14, 15.
28. Forman's note about Emilia Lanier: Rowse, 1974, p. 100.
29. 'halek': C. Nicholl, *The Lodger. Shakespeare on Silver Street*, Allen Lane, London, 2007, pp. 115-16, 325-6, Note 45.
30. Phillips' distaste: Cook, p. 212, Section 3, Note 5.
31. Emilia Lanier and Simon Forman: Cook, pp. 108, 140-1.
32. Forman's last reference to Emilia Lanier: Rowse, 1974, p. 102; Cook, p. 140.
33. Her religious conversion: Rowse, 1978, p. 17.
34. The dedication to *Salve Deus* ...: Rowse, 1978, p. 77.
35. Biblical women: Cook, p. 140.
36. Death of Emilia Lanier: Cook, p. 141; Wilson, I., p. 416.
37. As the Dark Lady: S. Woods, *Lanyer. A Renaissance Woman Poet*, Oxford University Press, 1999, p. 97.

7. Lucy Morgan: Royal Maid of Honour; Madam of Dishonour

1. 'fallen woman': Quennell, p. 131. 'Lucy': *Dictionary of First Names*, 1990, pp. 157-8.
2. 'Embarrassing Phantom': Brown. 1968, p. 196.
3. Weever, *Epigrams*, 1599, Third Week, Epigram 12, *In Byrrham*. Lucy Morgan as the Dark Lady: Harrison, 1933b, pp. 64, 310-11.
4. Disagreement with Harrison: Hotson, 1964, pp. 244-5.
5. Lucy Morgan's early background: Brown, 1968, pp. 194-5; Hotson, p. 248; A. & V. Palmer, 2000, p. 168.
6. Dancing and Stubbes: Picard, p. 215.
7. Playing the virginals: Sonnet, 128, lines 1-3.
8. Grosgrain: Hotson, p. 246.
9. The monetary value of velvet: Tames, pp. 29, 99-100.
10. Presents to Morgan and her servant: Hotson, p. 246; Brown, 1968, p. 194.
11. The royal court and seduction: Wraight, p. 227.
12. Greene's story: R. Greene, *A Disputation between a He Conny-Catcher and a Shee Conny-Catcher*, T. G., London, 1592. Reprint: Edinburgh University Press, ed. Harrison, 1966, pp. 55-9.
13. 'The fraud of men ...': Balthasar in *Much Ado About Nothing*, II, 3, 61-3.
14. 'Daughter of the game': Brown, 1968, p. 194.
15. The new calendar: D. E. Duncan, *The Calendar. The 5000-Year Struggle to Align the Clock and the Heavens – and What Happened to the Missing Ten Days*, Forth Estate, London, pp. 288-300, 306-7, 311.
16. 'Black Lucy': Haynes, p. 43; A. & V. Palmer, p. 168; Brown, 1968, pp. 194-6; Schoenbaum, 1987, p. 125.
17. John Davies: *The Scourge of Folly*, 1610, 'Upon English Proverbs', no. 281.
18. London brothels: Dekker's complaint, Salgado, pp. 53-4; Nashe's criticism, Porter, p. 152.
19. Turnmill brook: Stow, 1598, pp. 34-5.
20. 'Rose alley': Partridge, 1961, pp. 706-7; Salgado, p. 55.
21. Lucy Morgan as the madam of a brothel: Wood, p. 251; Hotson, pp. 253-4.
22. The area of Islington: R. Tames, 2009, pp. 137-8.
23. Elizabeth Holland: Hotson, pp. 252-3.
24. Elizabeth Holland's 'house' in Paris Gardens: F. Linane, *Madams. Bawds & Brothel-Keepers of London*, Sutton, Thrupp, 2005, p. 12.

25. Prostitutes: F. Linnane, *London. The Wicked City*, Robson, London, 2007, pp. 215.
26. The queen and the carter: Harrison, 1928, p. 284.
27. 'Thine eyes I love ...', Sonnet 132.
28. Colour prejudice: Wraight, p. 221.
29. Lucy Morgan at Gray's Inn: Bland, p. 17.
30. 'Cauda' et al: Bland, p. 95, notes 22-25.
31. 'Love is too young ...': Sonnet 151. 'Con': Blakemore Evans, pp. 253-4; Booth, p. 526; Burrow, p. 682. see also, *Love's Labour's Lost*, V, 2, 293-4.
32. 'Swart': *A Comedy of Errors*, III, 2, 96.
33. Two loves I have ...: Sonnet 144.
34. The housewife: Evans, pp. 145-6; 'hussif': Giroux, p. 290.
35. Salgado, pp. 54-6. Sonnet 153, lines 7, 8, 11, 12; Sonnet 154, lines 11-12.
36. 'Adultery': *King Lear*, IV, 5, 130-136.
37. Harrison, 1928: November 1594, pp. 330-1.
38. 'Mr Parker': Fido, p. 58.
39. Lucy Morgan in Bridewell: Hotson, p. 254. see also: Wraight, pp. 232-3.

8. Penelope Devereux, Lady Rich

1. The reality of the Dark Lady: Bate, 2008,p. 209.
2. 1595: Harrison, 1931, pp. 1-69.
3. Massey: *The Secret Drama of Shakespeare's Sonnets*, 1888.
4. Schoenbaum, 1991, p. 328; 'madness', ibid, p. 329.
5. Penelope, Lady Rich, as the Dark Lady: Holden p. 121.
6. Her marriage to Rich: Varlow, p. 72.
7. Sidney's 'Fool': Harrison, 1931, p. 46.
8. The sonnet sequence: Wraight, p. 3.
9. Sidney's published poetry: Wilson, I., p. 138.
10. Florio and Montaigne's Essays, Varlow, p. 168.
11. A self-indulgent life: Quennell, p. 27.
12. Barnfield: Varlow, p. 166.
13. Smallpox: *Dictionary of National Biography*, II, OUP, 1975, 1763.
14. Penelope and the Lord Chamberlain's Men: Varlow, p. 170.
15. Antonio Pérez: Varlow, pp. 138-9; Haynes, p. 127.
16. Armado's lack of a shirt: *Love's Labours Lost*: V, 2, 686-708.
17. Two sonnets for Penelope Devereux: numbers 127 and 132.
18. Sonnet 138: quoted from the 1609 Quarto edition. The wording is a little different from that of the *Passionate Pilgrime*, 1599.
19. Massey's protest: pp. 190-1, 204.
20. 'Will': Partridge, 1968, p. 284.
21. Sonnets 135 and 136.
22. Sonnet 140.
23. The 1584 earthquake: *Romeo and Juliet*, I, 3, 20-1.
24. The bitter Dark Lady sonnets: 127, 130, 132, 147.
25. Penelope Rich and Charles Blount: Quennell, pp. 27, 113.
26. Essex' rebellion: Baldwin Smith, pp. 239-76.
27. Essex's defiance: Baldwin Smith, p. 272.

9. Mary 'Mall' Fitton

1. Thomas Tyler, 1826–1902. *Dictionary of National Biography*, II, 2936.

2. On Tyler and the Dark Lady: Schoenbaum, 1987, pp. 329-30, 354.

3. Mary Fitton's appearance: A. & V. Palmer, pp. 83-4; Brown, 1968, p. 170; Saunders, pp. 330-1, Note 664.

4. Shaw's review of Tyler's *Sonnets*: Brown, 1949, p. 196.

5. Lee, *A Life of William Shakespeare*, 1898. Oracle Publishing reprint, Royston, 1996, 123, n. 1.

6. Lady Newdigate-Newdegate: Brown, 1968, pp. 40, 193.

7. The surname 'Fitton': J. W. Freeman, *Discovering Surnames*, Shire, 1968, p. 12.

8. 'Fickle', Sonnet 144; 'untrustworthy', Sonnet 137.

9. Nastiness of the sonnets: K. Duncan-Jones, *Shakespeare's Sonnets*, 2007, p. 51.

10. Hentzner on sugar and tobacco: J. B. Black, *The Reign of Elizabeth*, 1959, p. 274.

11. Shakespeare's purchase of New Place: Wells, 2002, pp. 33-5.

12. Ghosts and murders: C. Hamilton, *In Search of Shakespeare*, 1985, p. 98.

13. Shakespeare and local debts: Honan, p. 321; O'Connor, p. 141; Wilson, I., pp. 221-2.

14. Herbert, Fitton and 'Mr. W. H.': Wraight, p. 140.

15. Knollys, Mary Fitton and Anne Fitton.

16. 'Affection': Brown, 1968, p. 182; *Shakespeare's England*, I, p. 89; Lever, pp. 61-2, 64-9.

17. Kemp's name listed fifth in the *First Folio*, 1623, p. 15: 'William Kempt' between 'Augustine Phillips' and 'Thomas Poope'.

18. Kemp's jig and Mary Fitton: Brown, pp. 175-6.

19. 'William the Conqueror': First reported in T. Wilkes, *A General View of the Stage*, 1759. Manningham's Elizabethan *Diary* was not discovered until the nineteenth century: Honan, p. 263.

20. 'Argus were her eunuch and her guard': *Love's Labours Lost*, III, 1, 208-9.

21. Knollys' watchfulness: Lever, pp. 66-7; Brown, 1968, p. 180; E. K. Chambers, *Shakespeare's England*, I, p. 89. 'The mothers': N. Williams, pp. 249-50.

22. Knollys as 'Malvolio': Brown, 1968, pp. 180-1; Lever, pp. 66-8.

23. William Herbert and young women: Duncan-Jones, 2007, pp. 53-5.

24. Mary, Lady Pembroke: O. L. Dick, *Aubrey's Brief Lives*, 1949, p. 138.

25. Cecil about Mary Fitton: Brown, 1968, p. 181.

26. Ralegh and a maid of honour: Dick, *John Aubrey's Brief Lives*, 1949, pp. 255-6.

27. Laughter at Mary Fitton's pregnancy: *Twelfth Night*, I, 3, 93-4.

28. 'Woodman': a man who hunts game in a wood or forest, vulgar slang for a lecher pursuing a woman. see also: *Measure for Measure*, IV, 3, 145-6.

29. *Twelfth Night*, I, 3, 92-3; Brown, 1968, pp. 174-5.

10. Mrs Marie Mountjoy

1. John Marston: Linnane, 2007, pp. 57-8.

2. Hemming and Condell: Southworth, pp. 155-6.

3. Tire-making: Nicholl, 2007, pp. 139-42.

4. Tires: Brown, 1968, pp. 168-9; for prostitutes: Nicholl, 2007, pp. 231.

5. Jezebel: *Kings*, 2, IX, 30.

6. 'Dowry of a second head': *Merchant of Venice*, III, 2, 94, 97; 'A second time': Sonnet 68, lines 5-8.

7. False hair: Dekker, *The Shoemaker's Holiday*, III, 4, 47-50.

8. Mountjoy, Belott and Shakespeare: Nicholl, 2007, pp. 3-15; legal details, pp. 279-307.

9. Swan Alley: Stow, p. 176; Coleman Street: *ibid*, pp. 247-8. Henry Wood: Rowse,

1974, p. 183; Nicholl, 2007, pp. 123-5

10. Wood, in Forman's notebook: Nicholl, 2007, p. 123.

11. Marie Mountjoy's miscarriage: Cook, p. 109; Rowse, p. 98.

12. Forman's note: Nicholl, 2007, p. 125.

13. The Mountjoys' immorality: Nicholl, 2007, p. 117.

14. Jacqueline Field's move: Schoenbaum, 1987, pp. 260, 261-4.

15. Marie Mountjoy and the Woods: Cook, p. 116; Nicholl, 2007, p. 124; Rowse, 1974, p. 98.

16. Marie and Mrs Wood: Nicholl, 2007, p. 124.

17. The French and English languages: *Henry V*, III, 4, 1-8. With the English king: V, 2, 105-15.

18. 'In the old age …': Sonnet 127.

19. Argus the watchman: *Love's Labours Lost*, III, 1, 153-6.

20. Sonnets, complimentary: pp. 127, 130; insulting: pp. 131, 132, 147.

21. The *Mermaid* and other inns: Stow, p. 295. Its reputation: Schoenbaum, 1991, pp. 214-16.

22. Shakespeare's London inns: Speaight, p. 29.

23. Food and wine at the *Mermaid*: M. Chute, *Shakespeare of London*, p. 192.

11. Mrs Jane Davenant

1. Arthur Acheson, *Mistress Davenant, The Dark Lady of Shakespeare's Sonnets*, Bernard Quaritch, London. 1913.

2. The inaccuracies in Acheson: Schoenbaum, 1991, pp. 494-6.

3. Gossip about Jane Davenant and Shakespeare: Schoenbaum, 1987, p. 224

4. Thomas More's *Utopia*: Phoenix, London, 1996, p. 30.

5. Richard Lions: Stow, *A Survey of London, 1598*, pp. 220-1.

6. Doll Tearsheet and Falstaff: *Henry IV, Pt. II*, II, 4, 41-3.

7. Jane Davenant's children: Honan, pp. 318-19.

8. The tavern: Weis, p. 283; Schoenbaum, 1987, p. 224. The painted room: Cheetham, *On the Trail of William Shakespeare*, 2006, p. 114; Schoenbaum, 1991, pp. 60-1.

9. Sir William Davenant: John Aubrey, *Brief Lives*, p. 85.

10. John Davenant: Anthony á Wood, *Athenae Oxonienses, III*, pp. 802-3.

11. 'Godson': Weis, p. 302; *King Lear*, II, 1, 95.

12. William Davenant, Shakespeare's bastard?: Weis, pp. 302-3. The gossip: Greenblatt, pp. 330-1; Schoenbaum, 1991, pp. 62-3. Davenant's insult to his mother: Aubrey, p. 85. Jane Davenant: John Aubrey, *Brief Lives*, Dick, p. 85; Clark, I, p. 204.

13. 'a most sweet wench': Falstaff, in *Henry IV*, I, I, 2, 27-8.

14. George Bernard Shaw and Jane Davenant as the Dark Lady: Holden, p. 248.

15. 'If thy soul ...': Sonnet 136.

16. 'thou being rich in *Will* …' : Sonnet 135.

17. The neglected child: Sonnet 143.

12. The Elusive 'Mr. W. H.'

1. The identity of 'Mr. W. H' is of no importance: Kerrigan, pp. 10-11. But; wholly successful': Dobson & Wells, *The Oxford Companion to Shakespeare*, 306.

2. 'Who He?': Edmundson & Wells, p. 25.

3. 'Weariness of the flesh': *Ecclesiastes*, XII, 12-13.

4. Aubrey's note about Herbert: *Brief Lives*, Dick, p. 145.

5. William Herbert as 'Mr. W. H.': Duncan-Jones, 1997, pp. 45-69; Schoenbaum, 1987,

pp. 194, 269-70.

6. Sams, 1997, p. 111.

7. A second William Herbert: Dover Wilson, I., *The Sonnets*, 1969, xci.

8. Southampton not 'Mr. W. H.': Duncan-Jones, 1997, p. 52.

9. Nathan Drake, *Shakespeare and His Times*, II, p. 69.

10. Drake as a pioneer: Schoenbaum, 1991, pp. 193-9. Southampton as the 'fair youth' and 'Mr. W. H.': Burrow, pp. 100-3.

11. Sonnet 104.1: wishful thinking: Sams, pp. 111-12.

12. William Hall: S. Lee, *A Life of William Shakespeare*, Spottiswode, London, 1898; A. & V. Palmer, p. 103. Quennell, pp. 123-4.

13. Farmer's indolence: *Dictionary of National Biography*, I, 662.

14. Farmer and William Hart: A. & V. Palmer, p. 106; Schoenbaum, 1991, p. 119; Colin Burrow, in Schoenfeldt, 2010, p. 152; Stopes, 1901, pp. 109, 112.

15. Leslie Hotson, *Mr, W. H.*, Hart-Davis, London, 1564, pp. 118-36.

16. The coded sonnets: Hotson, pp. 145-62.

17. A. & V. Palmer, p. 108; Schoenbaum, 1987, p. 270.

18. 'Shakespeare's Wife: B. Everett, *Review of Books 8*. 1986, pp. 7-10.

19. The reaction: Schoenbaum, 1991, p. 565; S. Wells, *Is It True What They Say About Shakespeare?*, Long Barn Books, Ebrington, n. d., 127-8; Rowse, *New York Times*, 3 March 1987; Duncan-Jones, 2007, p. 52.

20. William Houghton: Berryman, pp. 269, 275-9; Lee; p. 418; A. & V. Palmer, p. 110.

21. 'William Himself': Schoenbaum, 1991, p. 319.

22. 'W. H', a careless mistake: J. M. Nosworthy, 'Shakespeare and Mr. W. H.', *The Library, 5th Series*, XVIII, 1963, pp. 294-8.

23. William Hole as 'Mr W. H.': Levi, 1998, p. 94.

24. Tyrwhitt: Schoenbaum 1991, p. 119.

25. Bishop of St Asaph: Fido, p. 51.

26. *Notes & Queries V*, 5th Series, p. 443; Fido, p. 50.

27. Samuel Butler and 'William Hughes': The10 Sonnets Reconsidered, and in Part Rearranged with Introductory Chapters, Notes and a Reprint of the Original 1609 Edition, [No Index], Longmans, Green, London 1899, pp. 7-9; Hotson, *Mr. W. H.*, p. 108.

28. Oscar Wilde's 'Willie Hughes' was a fiction: Wells, 2002, p. 314; Schoenbaum, 1991, pp. 320-4.

29. 'Harvey' or 'Hervey'?: *Dictionary of National Biography*, I, 963, 'Hervey'.

30. Sir William Hervey: Quentin, pp. 124-6; Sams, pp. 112-13; Rowse, 1973, *Shakespeare the Man*, pp. 240-1; Schoenbaum, 1987, pp. 194, 270-1; Schoenbaum, 1991, pp. 320-4.

13. The Rival Poet: Nine Sonnets & a Name

1. 'T. T. the sly one': Wraight, *The Story that the Sonnets Tell*, p. 3.

2. Auden and the sonnets: Burto, *William Shakespeare. The Sonnets*, xxi.

3. The sonnet sequence: Duncan-Jones, *Shakespeare's Sonnets*, 1997, xiii.

4. The year 1603: Schoenbaum, 1991, p. 379.

5. The 'mortal moon': Harrison, *Shakespeare Under Elizabeth*, 1933, p. 93; Booth, *Shakespeare's Sonnets*, 2000, p. 343.

6. The inconstant moon: *Romeo and Juliet*, II, 1, 158.

7. Date of the sonnets: final shape, post-1603, Duncan-Jones, *Shakespeare's Sonnets*, xiii. Written in the early 1590s: Bate, pp. 129-32; Giroux, p. 191; Greenblatt, p. 233; Kermode, p. 68.

8. Sonnet 80, lines 1-4.

9. The Rival Poet: Schoenbaum, 1991, p. 330. see also: pp. 201, 316, 377.

10. 'a composite figure': Duncan-Jones, *Shakespeare's Sonnets*, pp. 65-6.

11. Speculation about the rival poet: Boyce, 5, 1996, p. 609.

12. Barnabe Barnes: Chute, pp. 114, 154; Giroux, pp. 184-9; Lee, p. 132; Schoenbaum, 1991, p. 377.

13. Gervase Markham: M. Chute, 1997, p. 113; Dobson & Wells, *The Oxford Companion to Shakespeare*, pp. 278-9; Lee, *Life*, p. 131; A. & V. Palmer, p. 159; Schoenbaum, 1991, pp. 352-3, 537.

14. Daniel as the rival poet: A. & V. Palmer,, 59-60; Schoenbaum, 199-202; Dobson & Wells, *Oxford Companion …*, p. 393; Duncan-Jones, *Shakespeare's Sonnets*, 2007, pp. 65-6.

15. Davison as the Rival Poet: Duncan-Jones, *Shakespeare's Sonnets*, 2007, p. 65.

16. Davis, Jonson and Chapman: Duncan-Jones, *Shakespeare's Sonnets*, 2007, p. 65.

17. Edmund Spenser: A. & V. Palmer, p. 240.

18. Thomas Watson: Fido, p. 62. see also: A. & V. Palmer, p. 262. The fight: D. Riggs, *The World of Christopher Marlowe*, Faber & Faber, 2004, p. 249.

19. Tasso: G. A. Leigh, *Westminster Review*, 1897; Schoenbaum, 1991, p. 330.

20. 'Joris Schampen': C. Nicholl, *Shakespeare and his Contemporaries*, National Portrait Gallery, London, 2005, pp. 62-3.

21. Holofornes: *Love's Labours Lost*, V, 1, 9-10.

22. 'envious windsucker': Lee, *A Life …*, 1996, pp. 135-6.

23. *Shadow of the Night*: 'chapmen's tongues': *Love's Labours Lost*, II, 1, 15-16.

24. 'Hero and Leander' and Chapman: Honan, *Christopher Marlowe. Poet & Spy*, Oxford University Press, 2005, pp. 318-19.

25. 'blouse and skirt': Maclure, M. ed., (1968) *The Poems. Christopher Marlowe*, Methuen, London xxix.

26. Mendenhall and Marlowe: E. Jones and R. Guy, *The Shakespeare Companion*, A Think Book, London, 2005, p. 143. Calvin Hoffman, *The Murder of the Man who was Shakespeare*, London, 1955.

27. Marlowe as the rival poet: Robert Cartwright, *The Sonnets of William Shakspeare Rearranged, and Divided into Four Parts, with an Introduction and Explanatory Notes'* John Russell Smith, London, 1859.

28. Giroux, pp. 187-91.

29. Theatrical props: C. Edwards, ed. *The London Theatre Guide, 1576–1642*, Burlington House, Foxton Royston,1979, p. 20.

30. *The Merry Wives of Windsor*: III, 1, 18-21.

31. A 'great reckoning': Touchtone in *As You Like It*, III, 3, 7-9; Weis, pp. 125-33.

32. 'Dead shepherd': It was a line from Marlowe's unfinished 'Hero and Leander', *Sestiad* I, 176; Maclure, M. ed., (1968) *The Poems. Christopher Marlowe*, Methuen, London; Weis, 'The Rival Poet', pp. 125-38.

14. The Dark Lady of the Sonnets

1. Jane Davenant as the Dark Lady: John Aubrey: Dick, *Brief Lives*, p. 85; Holden, p. 246.

2. Debatable date of the sonnets: around 1593, Giroux, pp. 184-191; mostly first half of the 1590s, Greenblatt, p. 233; mid-1590s, Kermode, p. 68; begun early 1590s but most are late 1590s, Bate, pp. 129-32.

3. The 'Dark Woman': W. Thomson, p. 52.

4. Dark women: Nicholl, *The Lodger*, 2007, p. 192. 'scut': Alice Ford: *The Merry Wives*

of Windsor, V, 5, 12.

5. 'Scut': *The First English Dictionary, 1604,* by Robert Cawdrey: Bodleian, Oxford, 2007, p. 138; Partridge, *A Dictionary of Slang,* pp. 740-1; Partridge, *Shakespeare's Bawdy,* p. 232.

6. In the old age': Sonnet 127, line 1.

7. 'her gentle fingers': Sonnet 128, lines 12-14.

8. 'My mistress' eyes …': Sonnet 130.

9. 'conscience doth make cowards': *Hamlet,* III, 1, 83.

10. 'Lust in action ...', Sonnet 129. Bernard Shaw: Giroux, pp. 175-6.

11. 'Black is fairest: Sonnet 131, lines 10-14.

12. 'Thou art twice forsworn …': Sonnet 152, lines 1-4.

13. 'Myself I'll forfeit': Sonnet 134, lines 3-5.

14. A black-haired woman: Brown, *Shakespeare,* 1949, p. 200.

15. Married with children: Sonnet 142, Sonnet 143.

16. 'Rose': quoted in sonnets 35, 54, 67, 99.

17. Rosaline's dark complexion: McConnell, p. 308.

18. 'her Will': *Love's Labours Lost,* II, 1, 212-13.

19. Rosaline's eyes: Sonnets 127 and 132.

20. The virtue of the colour black: *Love's Labours Lost,* IV, 3, 6-7, 253-4.

21. 'Alas, poor Romeo': *Romeo and Juliet,* II, 3, 12-13.

22. Mercutio and Rosaline's bright eyes: *Romeo and Juliet,* II, 1, 19-22.

23. 'white wench's black eye': Brown, *Shakespeare,* 1949, p. 201.

24. The Dark Lady: G. & B. Lloyd Evans, *Everyman's Companion to Shakespeare,* 1978, p. 23.

25. 'love's prick and Rosalind': *As You Like It,* III, 2, 84-5.

Postscript: The Fourth Forger

1. For books about William-Henry Ireland, see: Grebanier; Mair; Pierce.

2. His appearance: Pierce, pp. 31-2.

3. His forgeries: Grebanier, pp. 78-9; Pierce, pp. 41-3.

4. Queen Elizabeth: Mair, p. 43; Pierce, pp. 81-4.

5. Anne Hathaway: Mair, pp. 40-1; Pierce, pp. 77-9.

6. Malone: Pierce, pp. 202-3.

7. Ireland was a somebody!: Pierce, p. 232.

Bibliography

Acheson, A. (1903) *Shakespeare and the Rival Poet*, John Lane, The Bodley Head, London.

Acheson, A. (1913) *Mistress Davenant, The Dark Lady of Shakespeare's Sonnets*, Bernard Quaritch, London.

Appelbaum, S. ed. (1991) *Complete Sonnets. William Shakespeare*, Dover Thrift, New York.

Auden, W. H. see: Burto.

Baker, W. (2009) *William Shakespeare*, Continuum, London and New York.

Barron, C. (2008) 'Introduction': *A Detailed Street Map of the City of London, Five Hundred Years Ago, c. 1520*, Old House Books, Moretonhampstead.

Bate, J. (1997) *The Genius of Shakespeare*, Picador, London.

Bate, J. (2008a) 'The other Master W. H', *Times Literary Supplement*, 5498, p. 14-15.

Bate, J. (2008b) *Shakespeare. Soul of the Age*, Viking, London.

Bate, J. & Rassmussen, eds. (2007) *The RSC Shakespeare. William Shakespeare. Complete Works*, Macmillan, London.

Bate, J. & Rassmussen, eds. (2009) *The RSC Shakespeare*. William Shakespeare. *Sonnets and Other Poems*, Macmillan, London.

Bearman, R. (1994) *Shakespeare in the Stratford Records*, Sutton, Thrupp.

Berryman. See: Haffenden.

Bevington, D. (2002) *Shakespeare*, Blackwell, Oxford.

Bland, D. ed. (1968) *Gesta Grayorum. or The History of the High and Mighty Prince Henry Prince of Purpoole. Anno Domini 1594*, Liverpool University Press, Liverpool.

Booth, S. (2000) *Shakespeare's Sonnets*, Yale University Press, New Haven & London.

Boyce, C. (1996) *The Wordsworth Dictionary of Shakespeare*, Wordsworth Reference, Ware.

Brown, I. (1949) *Shakespeare*, Collins, London.

Brown, I. (1957) *Dark Ladies*, Collins, London.

Brown, I. (1968) *The Women in Shakespeare's Life*, Bodley Head, London.

Burgess, A. (1970) *Shakespeare*, Jonathan Cape, London.

Burrow, C. ed. (2002) *William Shakespeare. The Complete Sonnets and Poems*, Oxford University Press, Oxford.

Burto, W. ed. (1964) *William Shakespeare. The Sonnets*, Introduction, W. H. Auden, New English Library, London.

Cheetham, J. K. (2006) *On the Trail of William Shakespeare*, Luath, Edinburgh.

Cheney, P. ed. (2007) *The Cambridge Companion to Shakespeare's Poetry*, Cambridge University Press, Cambridge.

Chute, M. (1977) *Shakespeare of London*, Souvenir, London.

Cook, J. (2001) *Dr Simon Forman. A Most Notorious Physician*, Chatto & Windus, London.

Cook, T. intro (1994) *The Poems & Sonnets of William Shakespeare*, Wordsworth, Ware.

Dobson, M. & Wells, S. eds. (2001) *The Oxford Companion to Shakespeare*, Oxford University Press, Oxford.

Duncan-Jones, K. ed. (1997) *Shakespeare's Sonnets*, Arden Shakespeare, (Third Series), London.

Duncan-Jones, K. (1989) *Intro. The Sonnets, and, A Lover's Complaint*, Folio Society, London.

Duncan-Jones, K. (2001) *Ungentle Shakespeare. Scenes from His Life*, Arden Shakespeare, London.

Duncan-Jones, K. ed. (2010) *Shakespeare's Sonnets and A Lover's Complaint*, Methuen Drama, London.

Edmondson, P. & Wells, S. (2004) *Shakespeare's Sonnets*, Oxford University Press, Oxford.

Edwards, C. ed. (1979) *The London Theatre Guide, 1576–1642*, The Bear Gardens Museum and Arts Centre, London.

Evans, G. B. ed. 2nd ed. (2006) *The Sonnets*, Cambridge University Press, Cambridge.

Evans, G. & B. L. (1978) *Everyman's Companion to Shakespeare*, Dent, London.

Evans, M. (1977) *Elizabethan Sonnets*, Dent, London.

Evans, M. (1989) *The Narrative Poems by William Shakespeare*, Penguin, London.

Ferris, J. (2000) *Shakespeare's London. A Guide to Elizabethan London*, Kingfisher, New York.

Fido, M. (1978) *Shakespeare*, Galley, London.

Forman, Simon. see: Cook, J.; Rowse, 1974; Traister.

Gibson, R. ed. (1997) *Shakespeare. The Sonnets*, Cambridge University Press, Cambridge.

Giroux, R. (1982) *The Book Known as Q. A Consideration of Shakespeare's Sonnets*, Weidenfeld & Nicolson, London.

Grebanier, B. (1996) *The Great Shakespeare Forgery. A New Look at the Career of William-Henry Ireland*, Heinemann, London. [no index].

Greenblatt, S. (2005) *Will in the World. How Shakespeare Became Shakespeare*, Pimlico, London.

Greer, G. (2007) *Shakespeare's Wife*, Bloomsbury, London.

Greer, G. (2009) Intro. *William Shakespeare. Sonnets*, Vintage, London.

Haffenden, J. ed. (2001) *Berryman's Shakespeare. Essays, Letters, and Other Writings by John Berryman*, Tauris, Parke, London.

Harrison, G. B. (1926) *Willobie His Avisa*, Bodley Head, London.

Harrison, G. B. (1928) *An Elizabethan Journal. Being a Record of Those Things Most Talked about during the Years 1591–1594*, Constable, London.

Harrison, G. B. (1931) *Ibid, 1595–1598*, Constable, London.

Harrison, G. B. (1933a) *A Last Elizabethan Journal, Ibid, 1599–1603*, Routledge & Kegan

Paul, London.

Harrison, G. B. (1933b) *Shakespeare Under Elizabeth*, Henry Holt, New York.

Harrison, G. B. ed. (1966) *Ben Jonson: 'Discoveries' 1641*, pp. 85-106; *Conversations with William Drummond of Hawthornden, 1619*. Edinburgh University Press, Edinburgh.

Harrison, G. B. (1966) *Introducing Shakespeare*, 3rd ed., Penguin, Harmondsworth.

Harrison, M. & Royston, O. M. (1965) *How They Lived. An Anthology of Original Accounts Written Between 1485 and 1700*, Blackwell. Oxford.

Holden, A. (1999) *William Shakespeare. His Life and Work*, Little Brown, London.

Honan, P. (1998) *Shakespeare. A Life*, Oxford University Press, Oxford.

Honan, P. (2005) *Christopher Marlowe. Poet and Spy*, Oxford University Press, Oxford.

Hotson, J. L. (1925) *The Death of Christopher Marlowe*, Nonesuch Press, Cambridge; Harvard University Press.

Hotson, J. L. (1949) *Shakespeare's Sonnets Dated. And Other Essays*, Hart-Davis, London.

Hotson, J. L. (1954) *The First Night of Twelfth Night*, Hart-Davis, London.

Hotson, J. L. (1964) *Mr. W. H.*, Hart-Davies, London.

Kermode, F. (2004) *The Age of Shakespeare*, Weidenfeld & Nicolson, London.

Kerrigan, J. ed. (1986) *The Sonnets and A Lover's Complaint*, Penguin Classics, London.

Lee, S. (1898) *A Life of William Shakespeare*, Eyre & Spottiswood, London. (reprint, Oracle, Royston, 1996).

Lee, S. (1900) *Shakespeare's Life and Work*. Smith, Elder, London.

Levi, P. (1988) *The Life and Times of William Shakespeare*, Macmillan, London.

Linnane, F. (2007) *London the Wicked City. A Thousand Years of Vice in the Capital*, Robson, London.

McConnell, L. (2003) *Exit, pursued by a bear. Shakespeare's Characters, Plays, Poems, History and Stagecraft*, Bloomsbury, London.

Mair, J. (1938) *The Fourth Forger. William Ireland and the Shakespeare Papers*, Cobden-Sanderson, London.

May, R. (1974) *Who Was Shakespeare? The Man – The Times – the Works*, David & Charles, Newton Stewart.

Michell, J. (1996) *Who Wrote Shakespeare?*, Thames & Hudson, London.

Nicholl, C. (2005) *Shakespeare and His Contemporaries*, National Portrait Gallery, London.

Nicholl, C. (2007) *The Lodger. Shakespeare on Silver Street*, Allen Lane, London.

O'Connor, G. (1991) *William Shakespeare A Life*, Hodder & Stoughton, London.

O'Connor, E. M. (1978) *Who's Who and What's What in Shakespeare*, Gramercy, New York.

Onions. C. T. (1925) *A Shakespeare Glossary*, Clarendon Press, Oxford. See also: Eagleton, 1986.

Palmer, A. & V. (2000) *Who's Who in Shakespeare's England. Over 700 Concise Biographies of Shakespeare's Contemporaries*, Methuen, London.

Partridge, E. (1961) *A Dictionary of Slang and Unconventional English, I, II*, 5th ed., Routledge & Kegan Paul, London.

Partridge, E. (2000) *Shakespeare's Bawdy. A Literary and Psychological Essay and a Comprehensive Glossary*, 3rd ed. Routledge & Kegan Paul, London.

Paterson, D. (2010). *Reading Shakespeare's Sonnets. A New Commentary*, Faber & Faber, London.

Picard, L. (2004), *Elizabeth's London. Everyday Life in Elizabethan London*, Phoenix, London.

Pierce, P. (2004) *The Great Shakespeare Fraud. The Strange True Story of William-Henry Ireland*, Sutton, Thrupp.

Porter, S. (2009) *Shakespeare's London. Everyday Life in London 1580–1616*, Amberley, Chalford.

Pritchard, R. E. ed. & Intro. (2010) *Shakespeare's England. Life in Elizabethan and Jacobean Times*, History Press, Brimscombe Port.

Prockter, A. & Taylor, R. (1979) *The A to Z of Elizabethan London*, Harry Margary, Lympe Castle (in association with Guildhall Library,) London.

Quennell, P. & Johnson, H. (2006) *Who's Who in Shakespeare*, Routledge, London.

Rasmussen, E. (2011) *The Shakespeare Thefts. In Search of the First Folios*, Palgrave Macmillan, London.

See also: Bate & Rasmasson.

Razzell, P. (1990) *William Shakespeare: The Anatomy of an Enigma*, Caliban.

Robins, N. (2005) *Walking Shakespeare's London. 20 Original Walks in and Around London*, Interlink, Northampton, Mass.

Roud, S. (2008 *London Lore. The Legends and Traditions of the World's Most Vibrant City*, Random House, London.

Routh, C. R. N. (1956) *They Saw It Happen. An Anthology of Eye-Witness Accounts of Events in British History, 1485–1688*, Blackwell, Oxford.

Routh, C. R. N. (1990) *Who's Who in Tudor England*, revised by Peter Holmes, Blackwell, Oxford.

Rowse, A. L. (1964a) *Christopher Marlowe. A Biography*, Macmillan, London.

Rowse, A. L. ed. (1964b) *Shakespeare's Sonnets*, Macmillan, London.

Rowse, A. L. (1965) *Shakespeare's Southampton, Patron of Virginia*, Macmillan, London.

Rowse, A. L. (1971) *The Elizabethan Renaissance. The Life of the Society*, History Book Club, London.

Rowse, A. L. (1974) *Simon Forman. Sex and Society in Shakespeare's Age*, Weidenfeld & Nicolson, London.

Rowse, A. L. (1978) Introduction. *The Poems of Shakespeare's Dark Lady, Salve Deus Rex Judaeorum*, by Emilia Lanier, Jonathan Cape, London.

Rowse, A. L. (1989) *Discovering Shakespeare. A Chapter in Literary History*, Weidenfeld & Nicolson, London.

Salgãdo, G. (1997) *The Elizabethan Underworld*, Book Club Associates, London.

Sams, E. (1995) *The Real Shakespeare. Retrieving the Early Years, 1564–1594*, Yale University Press, New Haven & London.

Saunders, A. W. L. (2007) *The Master of Shakespeare. I. The Sonnets*, MoS Publishing, Tortola, British Virgin Islands.

Schoenbaum, S. (1987) *William Shakespeare. A Compact Documentary Life, Revised Edition with a New Postscript*, Oxford University Press, New York, Oxford.

Schenbaum, S. (1991) *Shakespeare's Lives. New Edition*, Clarendon Press, Oxford.

Schoenfeldt, M, ed. (2010) *A Companion to Shakespeare's Sonnets*, Wiley-Blackwell, Chichester.

Shapiro, J. (2005) *1599. A Year in the Life of William Shakespeare*, Faber & Faber, London.

Speaight, R. (1977) *Shakespeare. The Man and His Achievements*, Dent, London.

Bibliography

Stow, J. (1598) *A Survey of London. Written in the Year 1598*, A. Fraser, Intro., Sutton, Thrupp, 2005.

Tames, R. (2009) *Shakespeare's London on Five Groats a Day*, Thames & Hudson, London.

Thomson, W. (1938) *The Sonnets of William Shakespeare & Henry Wriothesley Third Earl of Southampton. Together with A Lover's Complaint and The Phoenix and The Dove*, Basil Blackwell, Oxford.

Traister, B. H. (2001) *The Notorious Astrological Physician of London. Works and Days of Simon Forman*, University of Chicago, Chicago and London.

Uden, G. (1965) *They Looked Like This*, Blackwell, Oxford.

Vendler, H. (1992) *Intro. The Sonnets and Narrative Poems*, Everyman, London.

Wait, R. J. C. (1972) *The Background to Shakespeare's Sonnets*, Chatto & Windus, London.

Weinreb, B, Hibbert, C., Keay, J. & K. (1983) *The London Encyclopaedia*, Macmillan, London.

Weis, R. (2007) *Shakespeare Revealed. A Biography*, Murray, London.

Wells, S. (1985) *Shakespeare. An Illustrated Dictionary*, Oxford University Press, Oxford.

Wells, S. & Shaw, J. (2005) *A Dictionary of Shakespeare*, Oxford University Press, Oxford.

West, D. (2007) *Shakespeare's Sonnets. With a New Commentary*, Duckworth Overlook, Woodstock.

Wilson, I. (1993) *Shakespeare: The Evidence. Unlocking the Mysteries of the Man and his Work*, Headline, London.

Wilson, F. P. (1927) *The Plague in Shakespeare's London*, Oxford University Press, London. [Reprint: Sandpiper Books, London, 1999].

Wood, M. (2003) *In Search of Shakespeare*, BBC Worldwide, London.

Woods, S. (1999) *Lanyer: A Renaissance Women Poet*, Oxford University Press, Oxford.

Wraight, A. D. (1994) *The Story that the Sonnets Tell*, Adam Hart, London.

Wraight, A. D. (1996). *Shakespeare. New Evidence*, Adam Hart, London.

Wyndham, G. ed. (1898) *The Poems of Shakespeare*, Methuen, London. [reprint, Senate, London, 1994].

Yates, F. (1934) *John Florio: The Life of an Italian in Shakespeare's England.*

Acknowledgements

The Shakespeare Centre, Henley Street, Stratford-upon-Avon.
The Shakespeare Institute, Church Street, Stratford-upon-Avon.
The Shakespeare Library, Central Library, Chamberlain Square, Birmingham.
The Library of the Society of Antiquaries of London, Burlington House, Piccadilly, London.
The Library of the University of Birmingham, Edgbaston, Birmingham.
And to Judith, my wife, without whose encouragement and insistence the visits to towns and villages, to great houses and churches, and all the other research for this book would never have been made.

List of Illustrations

1. © Jonathan Reeve JR1080b3p299 16001650.
2. © Stephen Porter.
3. © Jonathan Reeve JR1076b3fp166 16001650.
4. © Jonathan Reeve JR1062b10prelims 16001650.
5. © Jonathan Reeve JR1110b22p1486 15501600.
6. © Brandon & Brooke.
7. © Brandon & Brooke.
8. © Jonathan Reeve JR1095b20p952-3 15001600.
9. © Stephen Porter.
10. © Stephen Porter.
11. © Stephen Porter.
12. © Stephen Porter.
13. © Jonathan Reeve JR149b3fp258 15501600.
14. © Jonathan Reeve JR1130b40p204 15501600.
15. © Jonathan Reeve JR1078b3p213 15501600.
16. © Jonathan Reeve JR1083b3fp472 15501600.
17. © Aubrey Burl
18. © Aubrey Burl.
19. © Aubrey Burl.
20. © Jonathan Reeve JR1131b40p289 15501600.
21. © Stephen Porter.
22. © Jonathan Reeve JR1102b2p787 15501600.
23. © Jonathan Reeve JR1073b3fp108 15501600.
24. © Jonathan Reeve JR1072b3fp98 15501600.
25. © Jonathan Reeve JR1090b20p769 15501600.
26. © Stephen Porter.
27. © Jonathan Reeve JR1060b4p788T 16001650.
28. © Aubrey Burl.
29. © Stephen Porter.
30. © Brandon & Brooke.

Also available from Amberley Publishing

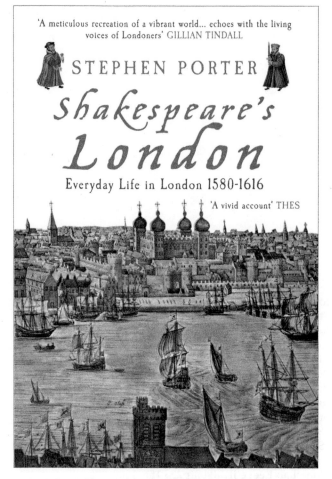

'A meticulous recreation of a vibrant world... echoes with the living voices of Londoners' GILLIAN TINDALL

STEPHEN PORTER
Shakespeare's London
Everyday Life in London 1580-1616
'A vivid account' THES

Everyday life in the teeming metropolis during William Shakespeare's time in the city (c.1580-1616), the height of Queen Elizabeth I's reign

'A vivid account' THES

'A lucid and cogent narrative of everyday life' SHAKESPEARE BIRTHPLACE TRUST

Shakespeare's London was a bustling, teeming metropolis that was growing so rapidly that the government took repeated, and ineffectual, steps to curb its expansion. From contemporary letters, journals and diaries, a vivid picture emerges of this fascinating city, with its many opportunities and also its persistent problems.

£9.99 Paperback
127 illustrations (45 colour)
304 pages
978-1-84868-200-9

Available from all good bookshops or to order direct
Please call **01453-847-800**
www.amberleybooks.com

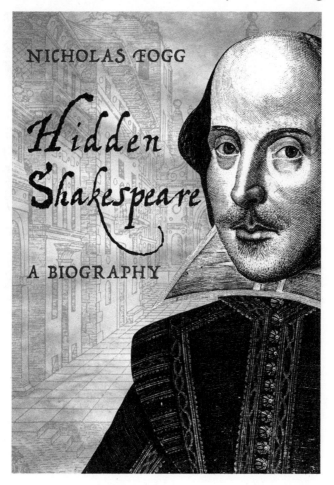

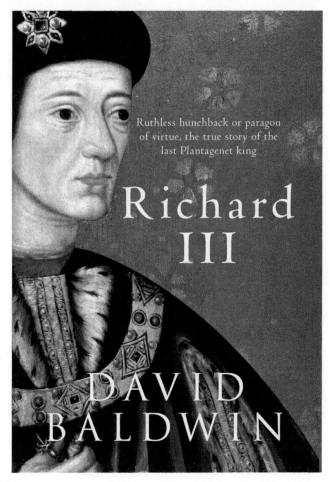

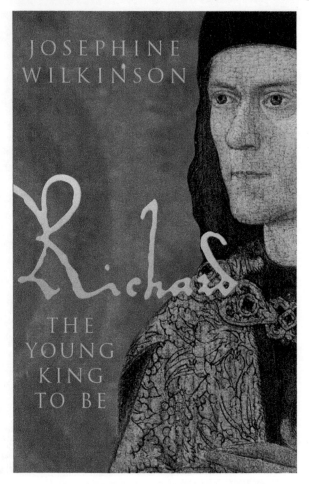

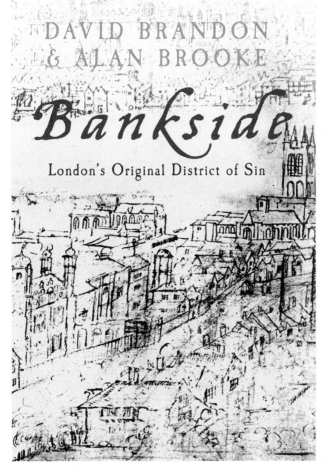

Also available from Amberley Publishing

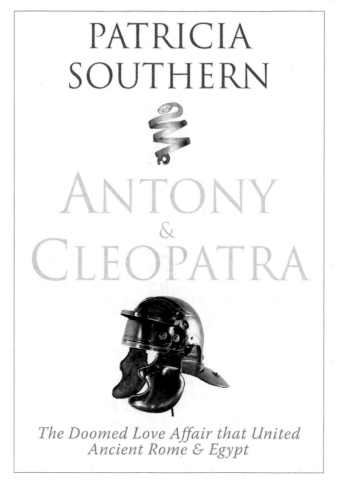

PATRICIA
SOUTHERN

ANTONY
&
CLEOPATRA

*The Doomed Love Affair that United
Ancient Rome & Egypt*

The story of one of the most compelling love affairs in history

The immortal lovers of novels, plays and films, Antony and Cleopatra were reviled by contemporary Romans, but history has transformed them into tragic heroes. Somewhere between their vilification by Augustus and the judgement of a later age there were two vibrant people whose destinies were entwined after the assassination of Julius Caesar in March 44 BC. Mark Antony's reputation for recklessness, hard drinking, and womanising overshadowed his talents for leadership and astute administration. Cleopatra was determined to reconstitute the ancient empire of the Ptolemies, and Antony as legally appointed ruler of the east gave her much, but not all, of what she desired.

£9.99 Paperback
38 illustrations
208 pages
978-1-4456-0576-0

Available from all good bookshops or to order direct
Please call **01453-847-800**
www.amberleybooks.com

Also available from Amberley Publishing

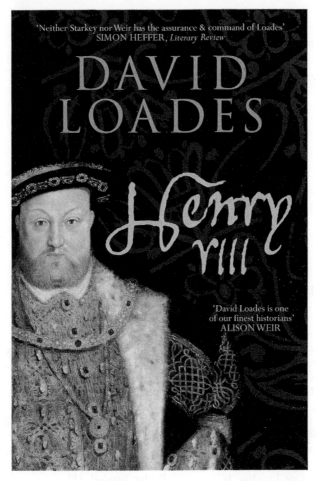

'Neither Starkey nor Weir has the assurance & command of Loades'
SIMON HEFFER, *Literary Review*

DAVID
LOADES

Henry
VIII

'David Loades is one
of our finest historians'
ALISON WEIR

A major new biography of the most infamous king of England

'A triumph' THE SPECTATOR

'The best place to send anyone seriously wanting to get to grips with alternative understandings of England's
most mesmerising monarch... copious illustrations, imaginatively chosen' BBC HISTORY MAGAZINE

'David Loades Tudor biographies are both highly enjoyable and instructive, the perfect combination'
ANTONIA FRASER

Professor David Loades has spent most of his life investigating the remains, literary, archival and archaeological, of
Henry VIII, and this monumental new biography book is the result. As a youth, he was a magnificent specimen of
manhood, and in age a gargantuan wreck, but even in his prime he was never the 'ladies man' which legend, and his
own imagination, created. Sexual insecurity undermined him, and gave his will that irascible edge which proved fatal
to Anne Boleyn and Thomas Cromwell alike.

£25 Hardback
113 illustrations (49 colour)
512 pages
978-1-84868-532-1

Available from all good bookshops or to order direct
Please call **01453-847-800**
www.amberleybooks.com

Index